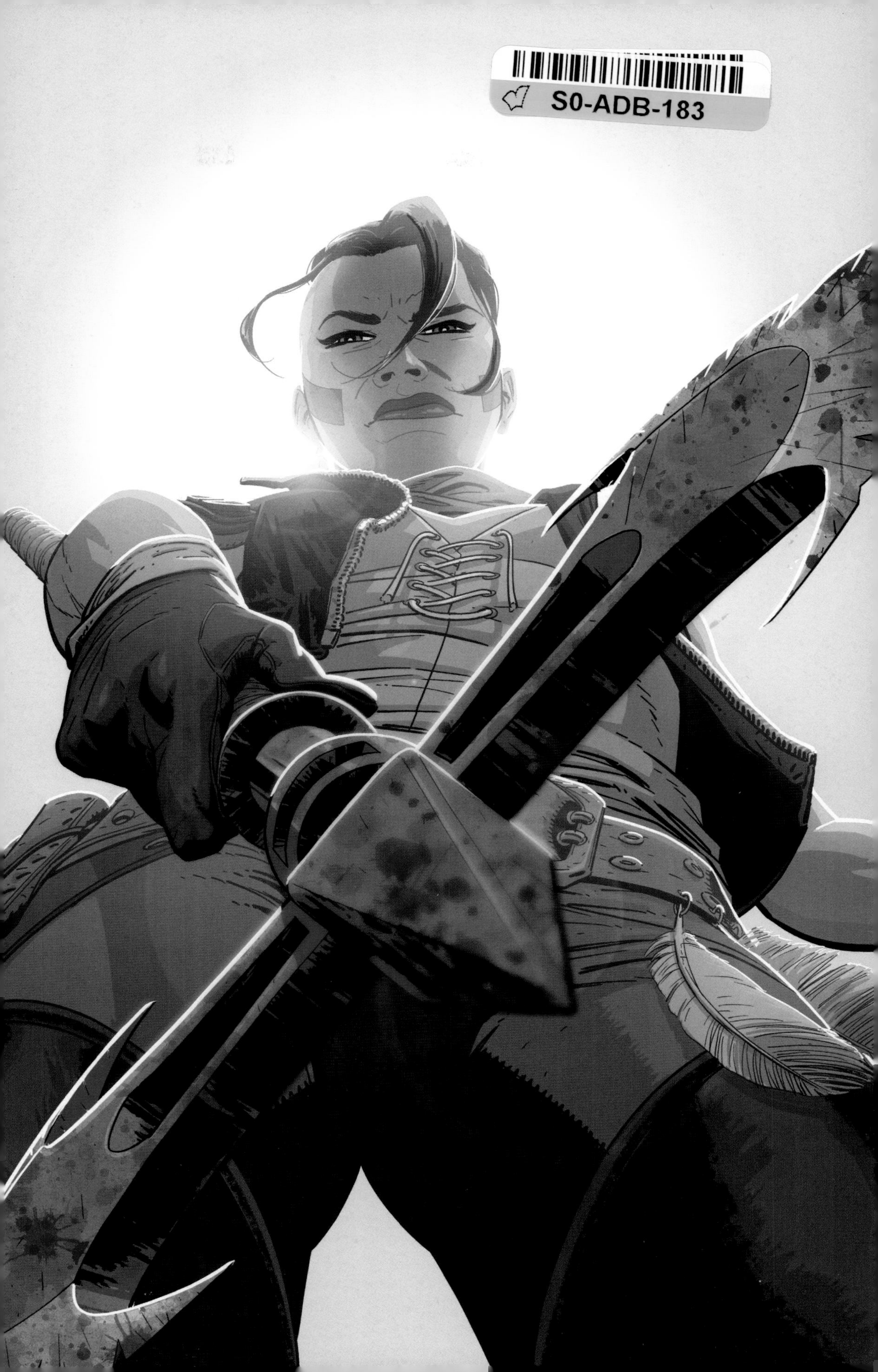

THE FORGOTTEN QUEEN™

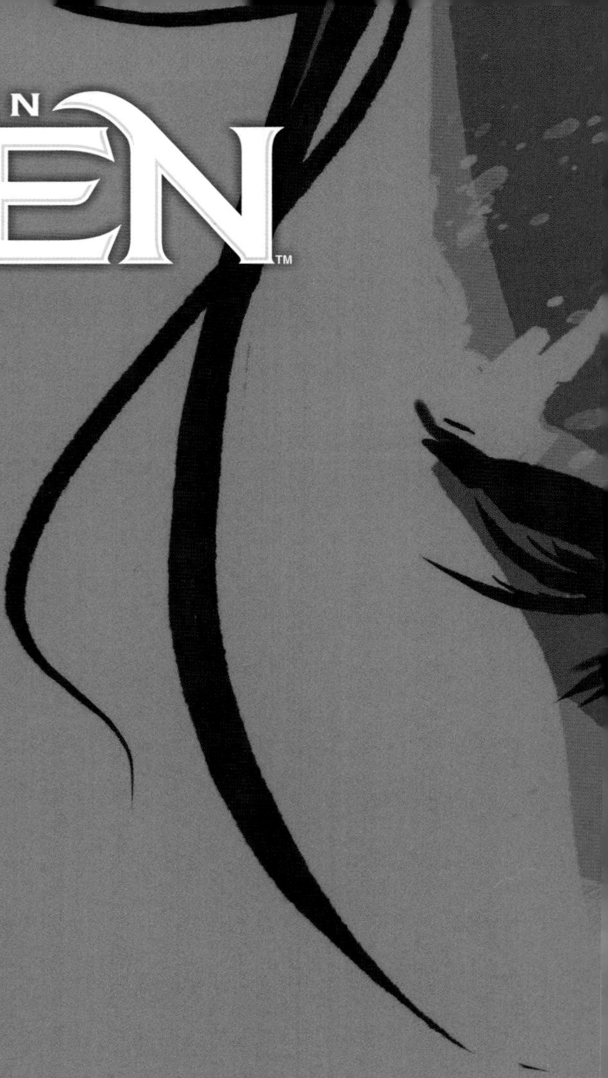

WRITER
TINI HOWARD

ARTIST
AMILCAR PINNA

COLOR ARTIST
ULISES ARREOLA

LETTERER
JEFF POWELL

COVERS BY
KANO

ASSISTANT EDITOR
DREW BAUMGARTNER

EDITOR
LYSA HAWKINS

GALLERY
MIRKA ANDOLFO
ULISES ARREOLA
GABE ELTAEB
VERONICA FISH
TINI HOWARD
VIKTOR KALVACHEV
AMILCAR PINNA
JEFF POWELL
HANNAH TEMPLER
DIEGO YAPUR

COLLECTION COVER ART
KANO

COLLECTION FRONT ART:
KANO
HANNAH TEMPLER

LOGO DESIGN
JEFF POWELL

COLLECTION EDITOR
IVAN COHEN

COLLECTION DESIGNER
STEVE BLACKWELL

VALIANT®

DAN MINTZ Chairman **FRED PIERCE** Publisher **WALTER BLACK** VP Operations **MATTHEW KLEIN** VP Sales & Marketing **ROBERT MEYERS** Senior Editorial Director **MEL CAYLO** Director of Marketing
TRAVIS ESCARFULLERY Director of Design & Production **PETER STERN** Director of International Publishing & Merchandising **KARL BOLLERS** Senior Editor **LYSA HAWKINS & HEATHER ANTOS** Editors
DAVID MENCHEL Associate Editor **DREW BAUMGARTNER** Assistant Editor **JEFF WALKER** Production & Design Manager **EMILY HECHT** Sales & Social Media Manager **KAT O'NEILL** Sales & Live Events Manager
DANIELLE WARD Sales Manager **CONNOR HILL** Sales Operations Coordinator **GREGG KATZMAN** Marketing Coordinator

THE FORGOTTEN QUEEN™. Published by Valiant Entertainment LLC. Office of Publication: 350 Seventh Avenue, New York, NY 10001. Compilation copyright © 2019 Valiant Entertainment LLC. All rights reserved. Contains materials originally published in single magazine form as The Forgotten Queen #1-4. Copyright © 2019 Valiant Entertainment LLC. All rights reserved. All characters, their distinctive likeness and related indicia featured in this publication are trademarks of Valiant Entertainment LLC. The stories, characters, and incidents featured in this publication are entirely fictional. Valiant Entertainment does not read or accept unsolicited submissions of ideas, stories, or artwork. Printed in the U.S.A. First Printing. ISBN: 9781682153246.

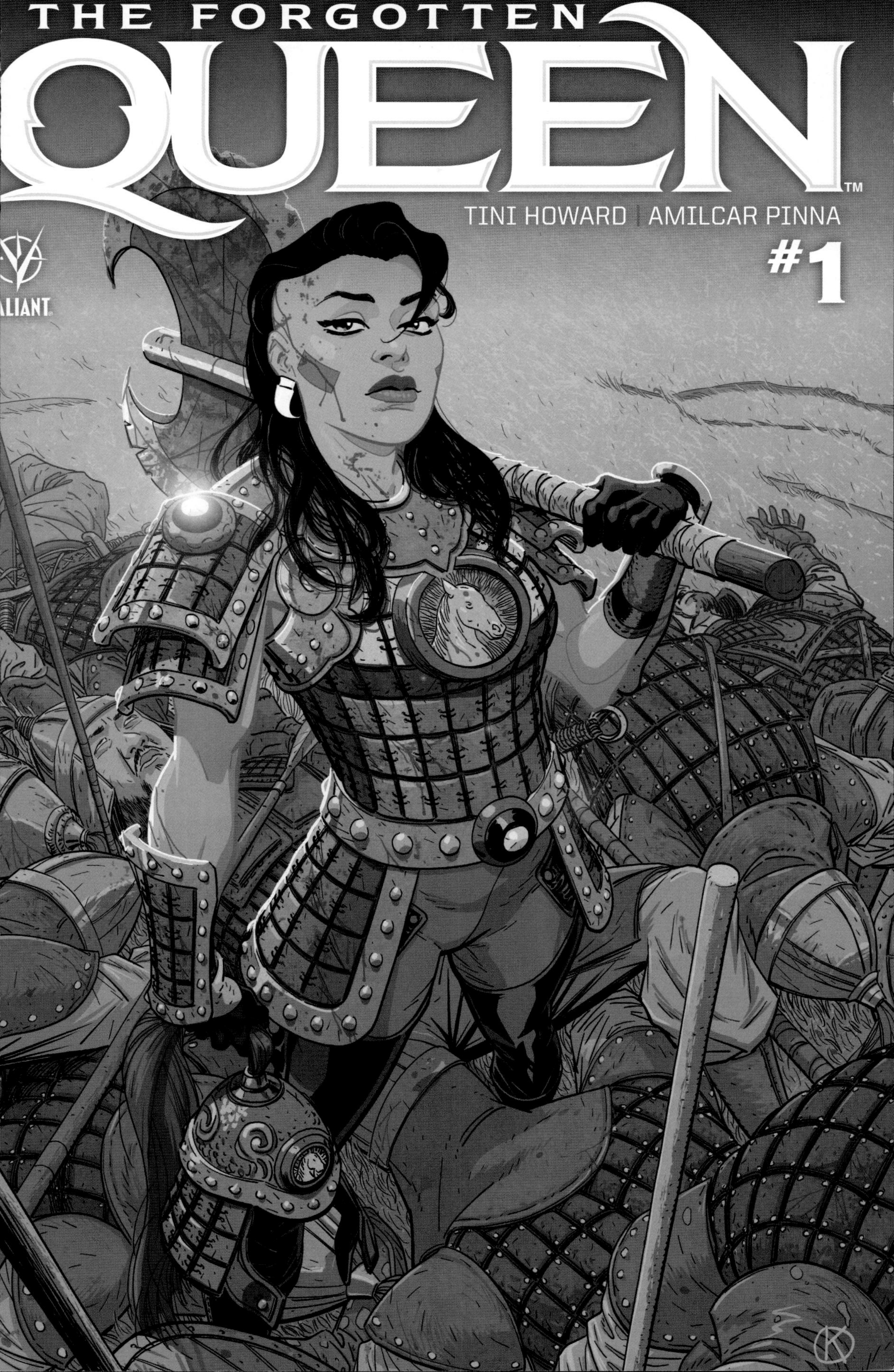
THE FORGOTTEN
QUEEN™
TINI HOWARD | AMILCAR PINNA
#1
ALIANT

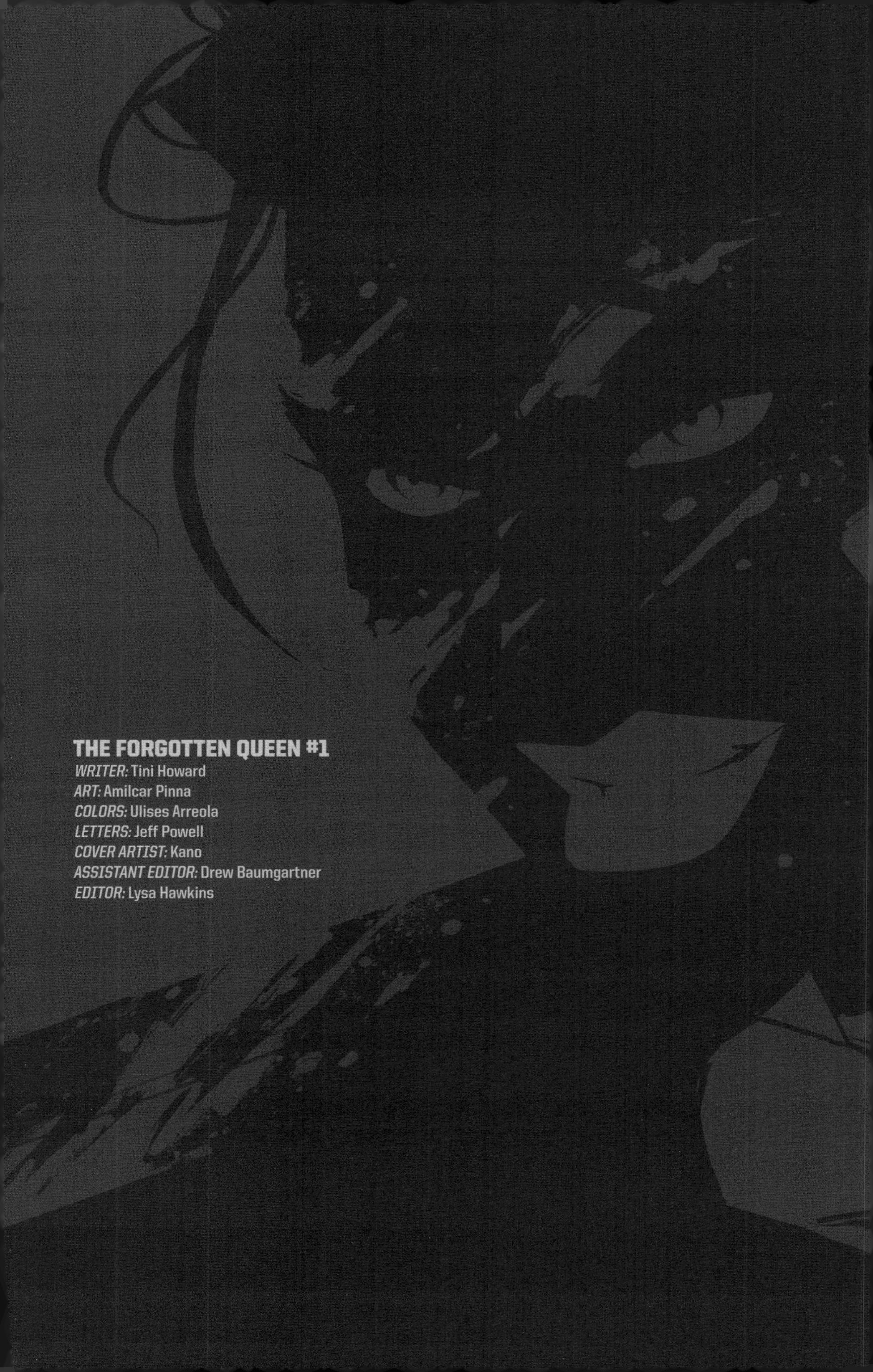

THE FORGOTTEN QUEEN #1

WRITER: Tini Howard
ART: Amilcar Pinna
COLORS: Ulises Arreola
LETTERS: Jeff Powell
COVER ARTIST: Kano
ASSISTANT EDITOR: Drew Baumgartner
EDITOR: Lysa Hawkins

THE WIDE, UNMARKED MIDDLE OF THE PACIFIC OCEAN.

14°57'52.1"S 152°58'04.6"W

ERIK?

THIS IS DR. LOLLI, OF THE RV LOHENGRIN...

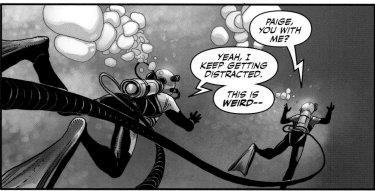

...ACCORDING TO WHAT I'M SEEING, YOU'RE WITHIN TWO HUNDRED FEET OF THE ATOLL.

ROGER.

PAIGE, YOU WITH ME?

YEAH, I KEEP GETTING DISTRACTED.

THIS IS WEIRD--

ERIK ZAFIROPOLOUS, VETERAN RESEARCH DIVER ON THE RESEARCH VESSEL *LOHENGRIN.*

YOU FEELING OKAY?

HOT...TIRED. YOU EVER JUST FEEL LIKE YOU DOVE WRONG?

MY GUTS FEEL ALL HOT FROM BREAKFAST.

PAIGE STEWART, SCUBA DIVING EXPERT, RESEARCH INTERN.

I THINK WE SHOULD HURRY.

EVERYTHING OKAY, TEAM?

STAND BY, LOHENGRIN.

WE'LL BE ALRIGHT.

JUST GONNA TAKE SOME SAMPLES FROM THE CAVE AND GET OUT.

RRRRRRRRRUUUUU

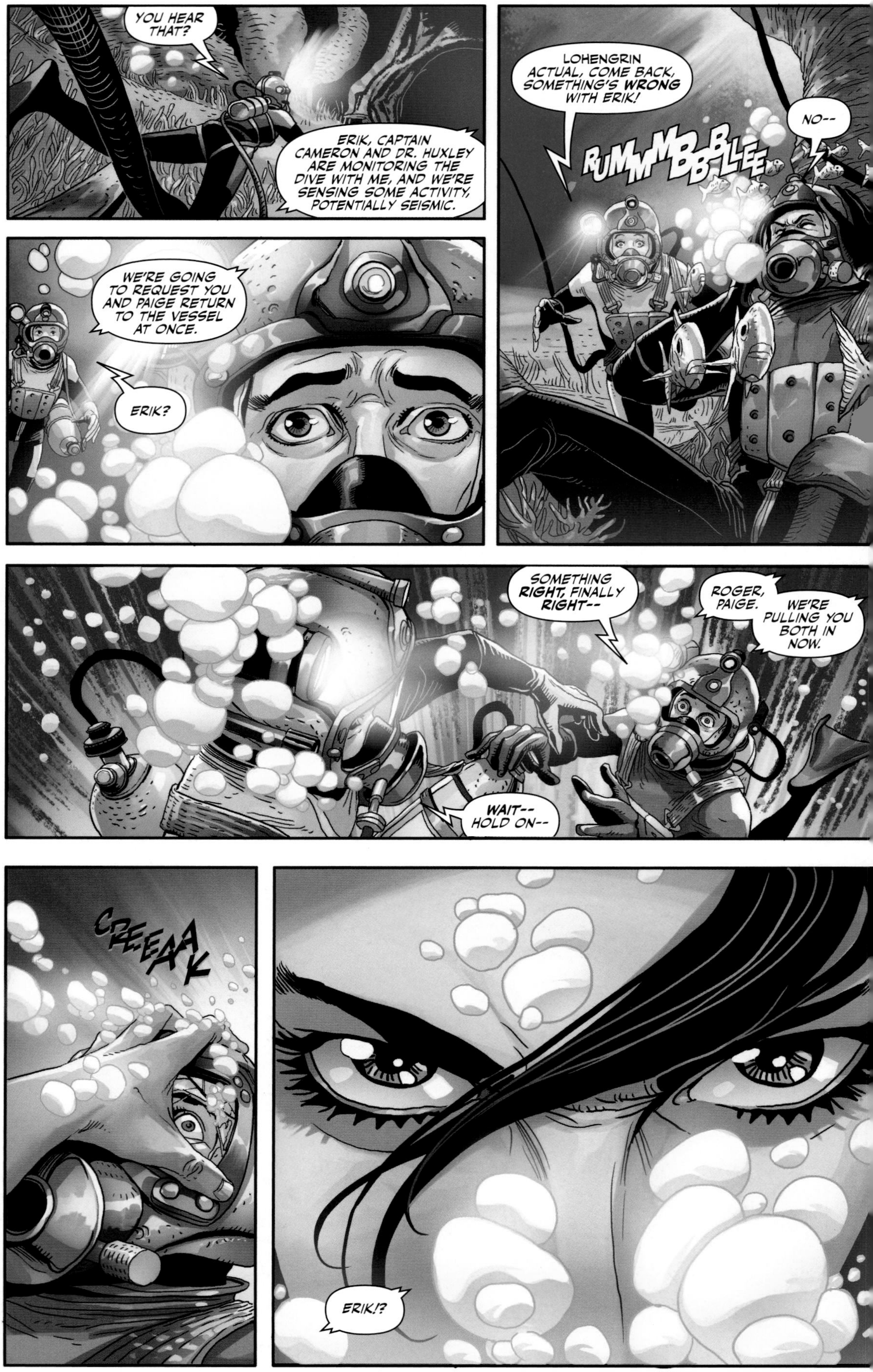
YOU HEAR THAT?
ERIK, CAPTAIN CAMERON AND DR. HUXLEY ARE MONITORING THE DIVE WITH ME, AND WE'RE SENSING SOME ACTIVITY, POTENTIALLY SEISMIC.
WE'RE GOING TO REQUEST YOU AND PAIGE RETURN TO THE VESSEL AT ONCE.
ERIK?
LOHENGRIN ACTUAL, COME BACK, SOMETHING'S WRONG WITH ERIK!
RUMMMBBBLLEE
NO--
SOMETHING RIGHT, FINALLY RIGHT--
ROGER, PAIGE.
WE'RE PULLING YOU BOTH IN NOW.
WAIT-- HOLD ON--
CREEAAK
ERIK!?

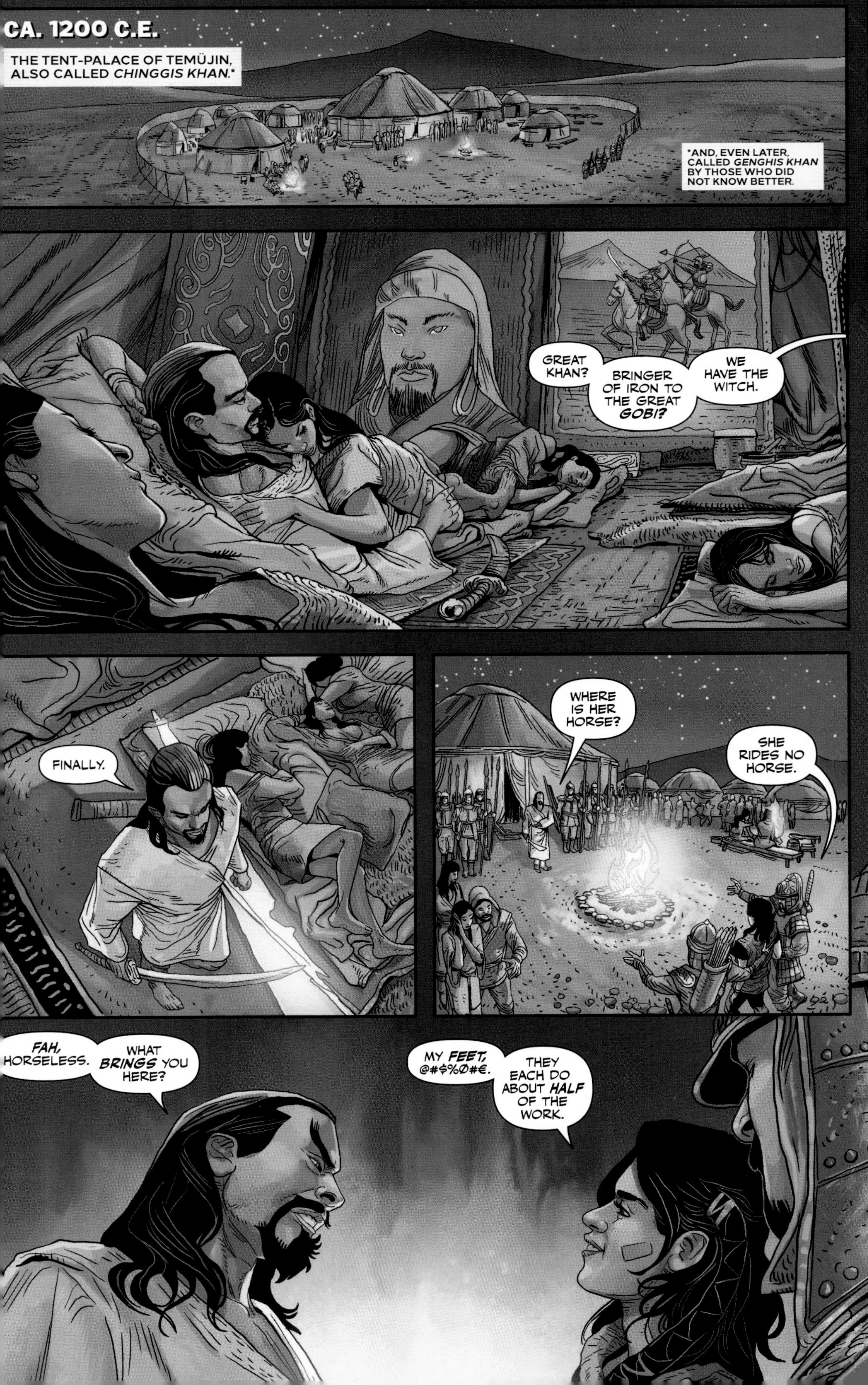
CA. 1200 C.E.
THE TENT-PALACE OF TEMÜJIN, ALSO CALLED *CHINGGIS KHAN.**
*AND, EVEN LATER, CALLED *GENGHIS KHAN* BY THOSE WHO DID NOT KNOW BETTER.
GREAT KHAN?
BRINGER OF IRON TO THE GREAT *GOBI?*
WE HAVE THE WITCH.
FINALLY.
WHERE IS HER HORSE?
SHE RIDES NO HORSE.
FAH, HORSELESS.
WHAT *BRINGS* YOU HERE?
MY *FEET,* @#$%Ø#€.
THEY EACH DO ABOUT *HALF* OF THE WORK.

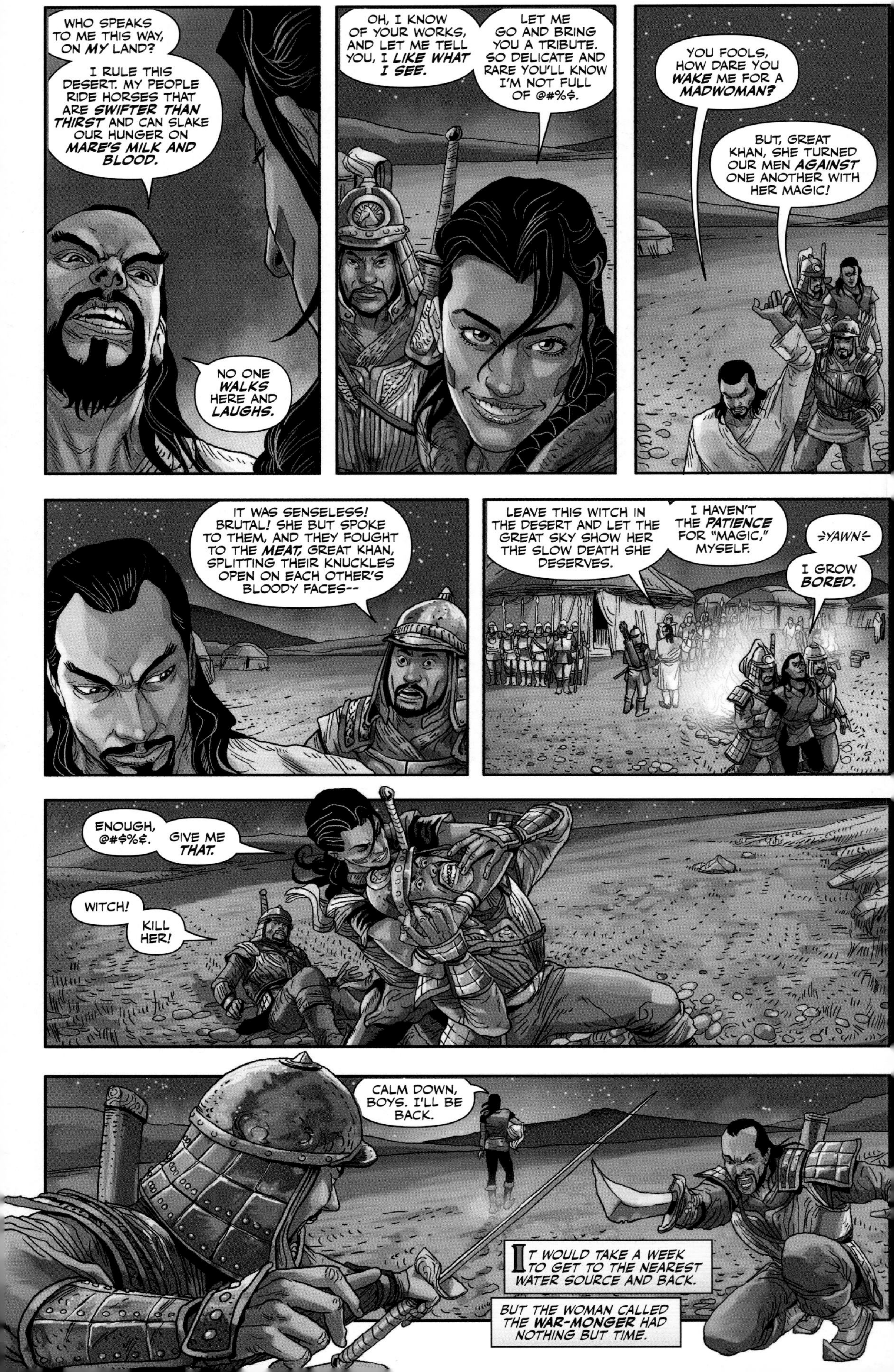
WHO SPEAKS TO ME THIS WAY, ON MY LAND?
I RULE THIS DESERT. MY PEOPLE RIDE HORSES THAT ARE SWIFTER THAN THIRST AND CAN SLAKE OUR HUNGER ON MARE'S MILK AND BLOOD.
NO ONE WALKS HERE AND LAUGHS.
OH, I KNOW OF YOUR WORKS, AND LET ME TELL YOU, I LIKE WHAT I SEE.
LET ME GO AND BRING YOU A TRIBUTE. SO DELICATE AND RARE YOU'LL KNOW I'M NOT FULL OF @#%$.
YOU FOOLS, HOW DARE YOU WAKE ME FOR A MADWOMAN?
BUT, GREAT KHAN, SHE TURNED OUR MEN AGAINST ONE ANOTHER WITH HER MAGIC!
IT WAS SENSELESS! BRUTAL! SHE BUT SPOKE TO THEM, AND THEY FOUGHT TO THE MEAT, GREAT KHAN, SPLITTING THEIR KNUCKLES OPEN ON EACH OTHER'S BLOODY FACES--
LEAVE THIS WITCH IN THE DESERT AND LET THE GREAT SKY SHOW HER THE SLOW DEATH SHE DESERVES.
I HAVEN'T THE PATIENCE FOR "MAGIC," MYSELF.
YAWN
I GROW BORED.
ENOUGH, @#$%¢.
GIVE ME THAT.
WITCH!
KILL HER!
CALM DOWN, BOYS. I'LL BE BACK.
IT WOULD TAKE A WEEK TO GET TO THE NEAREST WATER SOURCE AND BACK.
BUT THE WOMAN CALLED THE WAR-MONGER HAD NOTHING BUT TIME.

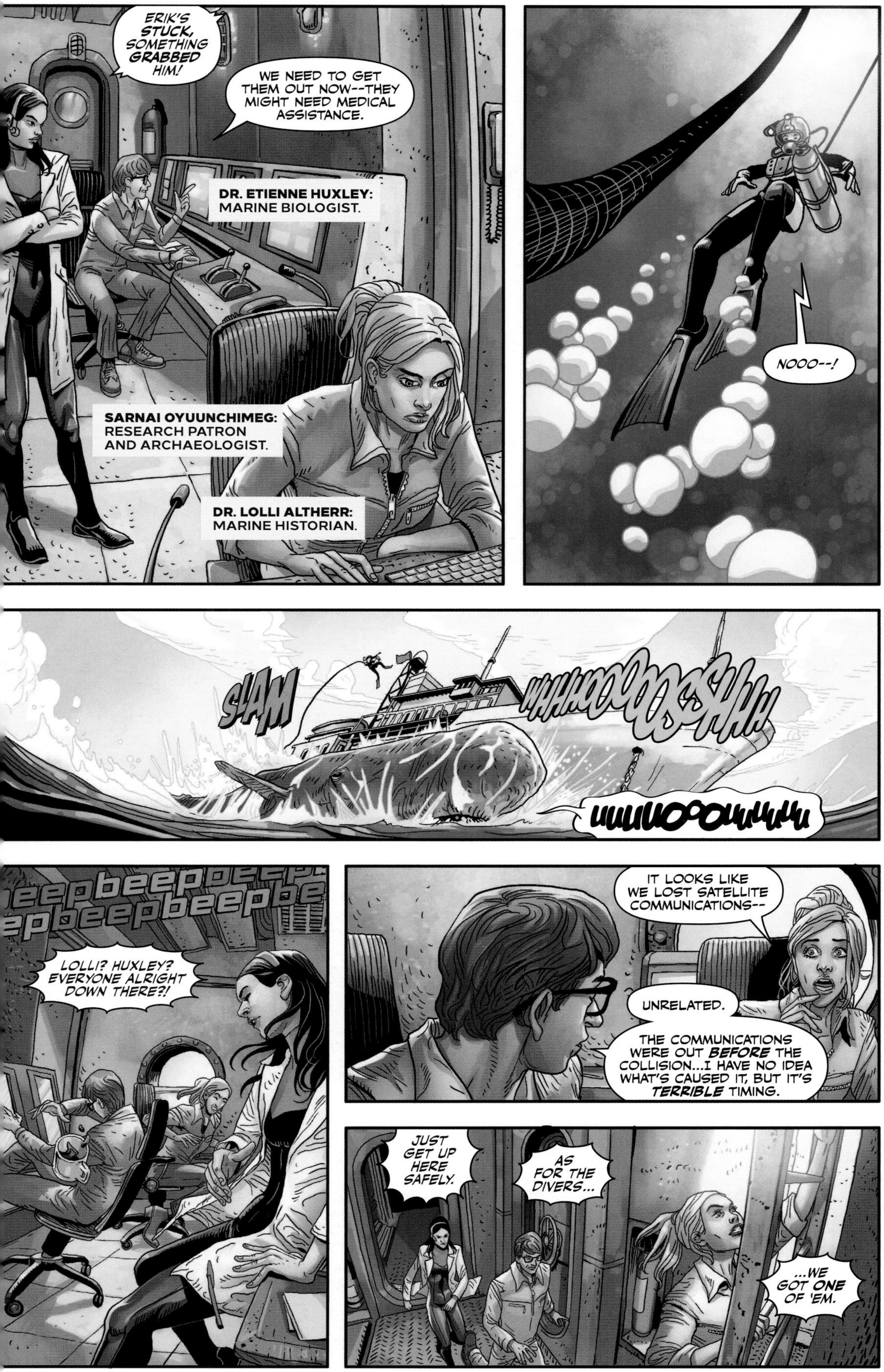
ERIK'S STUCK, SOMETHING GRABBED HIM!
WE NEED TO GET THEM OUT NOW--THEY MIGHT NEED MEDICAL ASSISTANCE.
DR. ETIENNE HUXLEY: MARINE BIOLOGIST.
SARNAI OYUUNCHIMEG: RESEARCH PATRON AND ARCHAEOLOGIST.
DR. LOLLI ALTHERR: MARINE HISTORIAN.
NOOO--!
SLAM
WHHHOOOOOOSHHH
UUUUUOOOUUUUUU
beepbeepbeepbeep
LOLLI? HUXLEY? EVERYONE ALRIGHT DOWN THERE?!
IT LOOKS LIKE WE LOST SATELLITE COMMUNICATIONS--
UNRELATED.
THE COMMUNICATIONS WERE OUT BEFORE THE COLLISION...I HAVE NO IDEA WHAT'S CAUSED IT, BUT IT'S TERRIBLE TIMING.
JUST GET UP HERE SAFELY.
AS FOR THE DIVERS...
...WE GOT ONE OF 'EM.

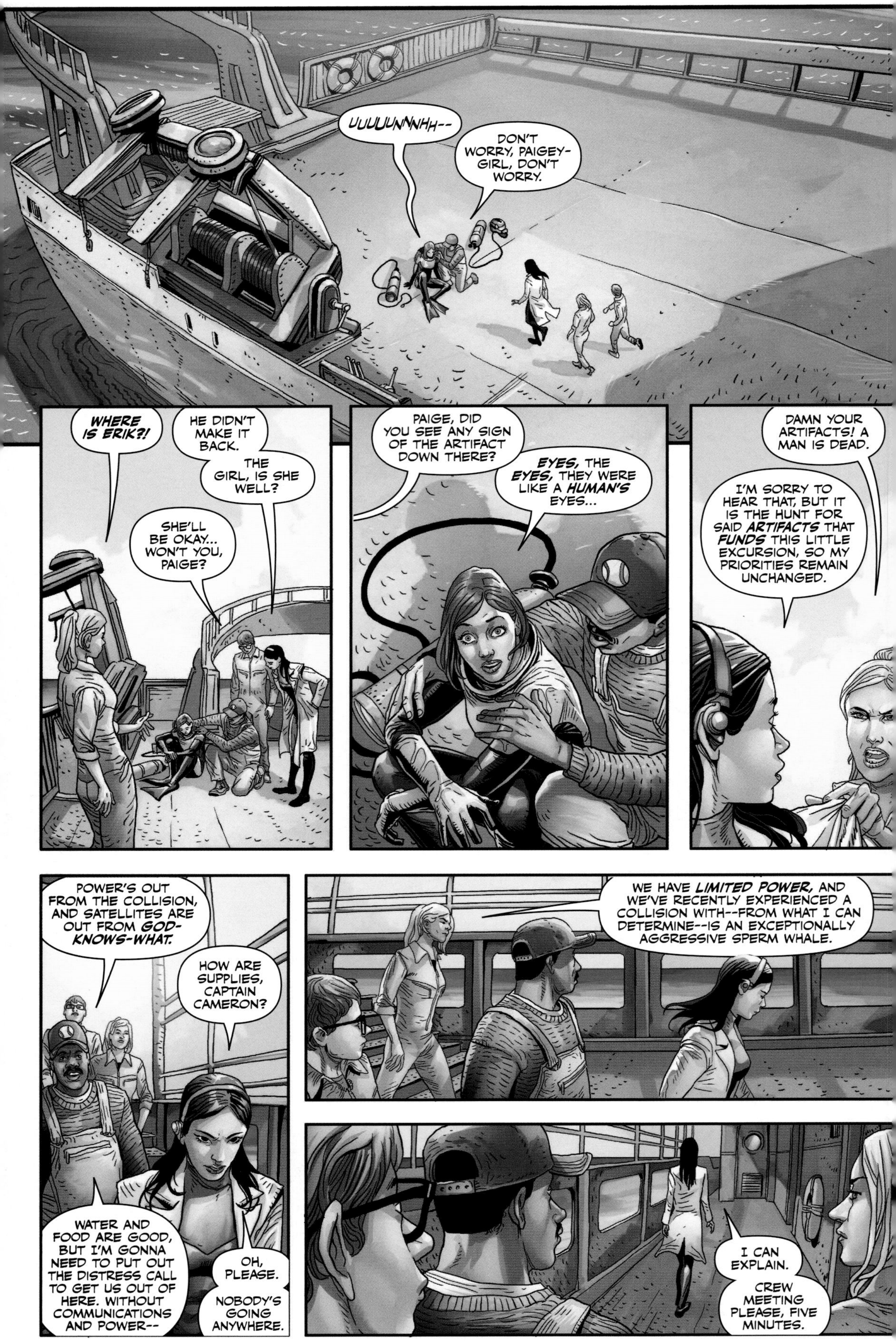
UUUUUNNHH--
DON'T WORRY, PAIGEY-GIRL, DON'T WORRY.
WHERE IS ERIK?!
HE DIDN'T MAKE IT BACK.
THE GIRL, IS SHE WELL?
SHE'LL BE OKAY... WON'T YOU, PAIGE?
PAIGE, DID YOU SEE ANY SIGN OF THE ARTIFACT DOWN THERE?
EYES, THE EYES, THEY WERE LIKE A HUMAN'S EYES...
DAMN YOUR ARTIFACTS! A MAN IS DEAD.
I'M SORRY TO HEAR THAT, BUT IT IS THE HUNT FOR SAID ARTIFACTS THAT FUNDS THIS LITTLE EXCURSION, SO MY PRIORITIES REMAIN UNCHANGED.
POWER'S OUT FROM THE COLLISION, AND SATELLITES ARE OUT FROM GOD-KNOWS-WHAT.
HOW ARE SUPPLIES, CAPTAIN CAMERON?
WATER AND FOOD ARE GOOD, BUT I'M GONNA NEED TO PUT OUT THE DISTRESS CALL TO GET US OUT OF HERE. WITHOUT COMMUNICATIONS AND POWER--
OH, PLEASE.
NOBODY'S GOING ANYWHERE.
WE HAVE LIMITED POWER, AND WE'VE RECENTLY EXPERIENCED A COLLISION WITH--FROM WHAT I CAN DETERMINE--IS AN EXCEPTIONALLY AGGRESSIVE SPERM WHALE.
I CAN EXPLAIN.
CREW MEETING PLEASE, FIVE MINUTES.

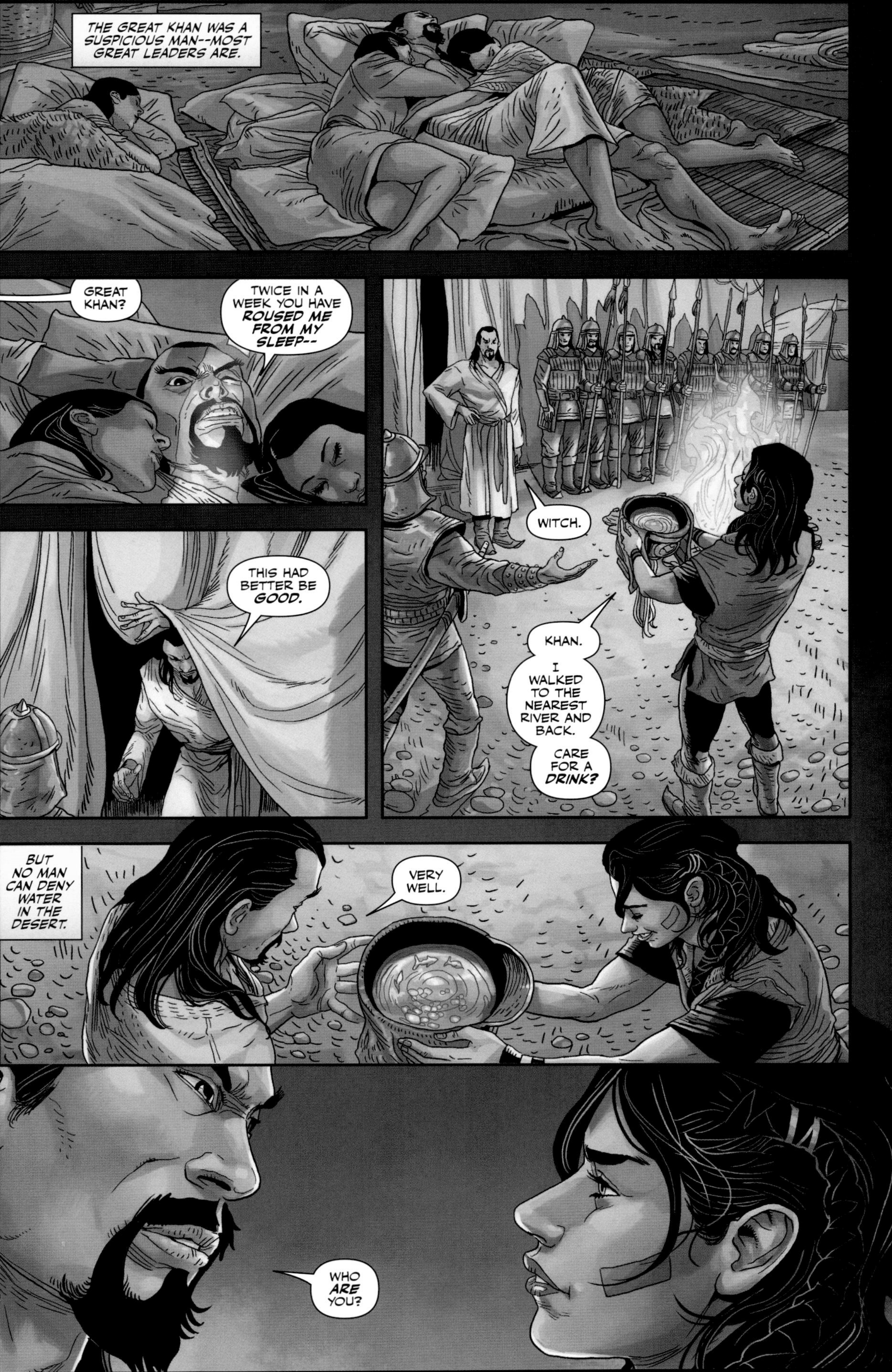
THE GREAT KHAN WAS A SUSPICIOUS MAN--MOST GREAT LEADERS ARE.
GREAT KHAN?
TWICE IN A WEEK YOU HAVE ROUSED ME FROM MY SLEEP--
THIS HAD BETTER BE GOOD.
WITCH.
KHAN.
I WALKED TO THE NEAREST RIVER AND BACK.
CARE FOR A DRINK?
BUT NO MAN CAN DENY WATER IN THE DESERT.
VERY WELL.
WHO ARE YOU?

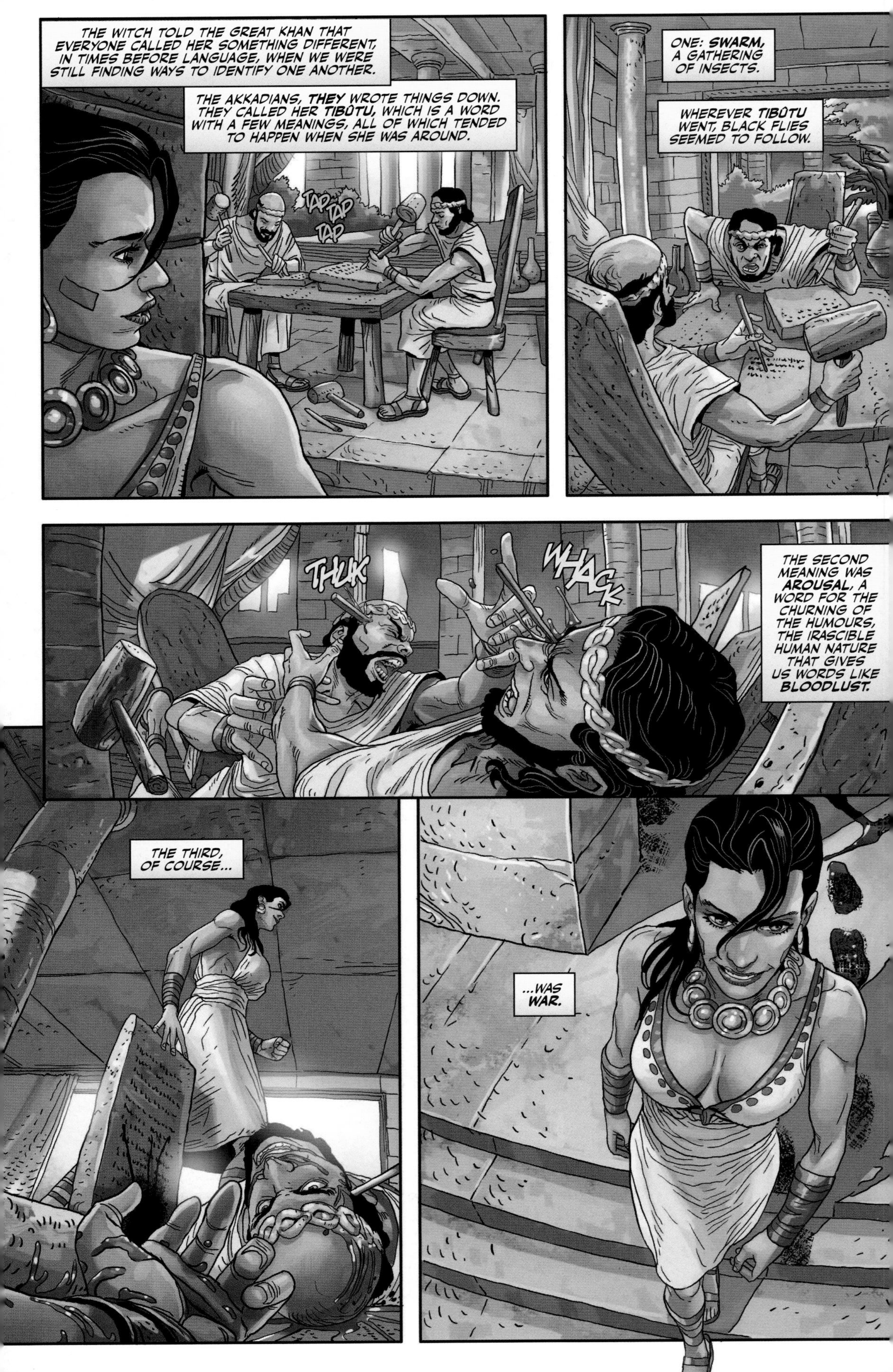
THE WITCH TOLD THE GREAT KHAN THAT EVERYONE CALLED HER SOMETHING DIFFERENT, IN TIMES BEFORE LANGUAGE, WHEN WE WERE STILL FINDING WAYS TO IDENTIFY ONE ANOTHER.
THE AKKADIANS, THEY WROTE THINGS DOWN. THEY CALLED HER TIBÛTU, WHICH IS A WORD WITH A FEW MEANINGS, ALL OF WHICH TENDED TO HAPPEN WHEN SHE WAS AROUND.
TAP TAP TAP
ONE: SWARM, A GATHERING OF INSECTS.
WHEREVER TIBÛTU WENT, BLACK FLIES SEEMED TO FOLLOW.
THUK
WHACK
THE SECOND MEANING WAS AROUSAL, A WORD FOR THE CHURNING OF THE HUMOURS, THE IRASCIBLE HUMAN NATURE THAT GIVES US WORDS LIKE BLOODLUST.
THE THIRD, OF COURSE...
...WAS WAR.

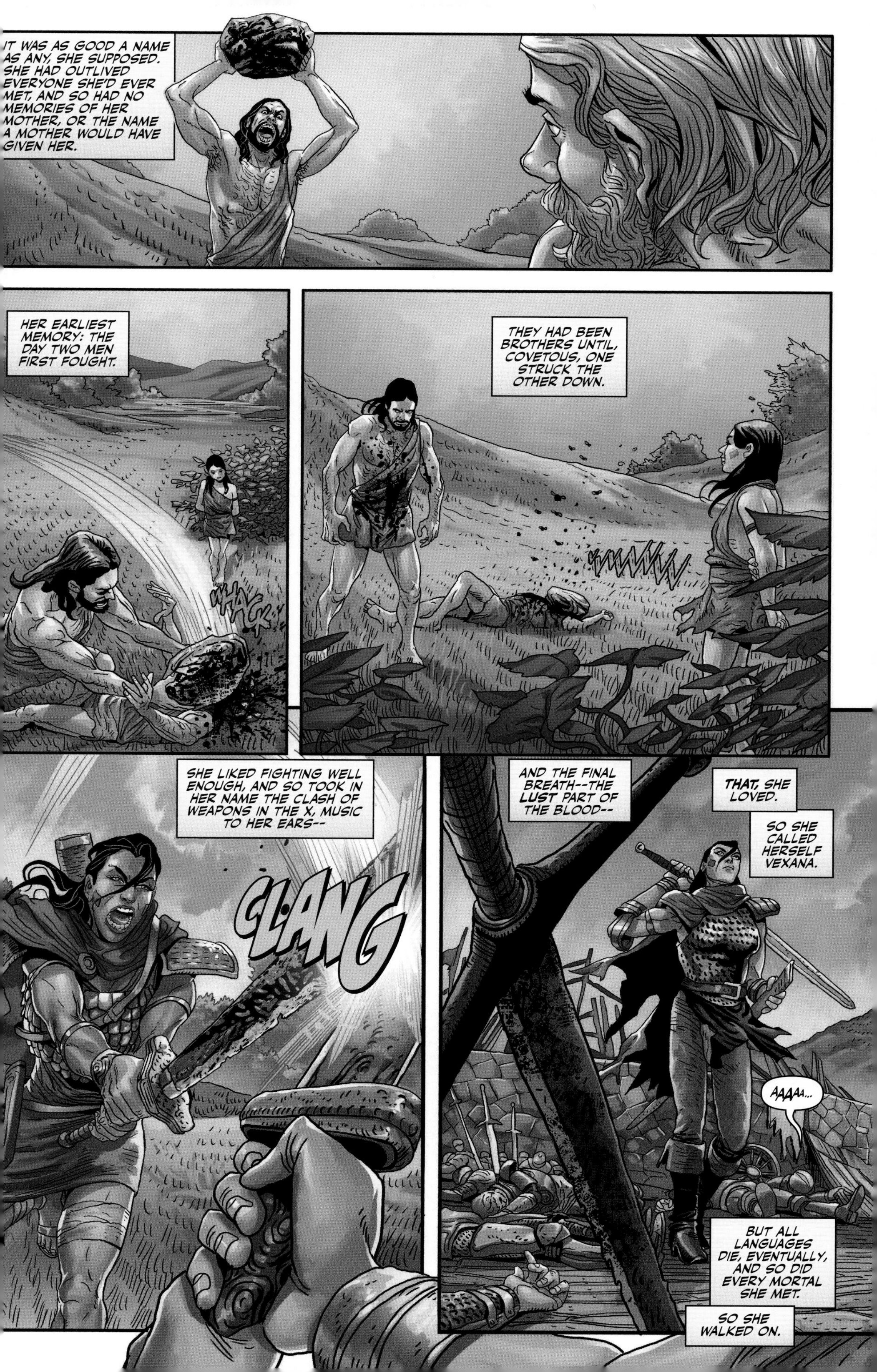
IT WAS AS GOOD A NAME AS ANY, SHE SUPPOSED. SHE HAD OUTLIVED EVERYONE SHE'D EVER MET, AND SO HAD NO MEMORIES OF HER MOTHER, OR THE NAME A MOTHER WOULD HAVE GIVEN HER.
HER EARLIEST MEMORY: THE DAY TWO MEN FIRST FOUGHT.
WHACK
THEY HAD BEEN BROTHERS UNTIL, COVETOUS, ONE STRUCK THE OTHER DOWN.
SHE LIKED FIGHTING WELL ENOUGH, AND SO TOOK IN HER NAME THE CLASH OF WEAPONS IN THE X, MUSIC TO HER EARS--
CLANG
AND THE FINAL BREATH--THE LUST PART OF THE BLOOD--
THAT, SHE LOVED.
SO SHE CALLED HERSELF VEXANA.
AAAAA...
BUT ALL LANGUAGES DIE, EVENTUALLY, AND SO DID EVERY MORTAL SHE MET.
SO SHE WALKED ON.

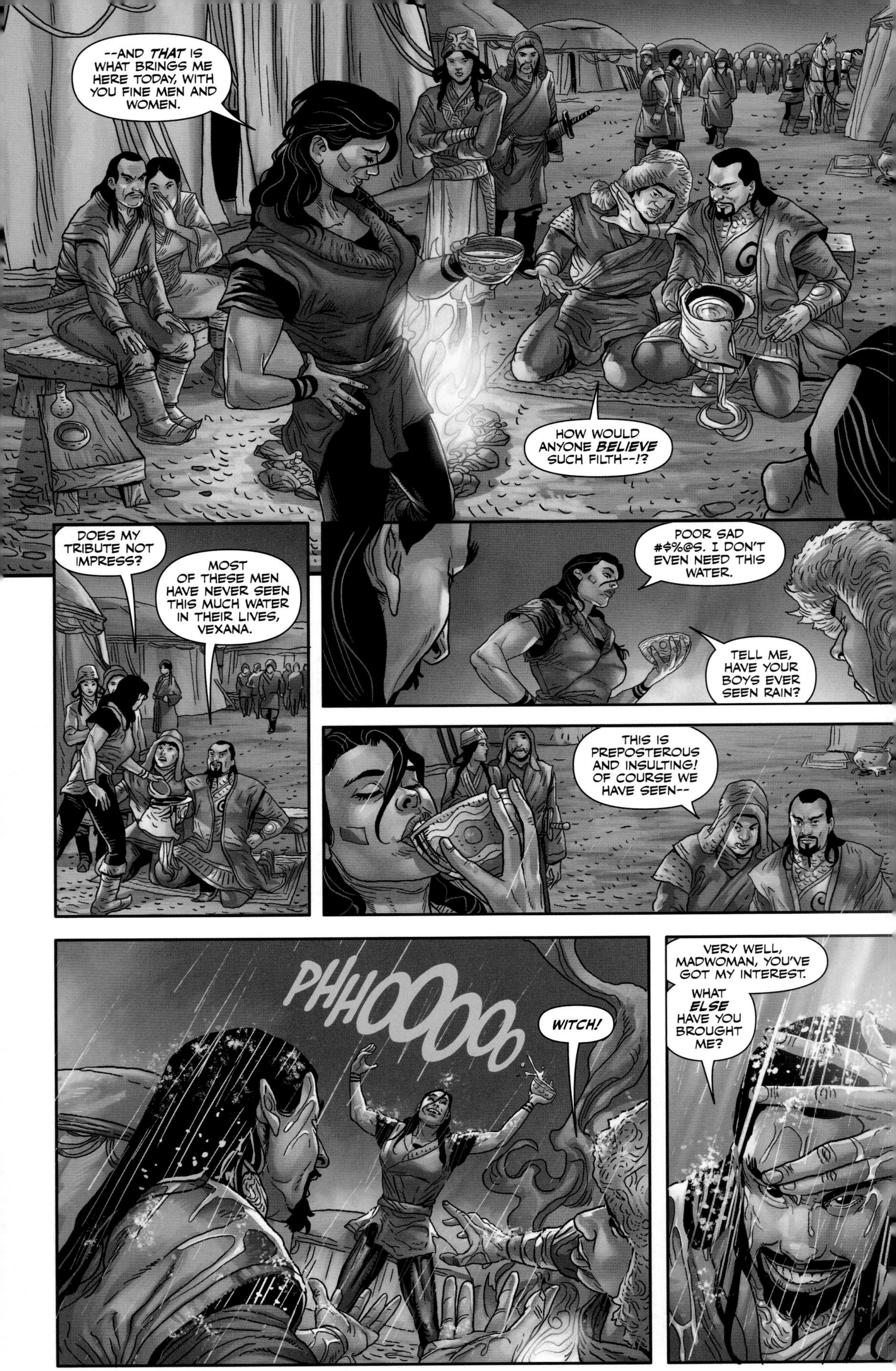
--AND THAT IS WHAT BRINGS ME HERE TODAY, WITH YOU FINE MEN AND WOMEN.
HOW WOULD ANYONE BELIEVE SUCH FILTH--!?
DOES MY TRIBUTE NOT IMPRESS?
MOST OF THESE MEN HAVE NEVER SEEN THIS MUCH WATER IN THEIR LIVES, VEXANA.
POOR SAD #$%@S. I DON'T EVEN NEED THIS WATER.
TELL ME, HAVE YOUR BOYS EVER SEEN RAIN?
THIS IS PREPOSTEROUS AND INSULTING! OF COURSE WE HAVE SEEN--
PHHOOOOO
WITCH!
VERY WELL, MADWOMAN, YOU'VE GOT MY INTEREST.
WHAT ELSE HAVE YOU BROUGHT ME?

FORGIVE ME, MA'AM, I'M JUST THE CAPTAIN, NOT A SCIENTIST LIKE Y'ALL, BUT ISN'T LOOKING FOR STUFF THAT CAME FROM THE *DESERT* IN THE *OCEAN* AWFULLY DUMB?

AN EXCELLENT QUESTION. CLASSIFIED INTELLIGENCE SUGGESTS THAT OUR ARTIFACTS, DESPITE THEIR ORIGIN IN THE GOBI DESERT, ARE RELATED TO THE RECENT REPORTS OF AGGRESSIVE SEALIFE.

WE'VE RETRIEVED THE HELMET AND BREASTPLATE, BUT THE BRACERS ARE SMALL AND REMAIN ELUSIVE.

ANY OTHER QUESTIONS?

YEAH, WHO EVEN *ARE* YOU AGAIN?

SARNAI OYUUNCHIMEG.

MY *ORGANIZATION* SPONSORS RESEARCH GRANTS SUCH AS THE ONE THAT FUNDS *THIS VESSEL,* IN EXCHANGE FOR THE ABILITY TO MAKE ARTIFACT DIVES PART OF YOUR ITINERARY.

OH. YOU'RE *PIRATES.*

HARDLY!

I AM NOT A PIRATE. I AM A *PRESERVATIONIST.*

THESE ARMOR PIECES ARE FROM THE ERA OF *TEMÜJIN,* HOW YOU ALL SAY, "GENGHIS KHAN," HIS DAUGHTERS AND GRANDDAUGHTERS. WHERE I AM FROM, WE *PROTECT* THAT LEGACY. AND ALL ITS MANY MYSTERIES.

WE'VE ACQUIRED THE HELMET AND THE BREASTPLATE. RECORDS INDICATE THE FINAL PIECE, THE BRACERS, ARE NEARBY.

WITH PAIGE UNWELL, AND OUR POOR ERIK DECEASED, I'M GOING TO NEED TO GO OUT AND DIVE FOR THE ITEMS MYSELF.

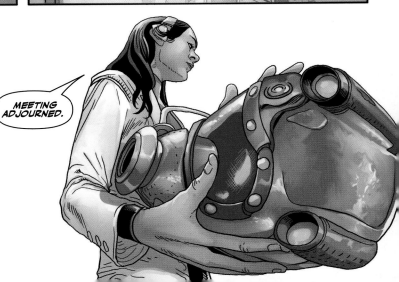

MEETING ADJOURNED.

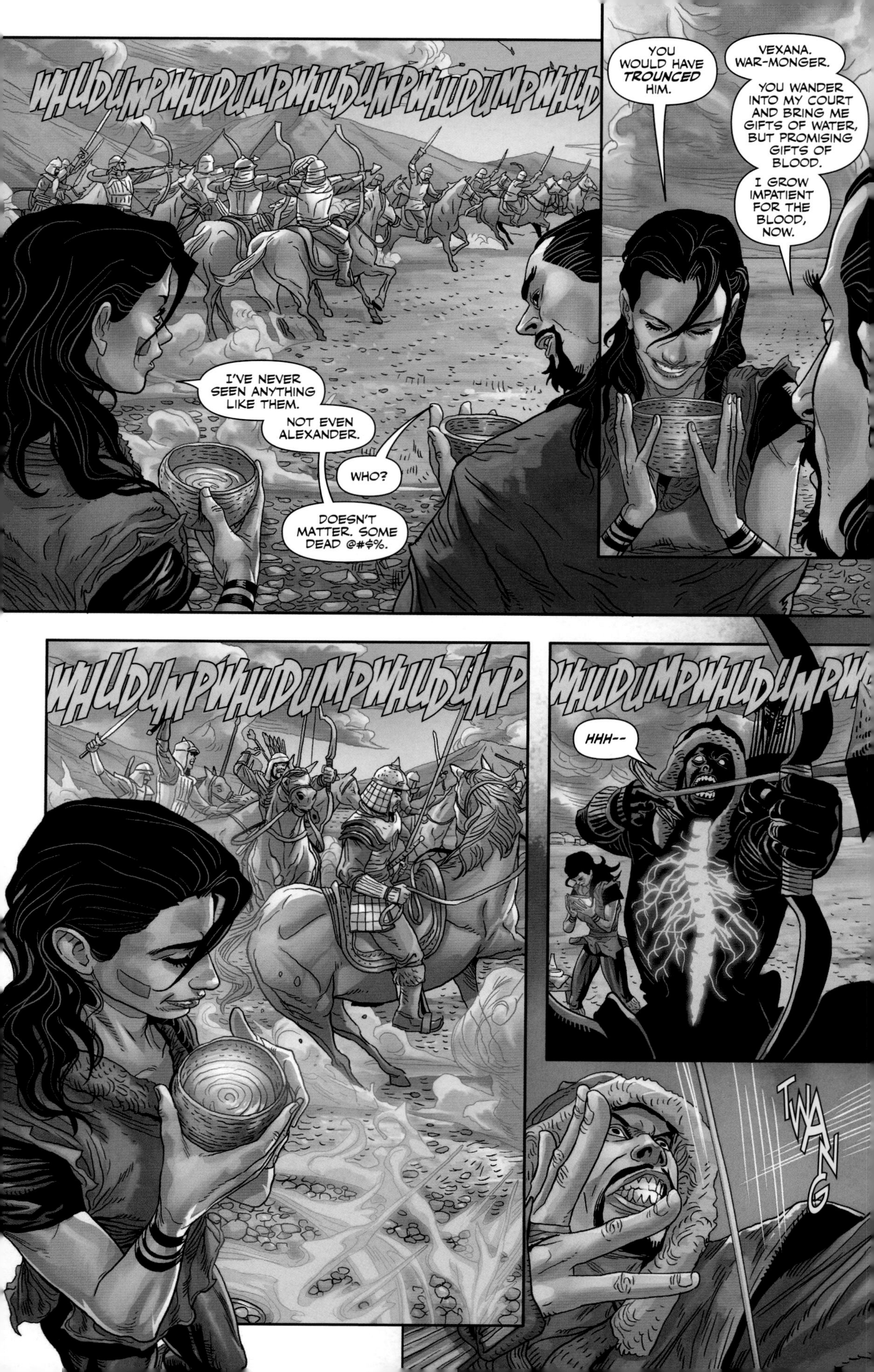
WHUDUMPWHUDUMPWHUDUMPWHUDUMPWHUD
I'VE NEVER SEEN ANYTHING LIKE THEM.
NOT EVEN ALEXANDER.
WHO?
DOESN'T MATTER. SOME DEAD @#$%.
YOU WOULD HAVE *TROUNCED* HIM.
VEXANA. WAR-MONGER.
YOU WANDER INTO MY COURT AND BRING ME GIFTS OF WATER, BUT PROMISING GIFTS OF BLOOD.
I GROW IMPATIENT FOR THE BLOOD, NOW.
WHUDUMPWHUDUMPWHUDUMP
WHUDUMPWHUDUMPWHUDUMPW
HHH--
TWANG

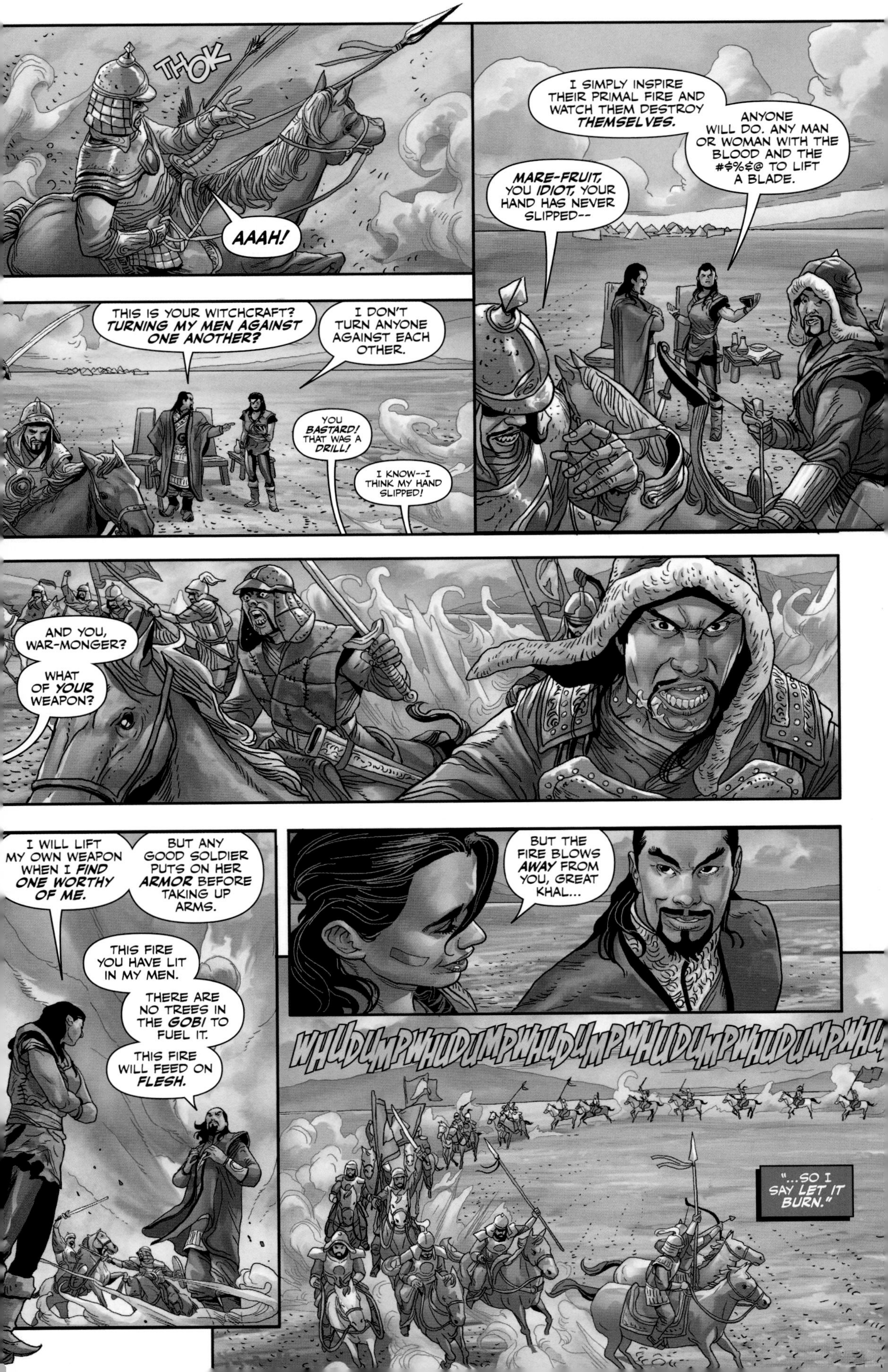
THOK
AAAH!
THIS IS YOUR WITCHCRAFT? TURNING MY MEN AGAINST ONE ANOTHER?
I DON'T TURN ANYONE AGAINST EACH OTHER.
YOU BASTARD! THAT WAS A DRILL!
I KNOW--I THINK MY HAND SLIPPED!
I SIMPLY INSPIRE THEIR PRIMAL FIRE AND WATCH THEM DESTROY THEMSELVES.
ANYONE WILL DO. ANY MAN OR WOMAN WITH THE BLOOD AND THE #$%&@ TO LIFT A BLADE.
MARE-FRUIT, YOU IDIOT, YOUR HAND HAS NEVER SLIPPED--
AND YOU, WAR-MONGER?
WHAT OF YOUR WEAPON?
I WILL LIFT MY OWN WEAPON WHEN I FIND ONE WORTHY OF ME.
BUT ANY GOOD SOLDIER PUTS ON HER ARMOR BEFORE TAKING UP ARMS.
THIS FIRE YOU HAVE LIT IN MY MEN.
THERE ARE NO TREES IN THE GOBI TO FUEL IT.
THIS FIRE WILL FEED ON FLESH.
BUT THE FIRE BLOWS AWAY FROM YOU, GREAT KHAL...
WHUDUMPWHUDUMPWHUDUMPWHUDUMPWHUDUMPWHU
"...SO I SAY LET IT BURN."

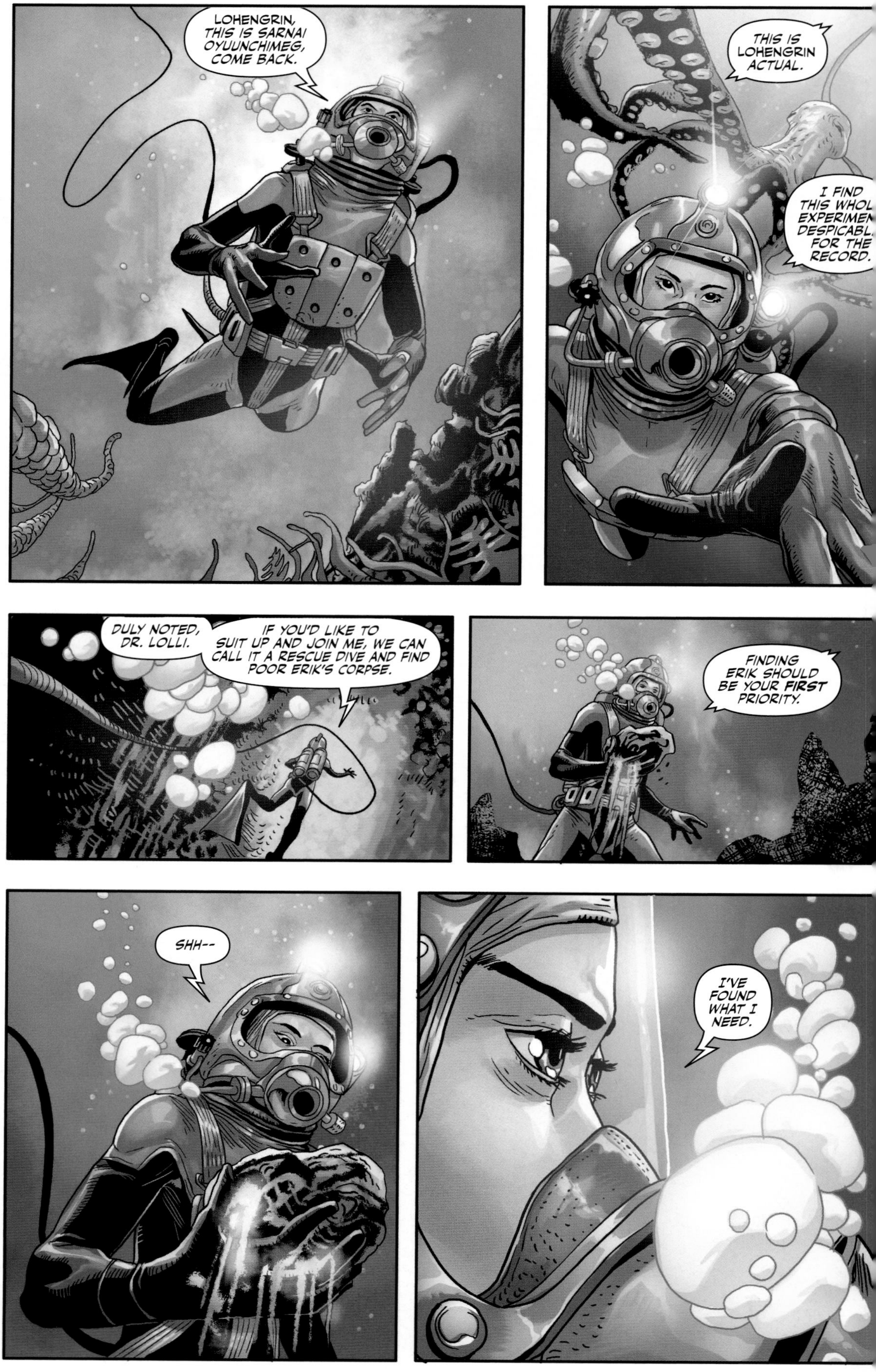
LOHENGRIN, THIS IS SARNAI OYUUNCHIMEG, COME BACK.
THIS IS LOHENGRIN ACTUAL.
I FIND THIS WHOL EXPERIMEN DESPICABL. FOR THE RECORD.
DULY NOTED, DR. LOLLI.
IF YOU'D LIKE TO SUIT UP AND JOIN ME, WE CAN CALL IT A RESCUE DIVE AND FIND POOR ERIK'S CORPSE.
FINDING ERIK SHOULD BE YOUR **FIRST** PRIORITY.
SHH--
I'VE FOUND WHAT I NEED.

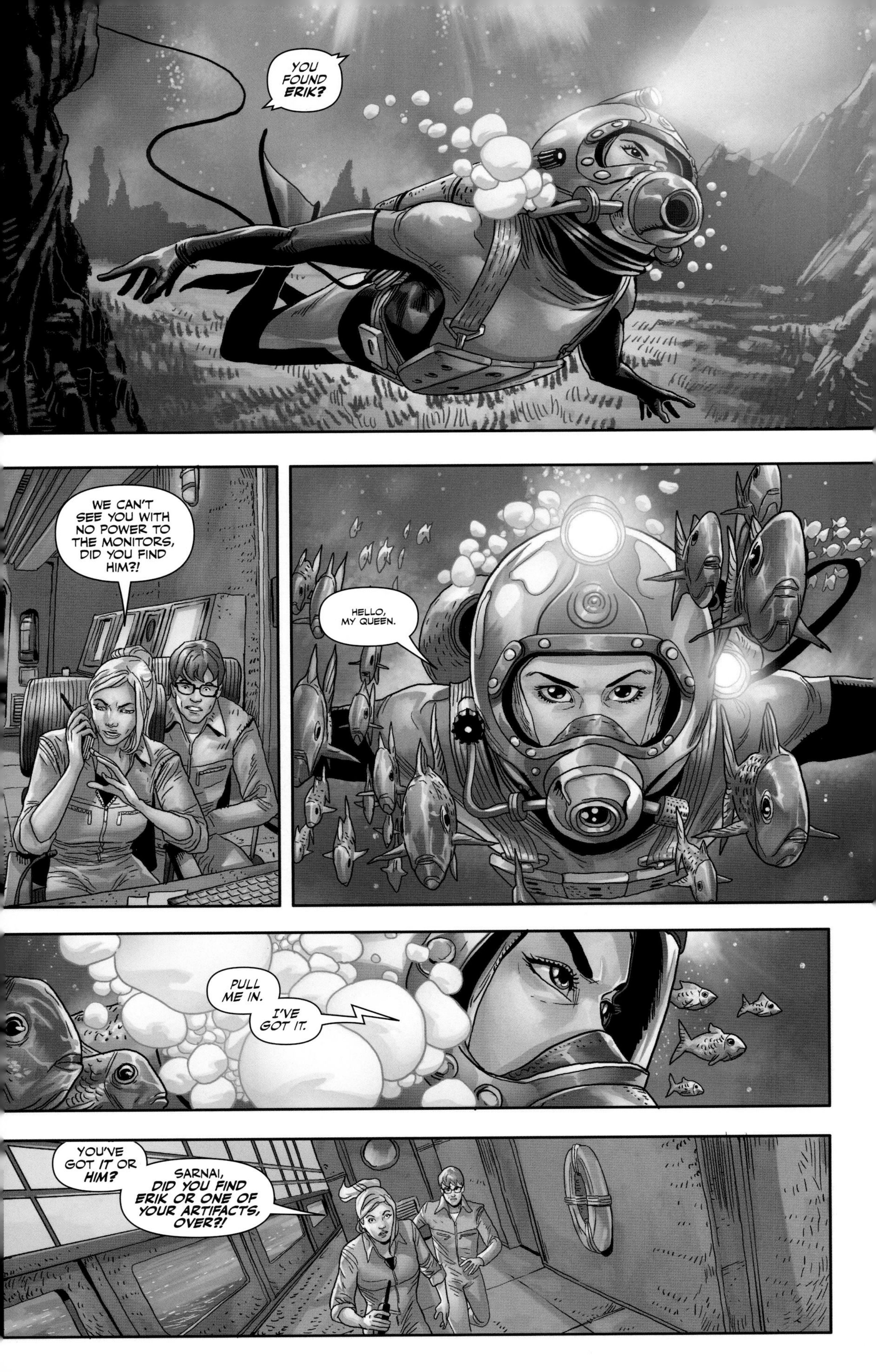
YOU FOUND ERIK?
WE CAN'T SEE YOU WITH NO POWER TO THE MONITORS, DID YOU FIND HIM?!
HELLO, MY QUEEN.
PULL ME IN.
I'VE GOT IT.
YOU'VE GOT IT OR HIM?
SARNAI, DID YOU FIND ERIK OR ONE OF YOUR ARTIFACTS, OVER?!

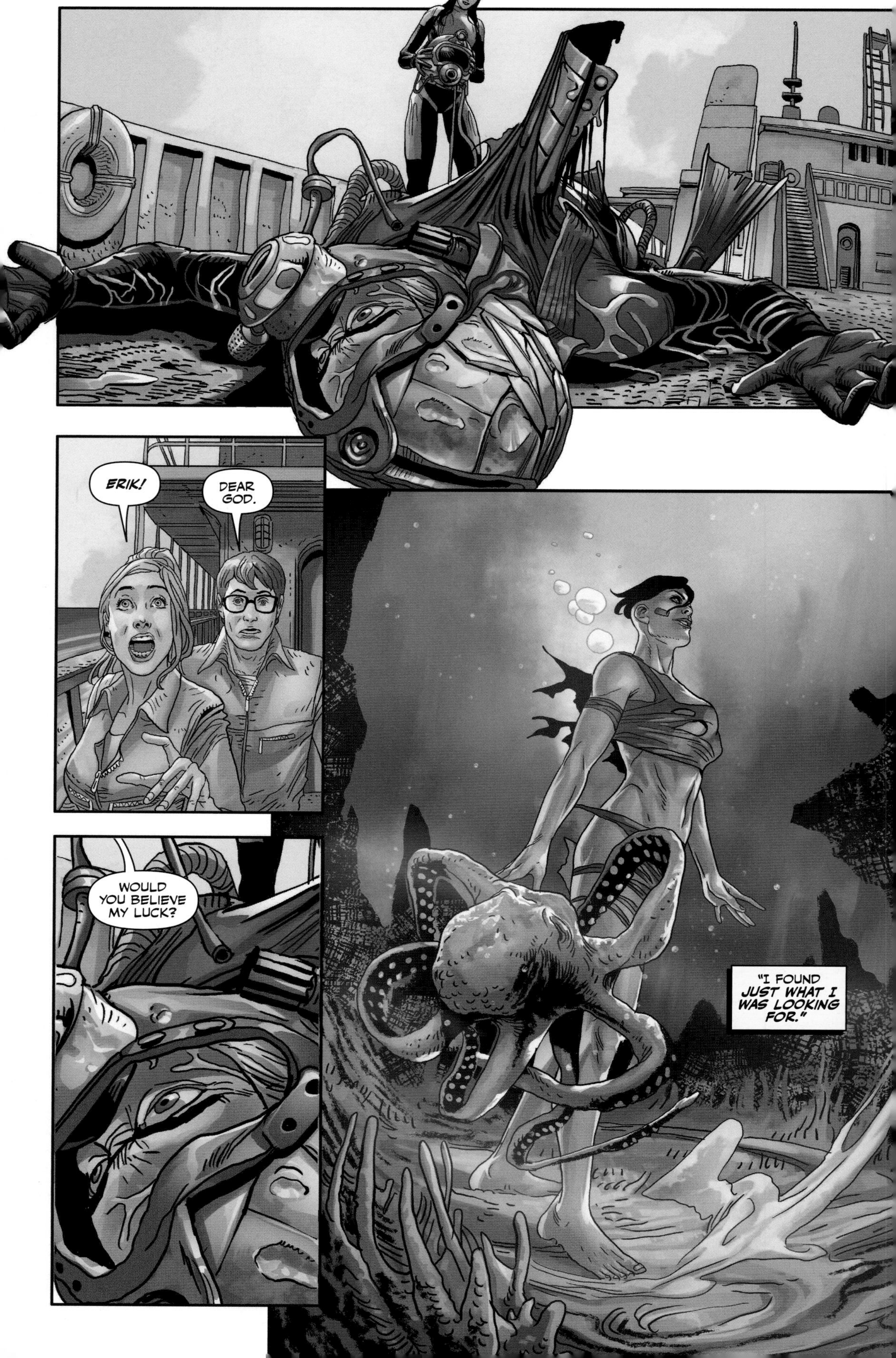
ERIK!
DEAR GOD.
WOULD YOU BELIEVE MY LUCK?
"I FOUND JUST WHAT I WAS LOOKING FOR."

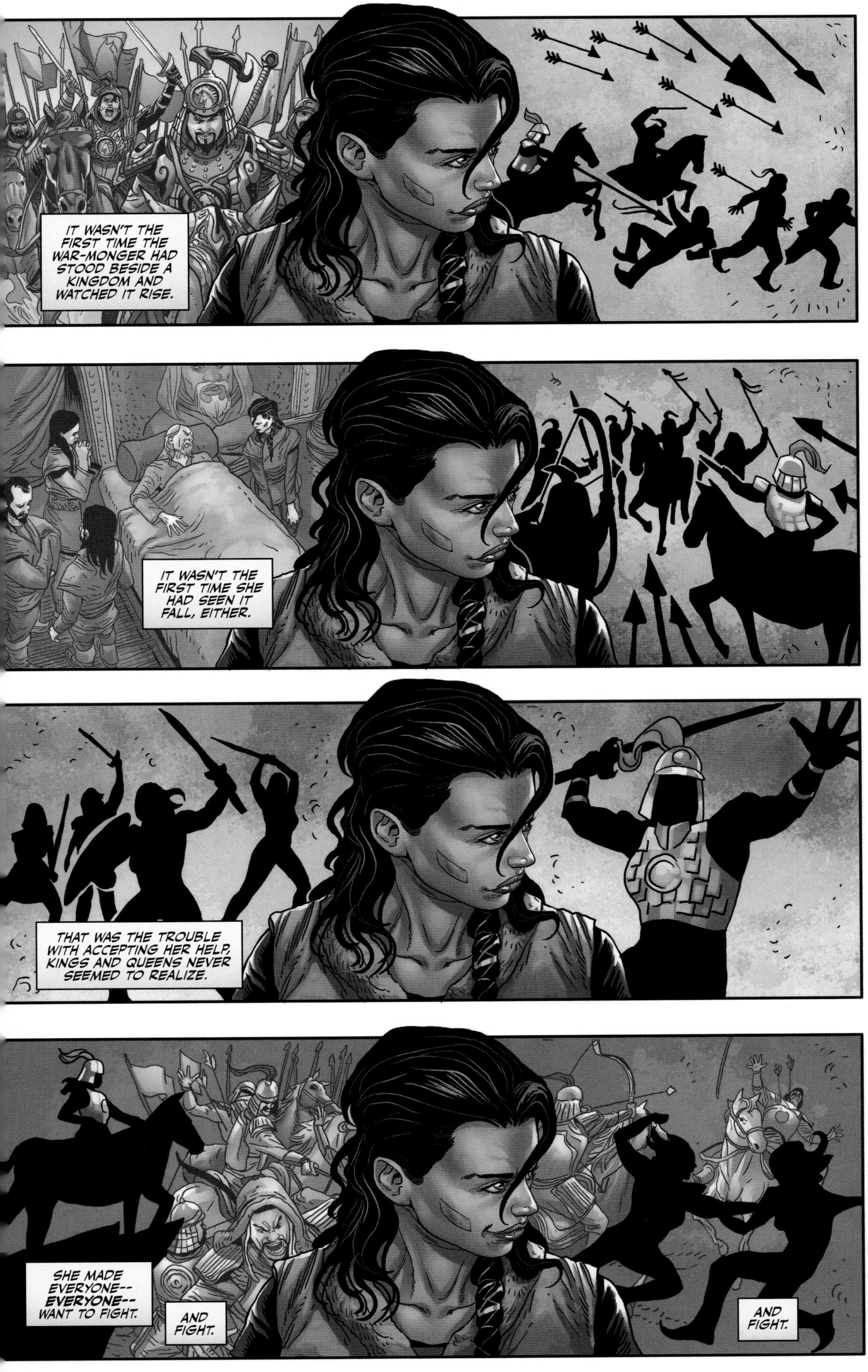
IT WASN'T THE FIRST TIME THE WAR-MONGER HAD STOOD BESIDE A KINGDOM AND WATCHED IT RISE.
IT WASN'T THE FIRST TIME SHE HAD SEEN IT FALL, EITHER.
THAT WAS THE TROUBLE WITH ACCEPTING HER HELP, KINGS AND QUEENS NEVER SEEMED TO REALIZE.
SHE MADE EVERYONE-- **EVERYONE--** WANT TO FIGHT.
AND FIGHT.
AND FIGHT.

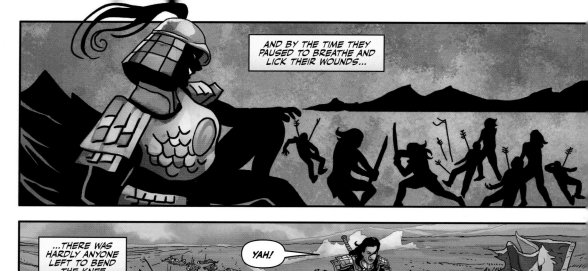

AND BY THE TIME THEY PAUSED TO BREATHE AND LICK THEIR WOUNDS...

...THERE WAS HARDLY ANYONE LEFT TO BEND THE KNEE.

YAH!

NOT A HUNDRED YEARS AGO, THE GREAT KHAN HAD OWNED EVERY INCH OF THIS DESERT, THE LARGEST EMPIRE **SHE'D** CERTAINLY SEEN WITH HER OWN EYES.

AND IT WAS BY HER HAND, BY HER STRANGE RED MAGIC THAT MADE MORTALS SWEAT AND WARPED THE VERY AIR AROUND HER, LIKE HEAT COMING OFF ARMORED BODIES, ROTTING IN THE SUN.

IT WAS THE FIRST TIME SHE HAD JOINED FORCES, APPLIED HER CHAOS TO AN ALREADY-RAGING BATTLE, AND SHE THOUGHT OFTEN OF HOW MUCH MORE FUN IT COULD BE...

IF ONLY HER SOLDIERS WOULD QUIT DYING SO EASILY.

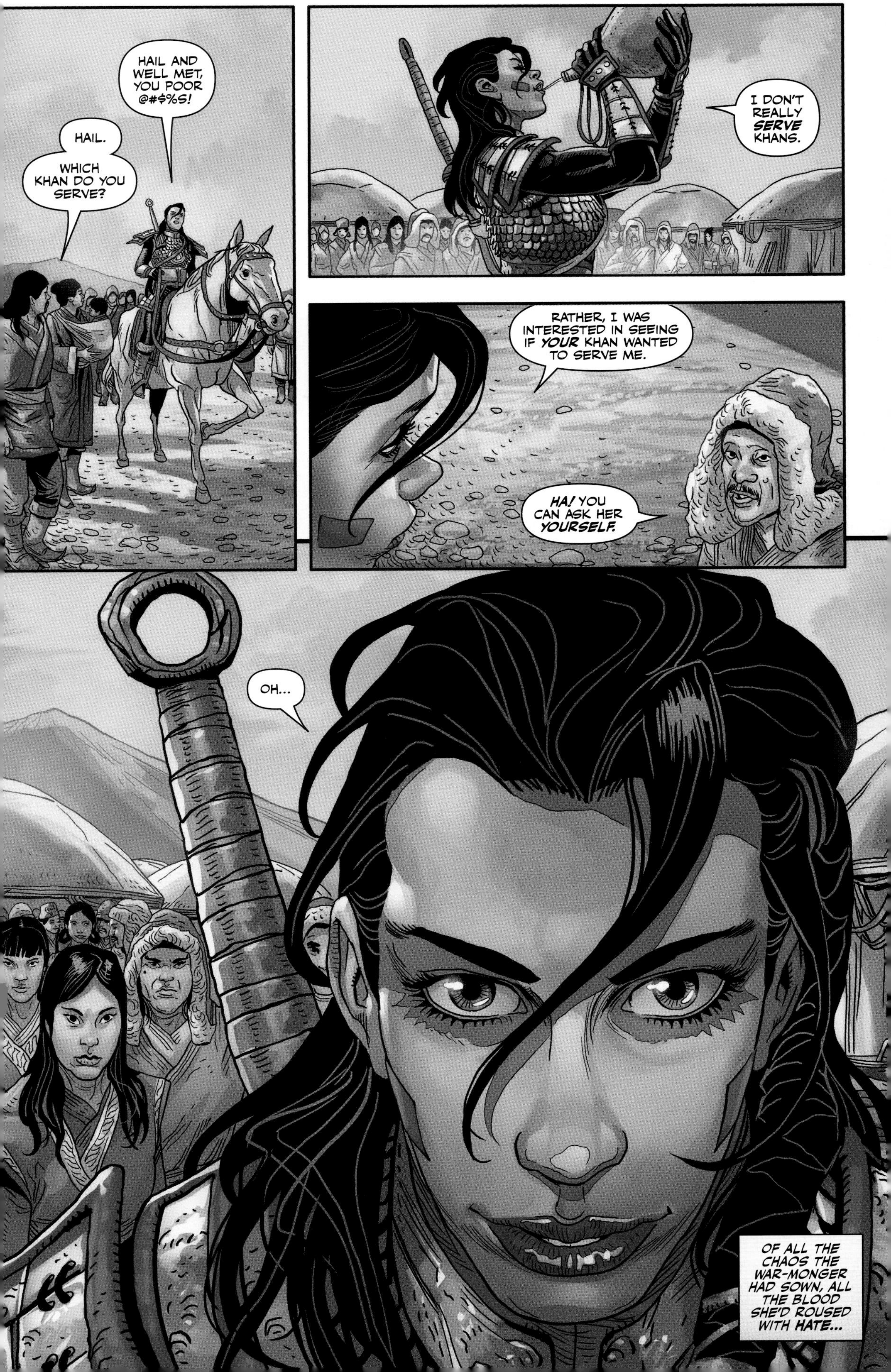

HAIL AND WELL MET, YOU POOR @#$%S!
HAIL.
WHICH KHAN DO YOU SERVE?
I DON'T REALLY *SERVE* KHANS.
RATHER, I WAS INTERESTED IN SEEING IF *YOUR* KHAN WANTED TO SERVE ME.
HA! YOU CAN ASK HER *YOURSELF.*
OH...
OF ALL THE CHAOS THE WAR-MONGER HAD SOWN, ALL THE BLOOD SHE'D ROUSED WITH **HATE...**

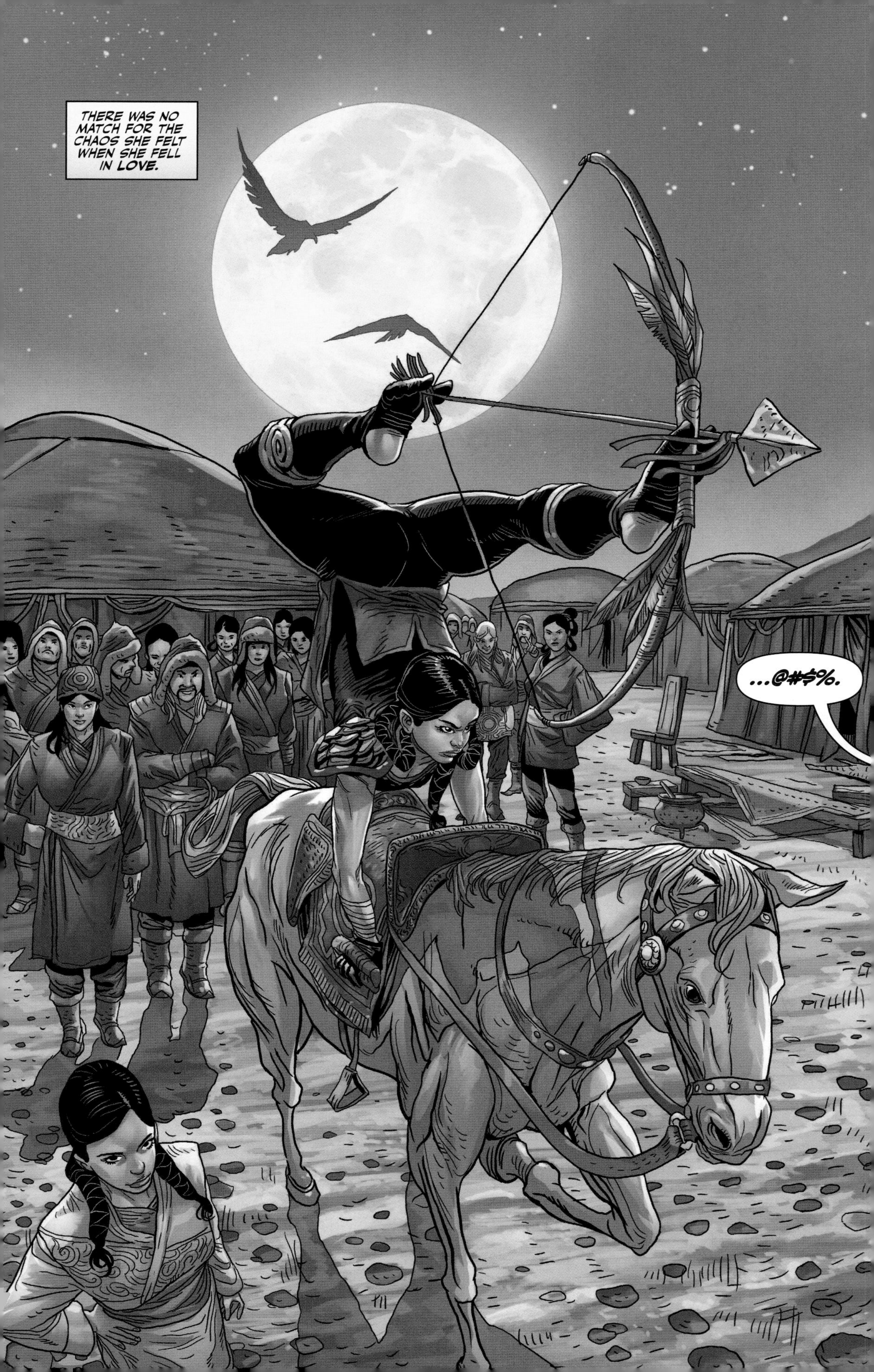
THERE WAS NO MATCH FOR THE CHAOS SHE FELT WHEN SHE FELL IN LOVE.
...@#$%.

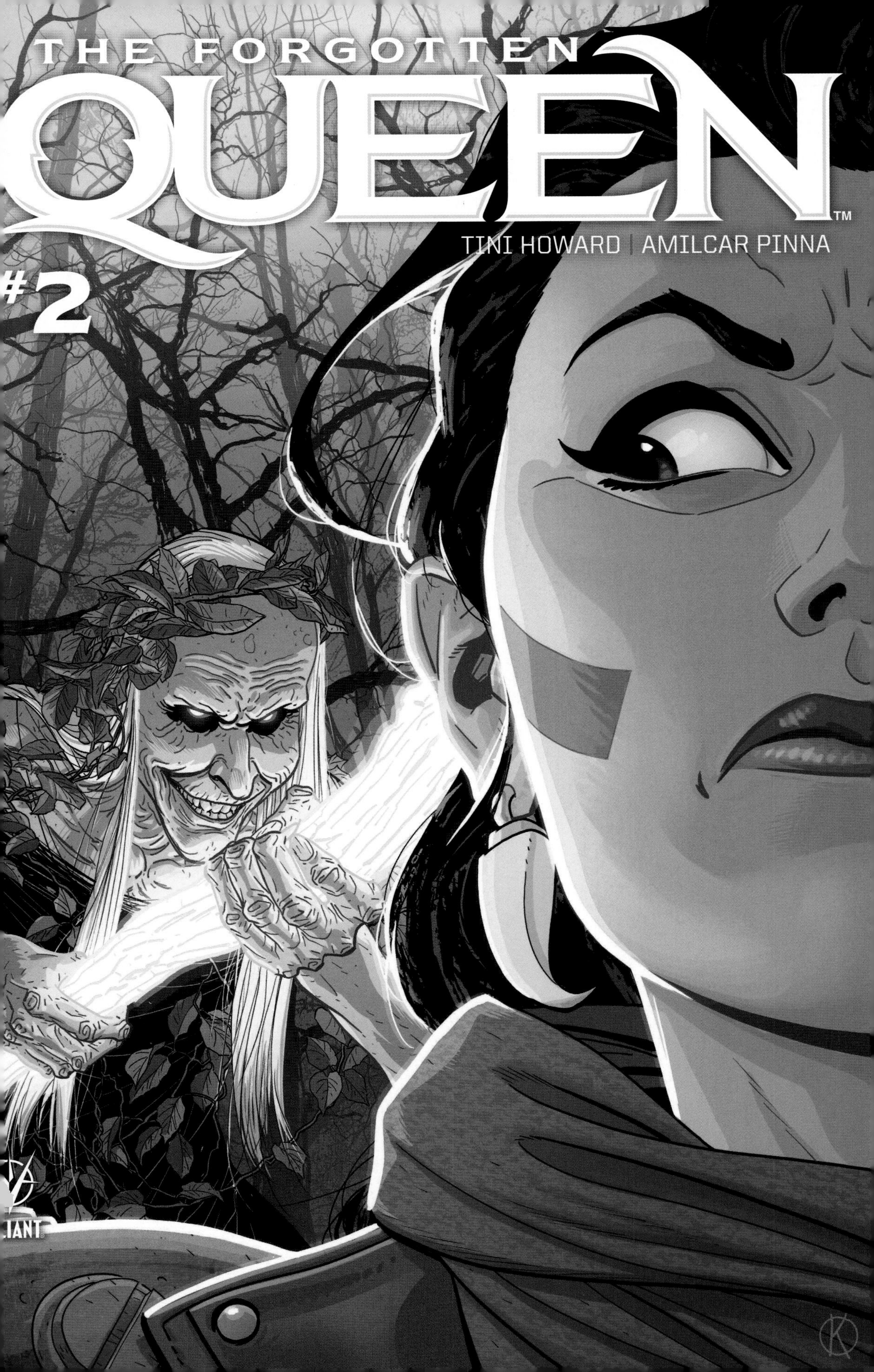
THE FORGOTTEN
QUEEN™
TINI HOWARD | AMILCAR PINNA
#2

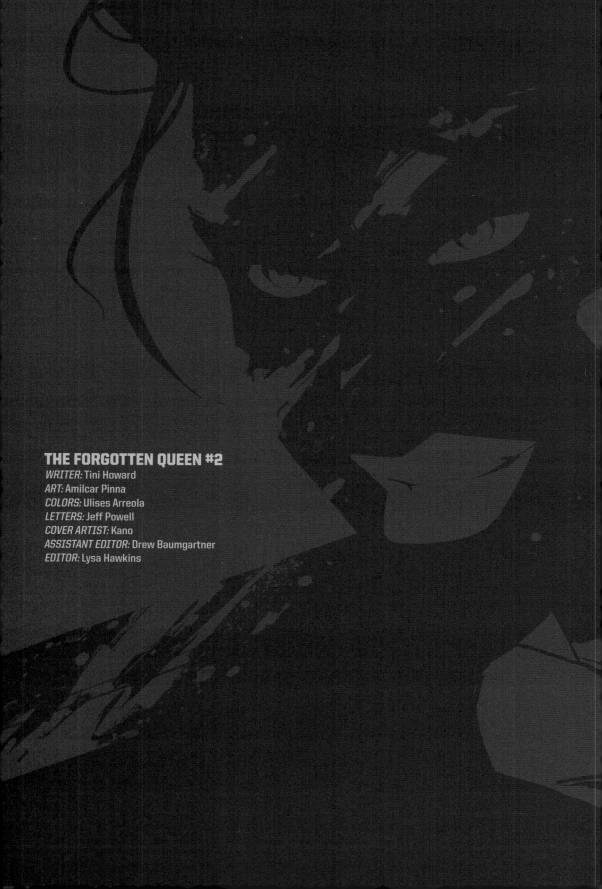

THE FORGOTTEN QUEEN #2

WRITER: Tini Howard
ART: Amilcar Pinna
COLORS: Ulises Arreola
LETTERS: Jeff Powell
COVER ARTIST: Kano
ASSISTANT EDITOR: Drew Baumgartner
EDITOR: Lysa Hawkins

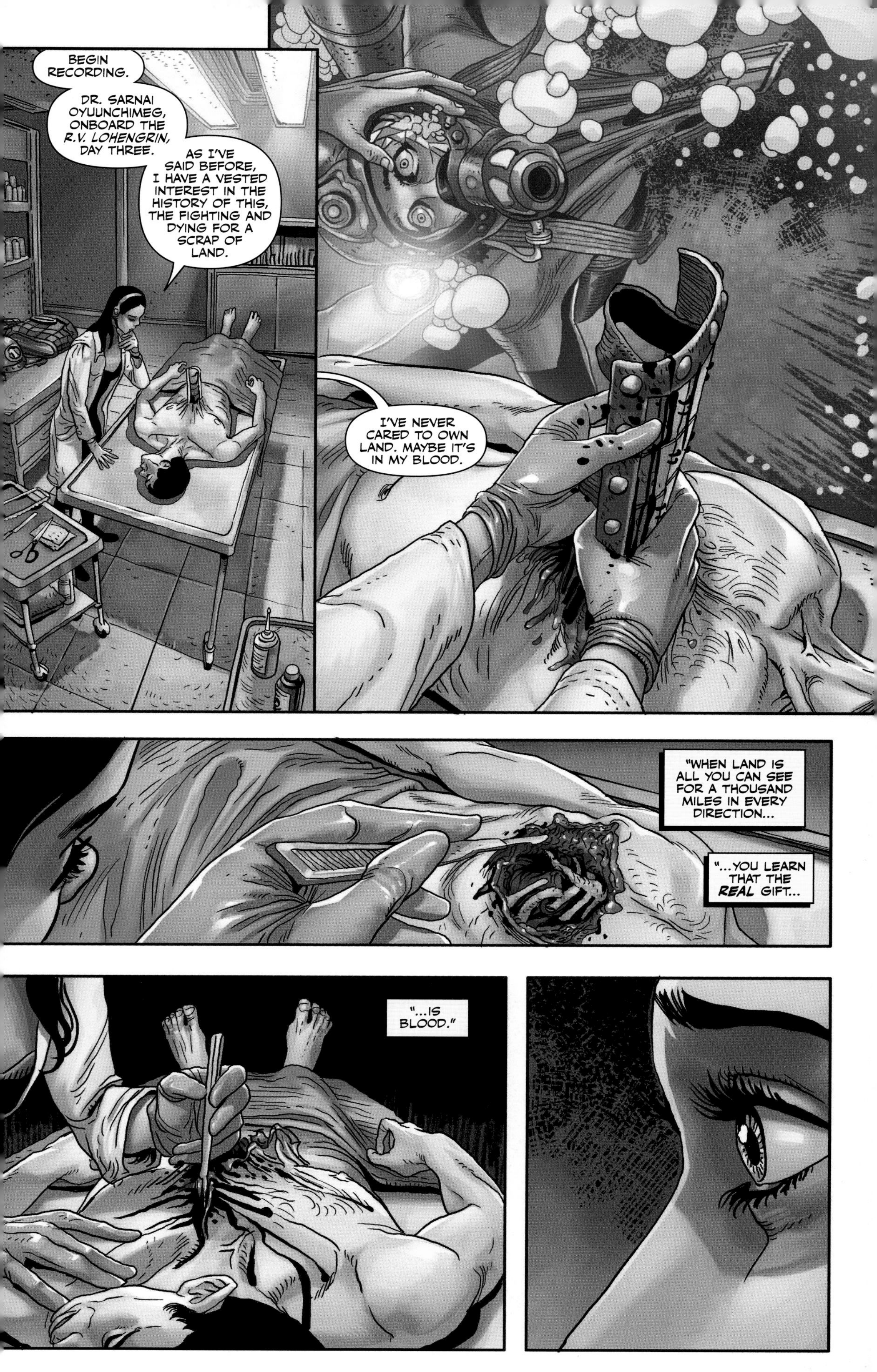
BEGIN RECORDING.
DR. SARNAI OYUUNCHIMEG, ONBOARD THE *R.V. LOHENGRIN,* DAY THREE.
AS I'VE SAID BEFORE, I HAVE A VESTED INTEREST IN THE HISTORY OF THIS, THE FIGHTING AND DYING FOR A SCRAP OF LAND.
I'VE NEVER CARED TO OWN LAND. MAYBE IT'S IN MY BLOOD.
"WHEN LAND IS ALL YOU CAN SEE FOR A THOUSAND MILES IN EVERY DIRECTION...
"...YOU LEARN THAT THE ***REAL*** GIFT...
"...IS BLOOD."

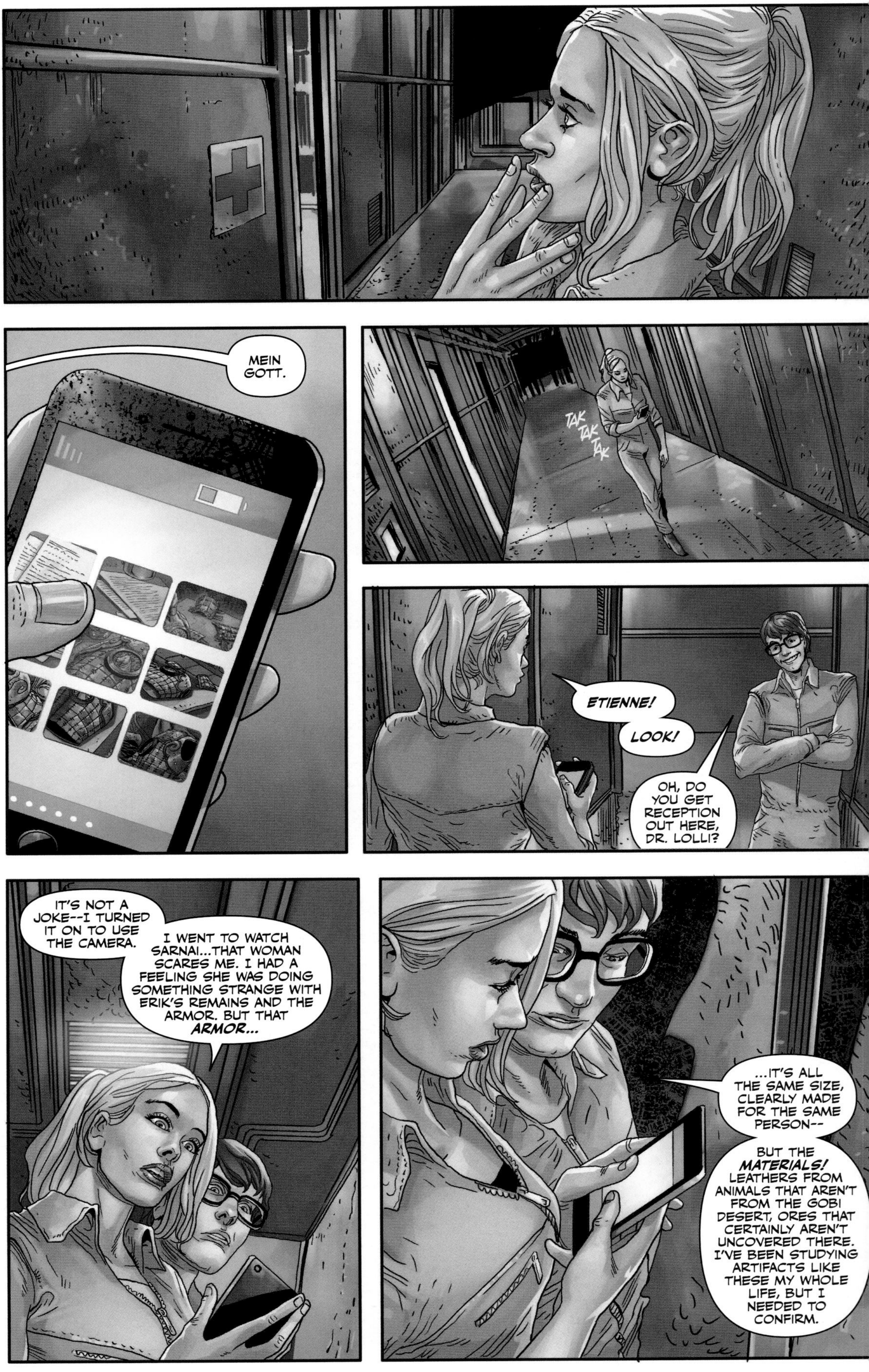
MEIN GOTT.
TAK TAK TAK
ETIENNE!
LOOK!
OH, DO YOU GET RECEPTION OUT HERE, DR. LOLLI?
IT'S NOT A JOKE--I TURNED IT ON TO USE THE CAMERA.
I WENT TO WATCH SARNAI...THAT WOMAN SCARES ME. I HAD A FEELING SHE WAS DOING SOMETHING STRANGE WITH ERIK'S REMAINS AND THE ARMOR. BUT THAT ARMOR...
...IT'S ALL THE SAME SIZE, CLEARLY MADE FOR THE SAME PERSON--
BUT THE MATERIALS! LEATHERS FROM ANIMALS THAT AREN'T FROM THE GOBI DESERT, ORES THAT CERTAINLY AREN'T UNCOVERED THERE. I'VE BEEN STUDYING ARTIFACTS LIKE THESE MY WHOLE LIFE, BUT I NEEDED TO CONFIRM.

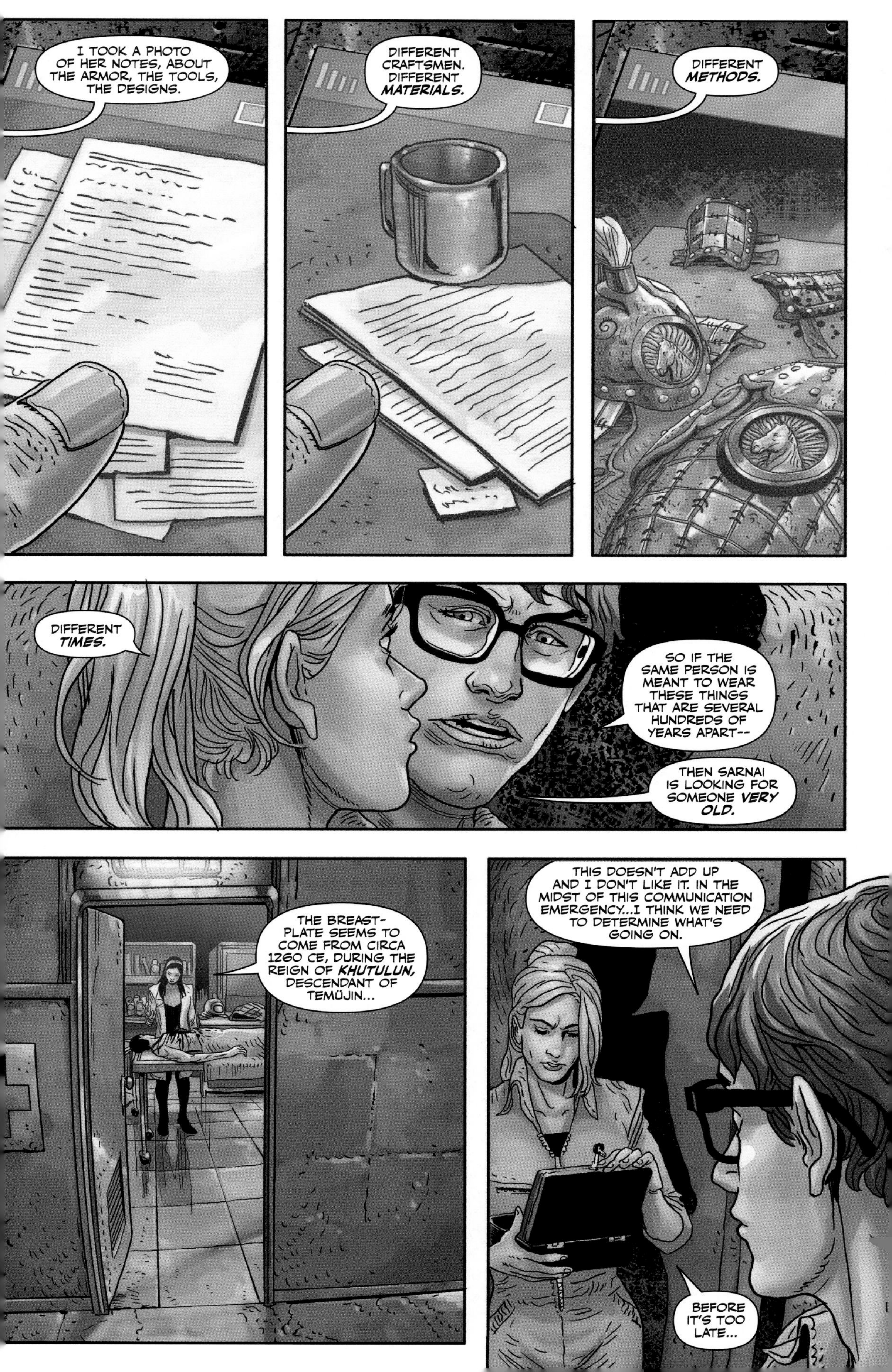
I TOOK A PHOTO OF HER NOTES, ABOUT THE ARMOR, THE TOOLS, THE DESIGNS.
DIFFERENT CRAFTSMEN. DIFFERENT MATERIALS.
DIFFERENT METHODS.
DIFFERENT TIMES.
SO IF THE SAME PERSON IS MEANT TO WEAR THESE THINGS THAT ARE SEVERAL HUNDREDS OF YEARS APART--
THEN SARNAI IS LOOKING FOR SOMEONE VERY OLD.
THE BREAST-PLATE SEEMS TO COME FROM CIRCA 1260 CE, DURING THE REIGN OF KHUTULUN, DESCENDANT OF TEMÜJIN...
THIS DOESN'T ADD UP AND I DON'T LIKE IT. IN THE MIDST OF THIS COMMUNICATION EMERGENCY...I THINK WE NEED TO DETERMINE WHAT'S GOING ON.
BEFORE IT'S TOO LATE...

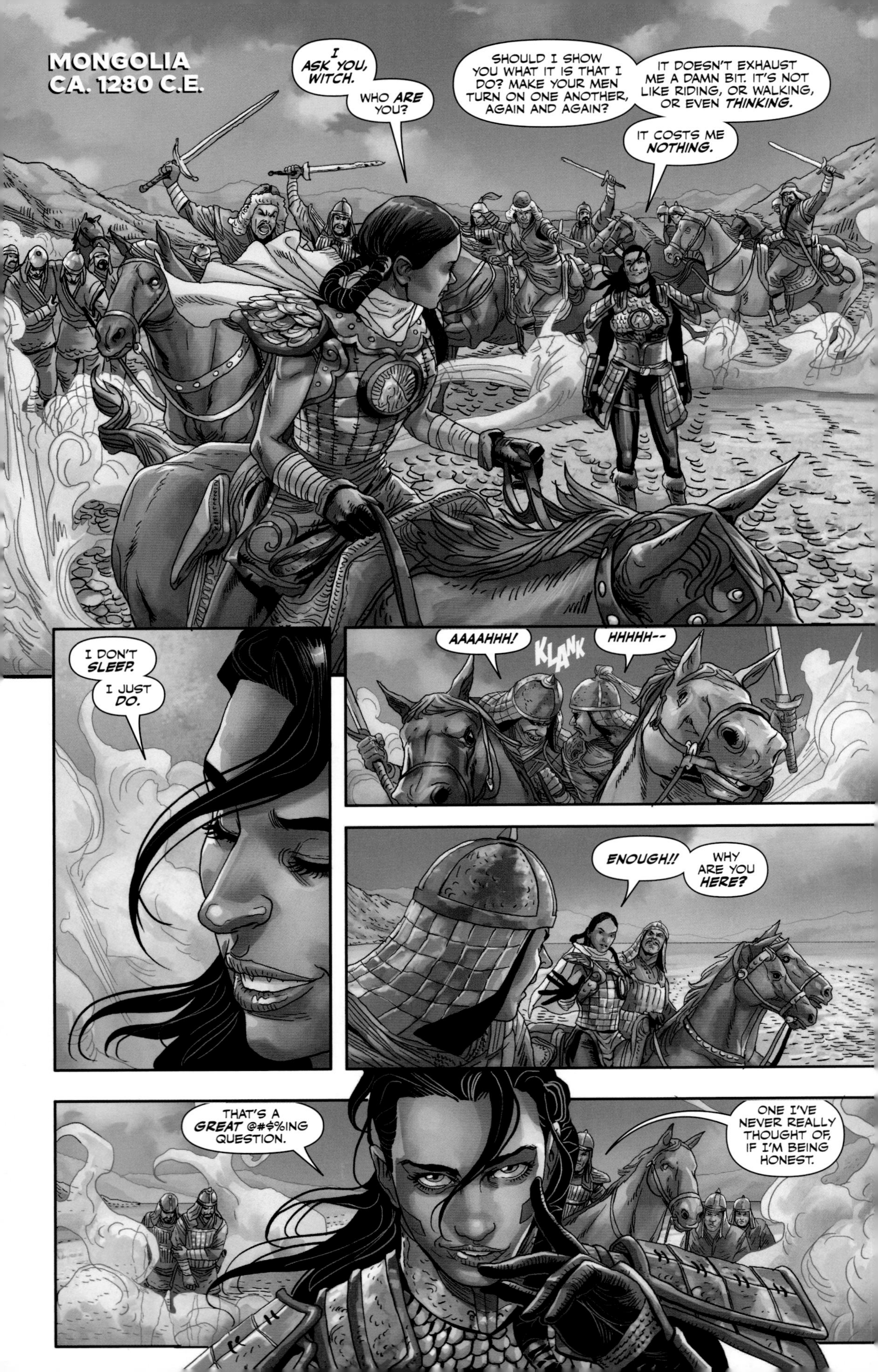

MONGOLIA
CA. 1280 C.E.
I ASK YOU, WITCH.
WHO ARE YOU?
SHOULD I SHOW YOU WHAT IT IS THAT I DO? MAKE YOUR MEN TURN ON ONE ANOTHER, AGAIN AND AGAIN?
IT DOESN'T EXHAUST ME A DAMN BIT. IT'S NOT LIKE RIDING, OR WALKING, OR EVEN THINKING.
IT COSTS ME NOTHING.
I DON'T SLEEP.
I JUST DO.
AAAAHHH!
KLANK
HHHHH--
ENOUGH!!
WHY ARE YOU HERE?
THAT'S A GREAT @#$%ING QUESTION.
ONE I'VE NEVER REALLY THOUGHT OF, IF I'M BEING HONEST.

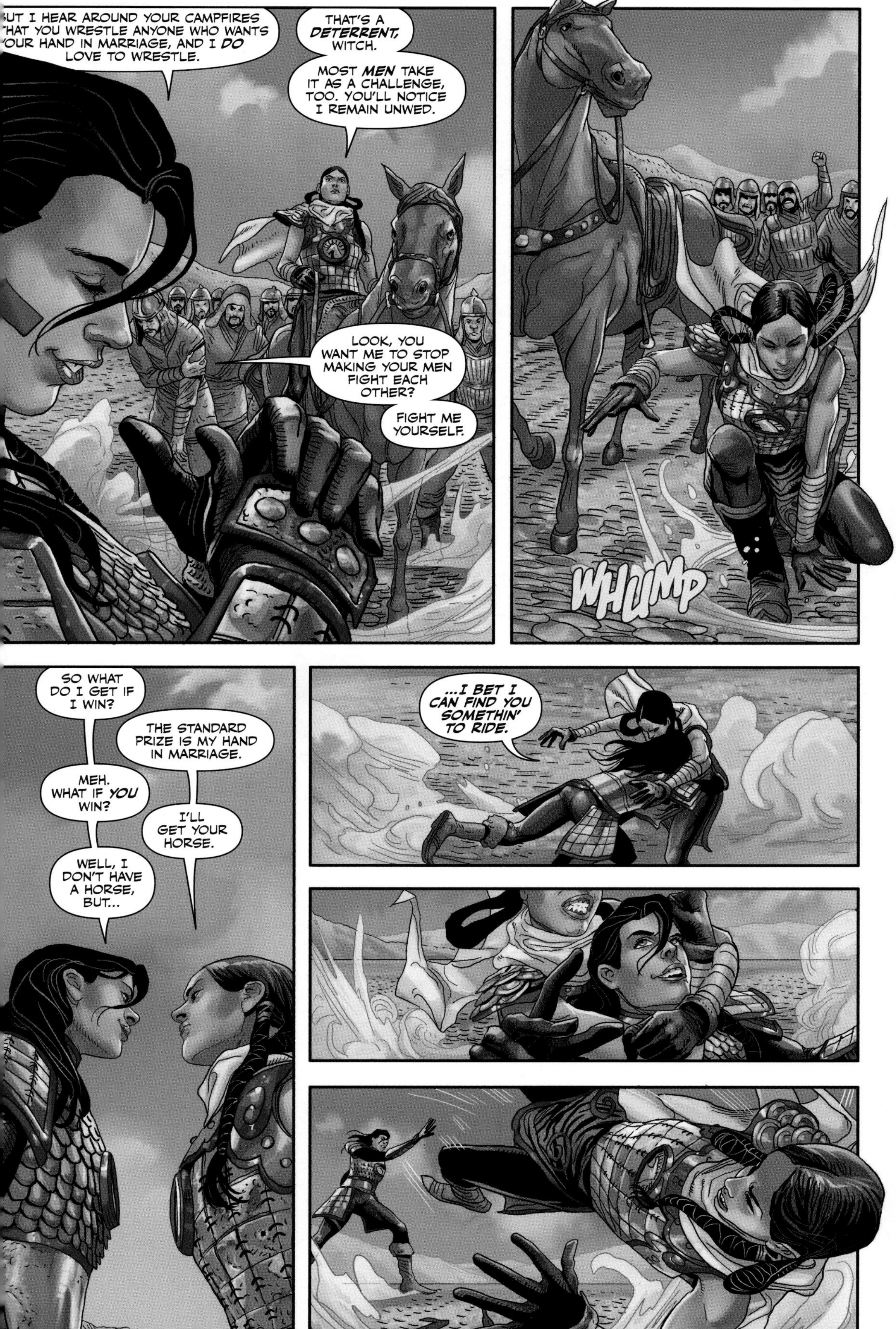
BUT I HEAR AROUND YOUR CAMPFIRES THAT YOU WRESTLE ANYONE WHO WANTS YOUR HAND IN MARRIAGE, AND I *DO* LOVE TO WRESTLE.
THAT'S A *DETERRENT,* WITCH.
MOST *MEN* TAKE IT AS A CHALLENGE, TOO. YOU'LL NOTICE I REMAIN UNWED.
LOOK, YOU WANT ME TO STOP MAKING YOUR MEN FIGHT EACH OTHER?
FIGHT ME YOURSELF.
WHUMP
SO WHAT DO I GET IF I WIN?
THE STANDARD PRIZE IS MY HAND IN MARRIAGE.
MEH. WHAT IF *YOU* WIN?
I'LL GET YOUR HORSE.
WELL, I DON'T HAVE A HORSE, BUT...
...I BET I CAN FIND YOU SOMETHIN' TO RIDE.

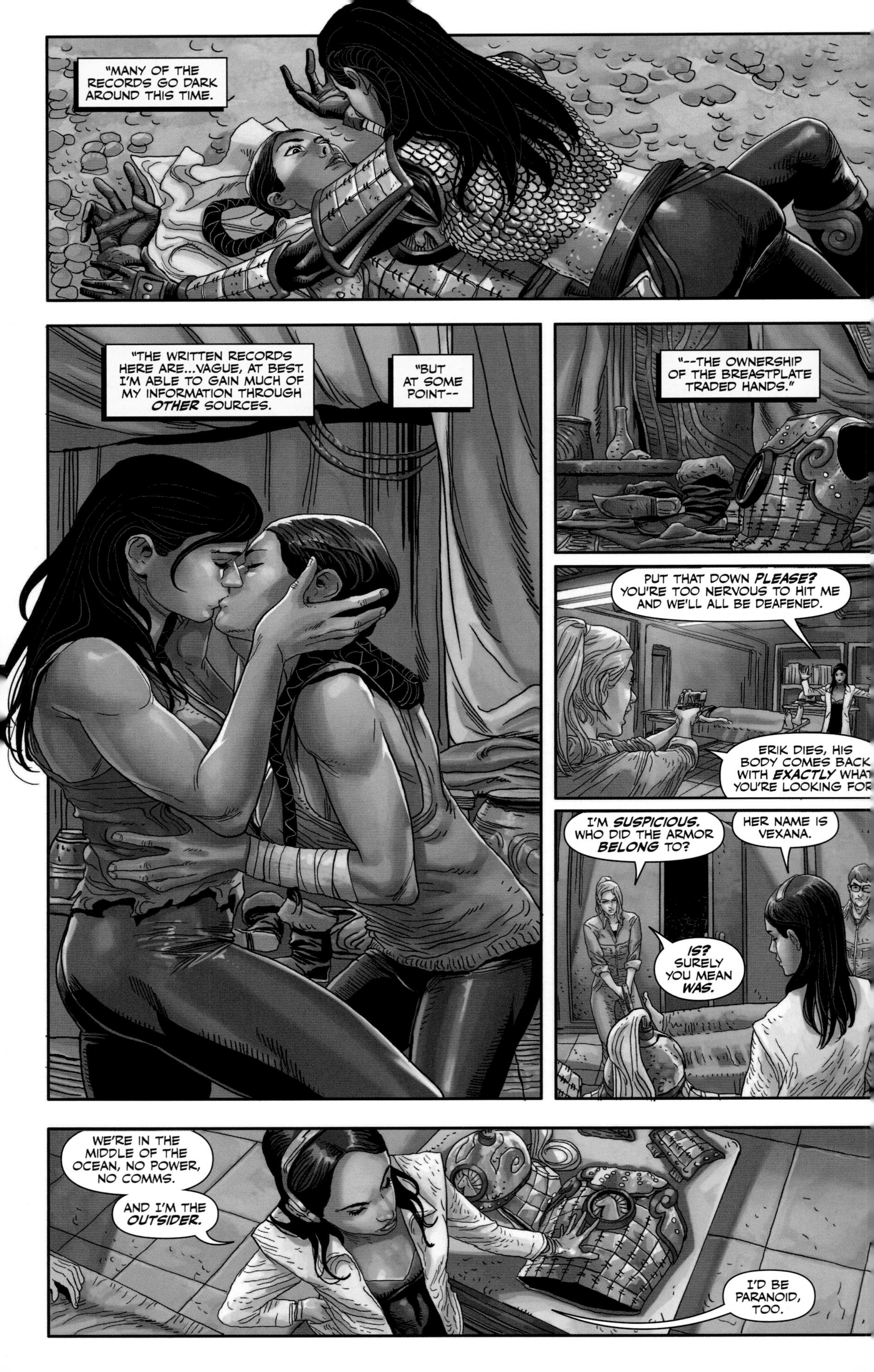
"MANY OF THE RECORDS GO DARK AROUND THIS TIME.
"THE WRITTEN RECORDS HERE ARE...VAGUE, AT BEST. I'M ABLE TO GAIN MUCH OF MY INFORMATION THROUGH OTHER SOURCES.
"BUT AT SOME POINT--
"--THE OWNERSHIP OF THE BREASTPLATE TRADED HANDS."
PUT THAT DOWN PLEASE? YOU'RE TOO NERVOUS TO HIT ME AND WE'LL ALL BE DEAFENED.
ERIK DIES, HIS BODY COMES BACK WITH EXACTLY WHAT YOU'RE LOOKING FOR
I'M SUSPICIOUS. WHO DID THE ARMOR BELONG TO?
HER NAME IS VEXANA.
IS? SURELY YOU MEAN WAS.
WE'RE IN THE MIDDLE OF THE OCEAN, NO POWER, NO COMMS.
AND I'M THE OUTSIDER.
I'D BE PARANOID, TOO.

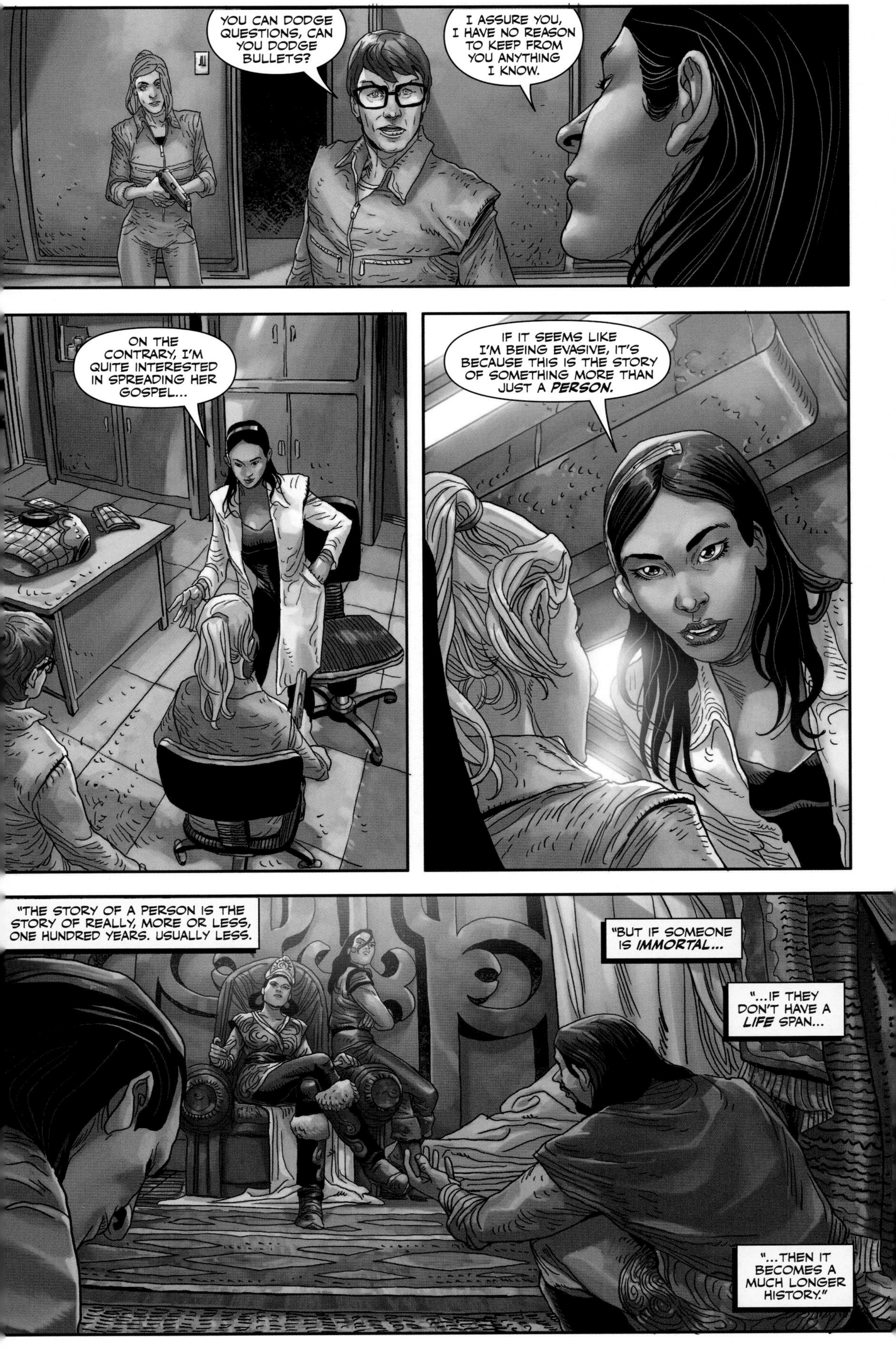

YOU CAN DODGE QUESTIONS, CAN YOU DODGE BULLETS?
I ASSURE YOU, I HAVE NO REASON TO KEEP FROM YOU ANYTHING I KNOW.
ON THE CONTRARY, I'M QUITE INTERESTED IN SPREADING HER GOSPEL...
IF IT SEEMS LIKE I'M BEING EVASIVE, IT'S BECAUSE THIS IS THE STORY OF SOMETHING MORE THAN JUST A *PERSON.*
"THE STORY OF A PERSON IS THE STORY OF REALLY, MORE OR LESS, ONE HUNDRED YEARS. USUALLY LESS.
"BUT IF SOMEONE IS *IMMORTAL...*
"...IF THEY DON'T HAVE A *LIFE* SPAN...
"...THEN IT BECOMES A MUCH LONGER HISTORY."

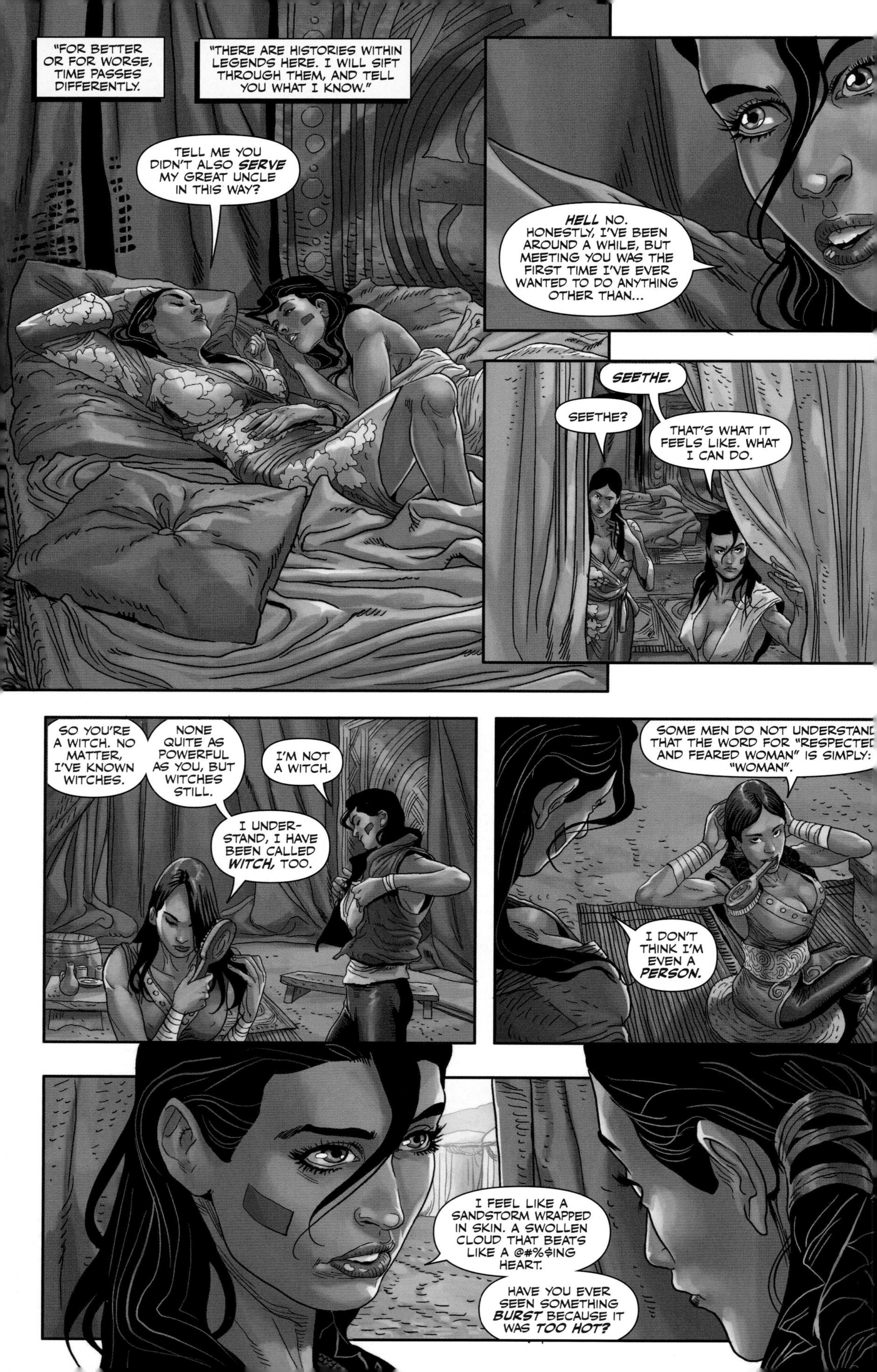
"FOR BETTER OR FOR WORSE, TIME PASSES DIFFERENTLY.
"THERE ARE HISTORIES WITHIN LEGENDS HERE. I WILL SIFT THROUGH THEM, AND TELL YOU WHAT I KNOW."
TELL ME YOU DIDN'T ALSO *SERVE* MY GREAT UNCLE IN THIS WAY?
HELL NO. HONESTLY, I'VE BEEN AROUND A WHILE, BUT MEETING YOU WAS THE FIRST TIME I'VE EVER WANTED TO DO ANYTHING OTHER THAN...
SEETHE.
SEETHE?
THAT'S WHAT IT FEELS LIKE. WHAT I CAN DO.
SO YOU'RE A WITCH. NO MATTER, I'VE KNOWN WITCHES.
NONE QUITE AS POWERFUL AS YOU, BUT WITCHES STILL.
I'M NOT A WITCH.
I UNDER-STAND, I HAVE BEEN CALLED *WITCH,* TOO.
SOME MEN DO NOT UNDERSTAND THAT THE WORD FOR "RESPECTED AND FEARED WOMAN" IS SIMPLY: "WOMAN".
I DON'T THINK I'M EVEN A *PERSON.*
I FEEL LIKE A SANDSTORM WRAPPED IN SKIN. A SWOLLEN CLOUD THAT BEATS LIKE A @#%$ING HEART.
HAVE YOU EVER SEEN SOMETHING *BURST* BECAUSE IT WAS *TOO HOT?*

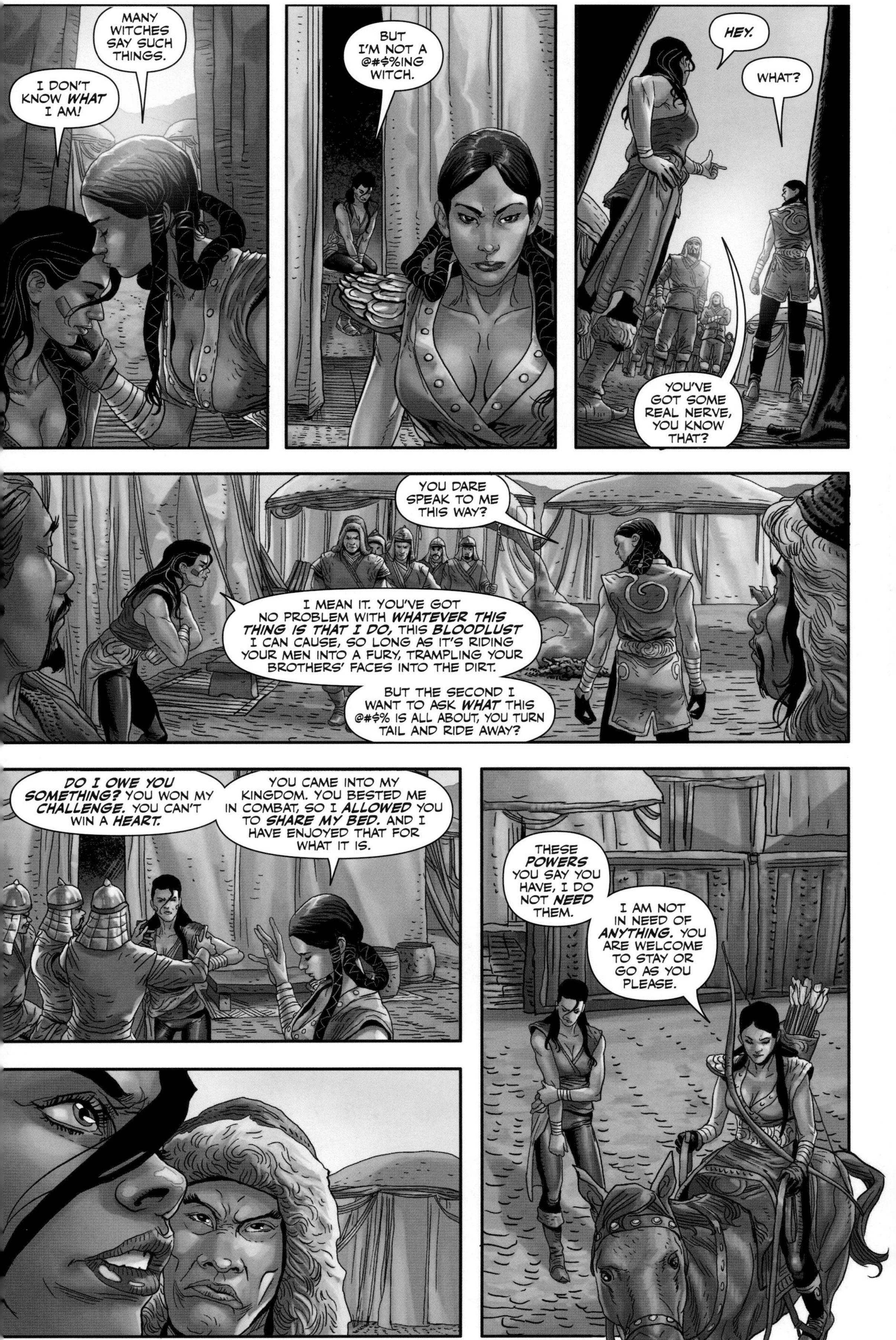

I DON'T KNOW *WHAT* I AM!
MANY WITCHES SAY SUCH THINGS.
BUT I'M NOT A @#$%ING WITCH.
HEY.
WHAT?
YOU'VE GOT SOME REAL NERVE, YOU KNOW THAT?
YOU DARE SPEAK TO ME THIS WAY?
I MEAN IT. YOU'VE GOT NO PROBLEM WITH *WHATEVER THIS THING IS THAT I DO,* THIS *BLOODLUST* I CAN CAUSE, SO LONG AS IT'S RIDING YOUR MEN INTO A FURY, TRAMPLING YOUR BROTHERS' FACES INTO THE DIRT.
BUT THE SECOND I WANT TO ASK *WHAT* THIS @#$% IS ALL ABOUT, YOU TURN TAIL AND RIDE AWAY?
DO I OWE YOU SOMETHING? YOU WON MY *CHALLENGE.* YOU CAN'T WIN A *HEART.*
YOU CAME INTO MY KINGDOM. YOU BESTED ME IN COMBAT, SO I *ALLOWED* YOU TO *SHARE MY BED.* AND I HAVE ENJOYED THAT FOR WHAT IT IS.
THESE *POWERS* YOU SAY YOU HAVE, I DO NOT *NEED* THEM.
I AM NOT IN NEED OF *ANYTHING.* YOU ARE WELCOME TO STAY OR GO AS YOU PLEASE.

"THERE'S AN ENTIRE FIELD OF US, YOU KNOW. HISTORIANS, WHO *ONLY* STUDY IMMORTALS.

"VERY CLEVER TO SUSS THAT OUT WITH THE ARMOR--IT INDEED BELONGED TO AN IMMORTAL. AND, YES, THERE ARE OTHERS.

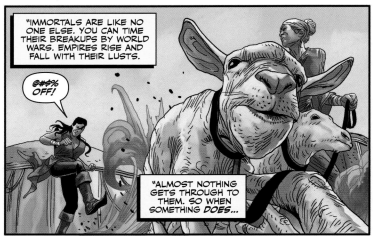

"IMMORTALS ARE LIKE NO ONE ELSE. YOU CAN TIME THEIR BREAKUPS BY WORLD WARS. EMPIRES RISE AND FALL WITH THEIR LUSTS.

@#$% OFF!

"ALMOST NOTHING GETS THROUGH TO THEM. SO WHEN SOMETHING *DOES*...

YOU'RE THE PRINCESS' BEDWARMER, YES?

IS IT TRUE YOU GET *EVERYONE* RILED UP?

IS THAT RIGHT, WITCH?

"...MAPS GET REWRITTEN.

OY!

"ENTIRE PEOPLE ARE WIPED OUT.

"BLOODLINES JUST STOP."

PERHAPS.

LET'S FIND OUT.

YAAAAH!

OOF!

WHAP

I'M FAIR ENOUGH IN A FIGHT. ENOUGH TO KICK YOU FOOLS AROUND.

WITCH--

"A LOT OF WHAT IMMORTALS CAN DO IS SIMPLY A MATTER OF TIME. THEY'RE BETTER AT THINGS THAN YOU OR I BECAUSE THEY'VE HAD LONGER TO WORK ON THEM. TO REFINE THEM.

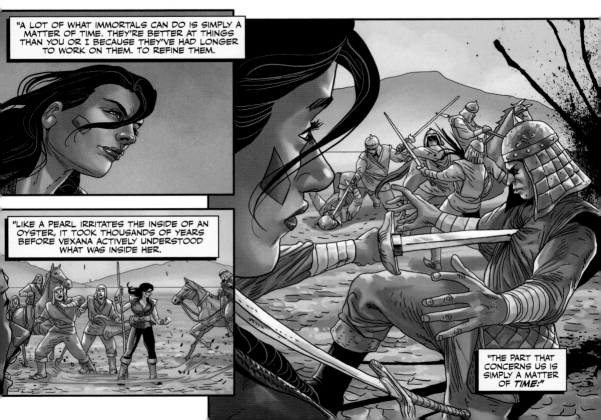

"LIKE A PEARL IRRITATES THE INSIDE OF AN OYSTER, IT TOOK THOUSANDS OF YEARS BEFORE VEXANA ACTIVELY UNDERSTOOD WHAT WAS INSIDE HER.

"THE PART THAT CONCERNS US IS SIMPLY A MATTER OF *TIME*."

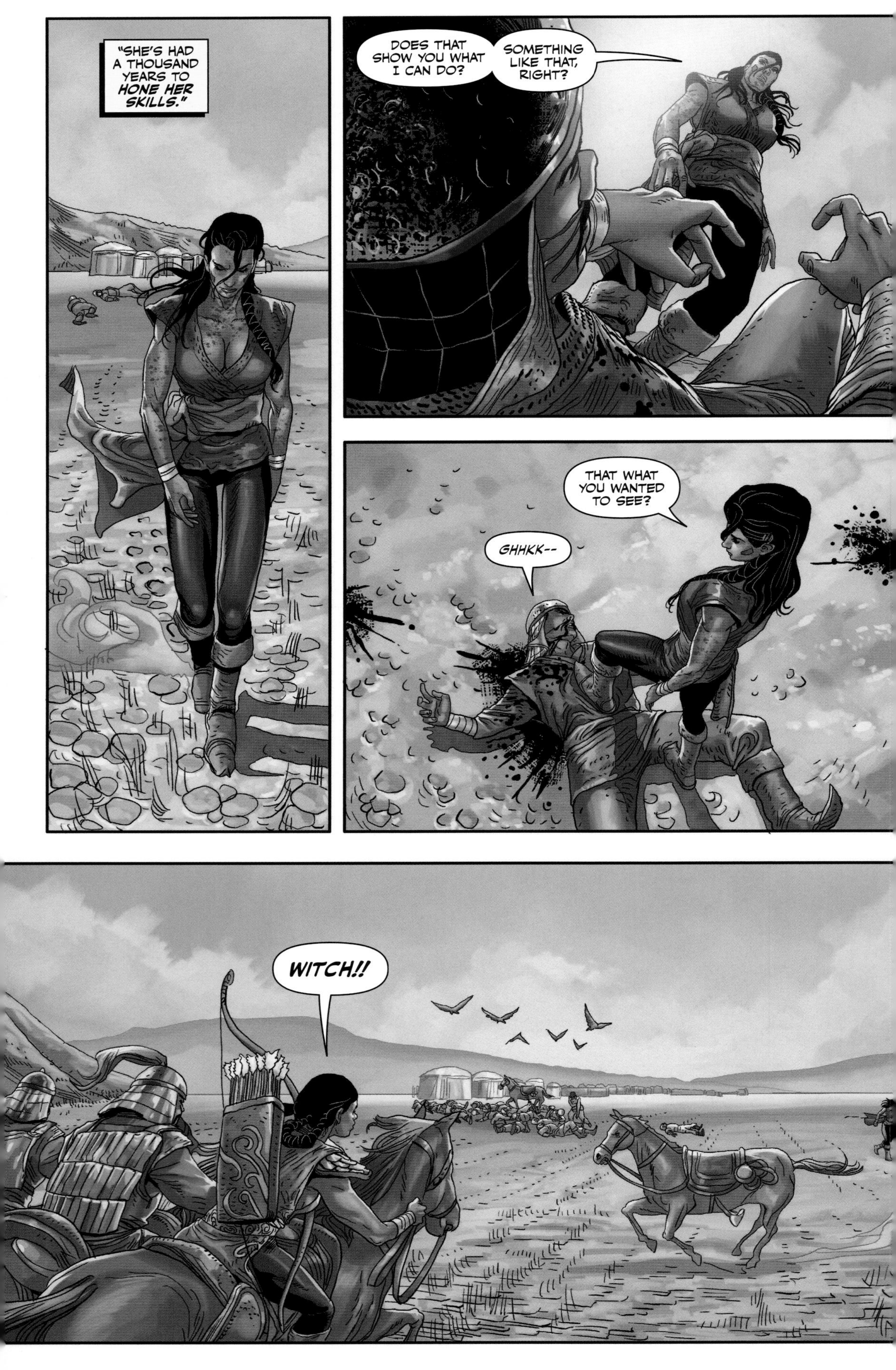
"SHE'S HAD A THOUSAND YEARS TO HONE HER SKILLS."
DOES THAT SHOW YOU WHAT I CAN DO?
SOMETHING LIKE THAT, RIGHT?
THAT WHAT YOU WANTED TO SEE?
GHHKK--
WITCH!!

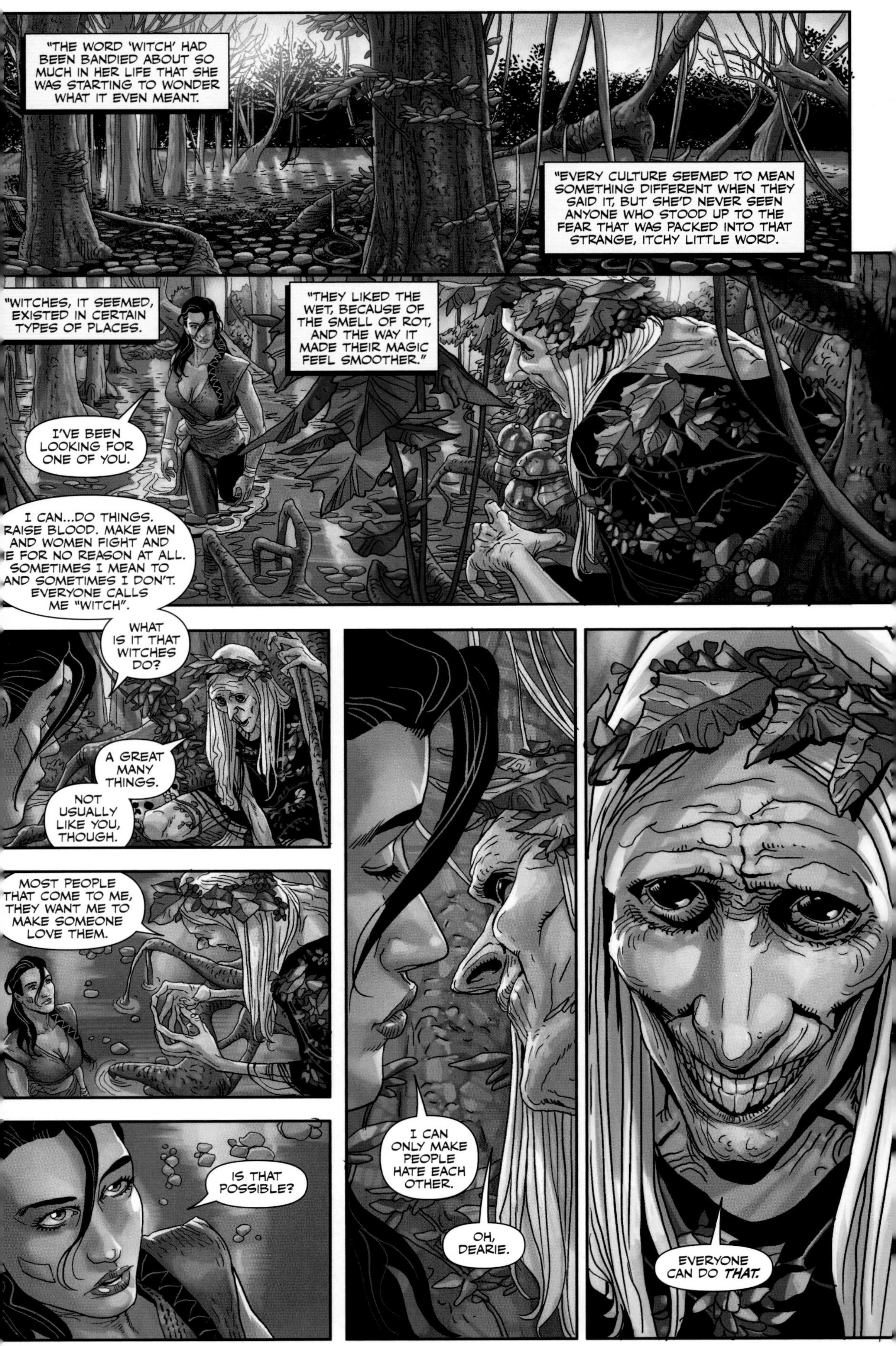
"THE WORD 'WITCH' HAD BEEN BANDIED ABOUT SO MUCH IN HER LIFE THAT SHE WAS STARTING TO WONDER WHAT IT EVEN MEANT.
"EVERY CULTURE SEEMED TO MEAN SOMETHING DIFFERENT WHEN THEY SAID IT, BUT SHE'D NEVER SEEN ANYONE WHO STOOD UP TO THE FEAR THAT WAS PACKED INTO THAT STRANGE, ITCHY LITTLE WORD.
"WITCHES, IT SEEMED, EXISTED IN CERTAIN TYPES OF PLACES.
"THEY LIKED THE WET, BECAUSE OF THE SMELL OF ROT, AND THE WAY IT MADE THEIR MAGIC FEEL SMOOTHER."
I'VE BEEN LOOKING FOR ONE OF YOU.
I CAN...DO THINGS. RAISE BLOOD. MAKE MEN AND WOMEN FIGHT AND E FOR NO REASON AT ALL. SOMETIMES I MEAN TO AND SOMETIMES I DON'T. EVERYONE CALLS ME "WITCH".
WHAT IS IT THAT WITCHES DO?
A GREAT MANY THINGS.
NOT USUALLY LIKE YOU, THOUGH.
MOST PEOPLE THAT COME TO ME, THEY WANT ME TO MAKE SOMEONE LOVE THEM.
IS THAT POSSIBLE?
I CAN ONLY MAKE PEOPLE HATE EACH OTHER.
OH, DEARIE.
EVERYONE CAN DO *THAT.*

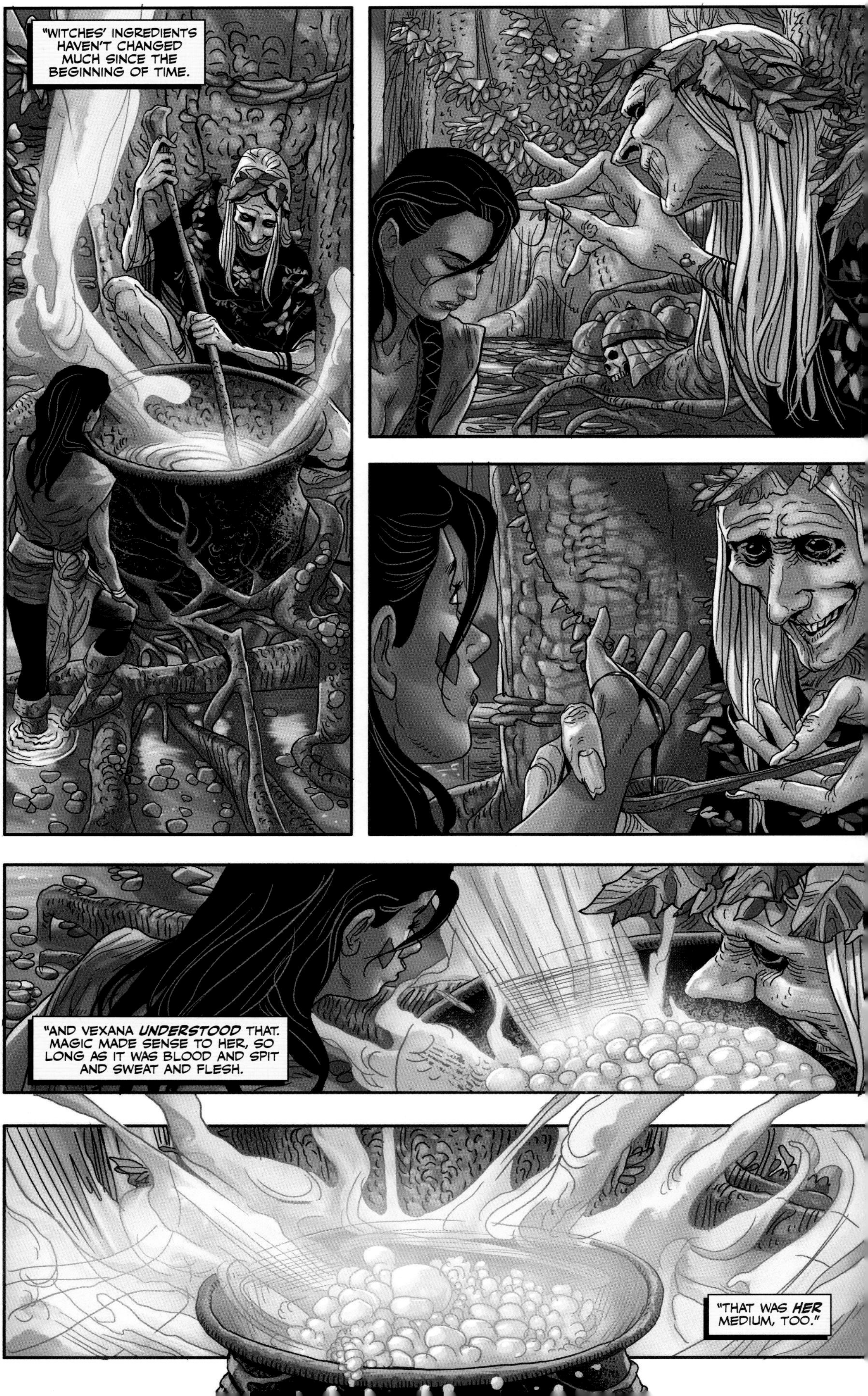
"WITCHES' INGREDIENTS HAVEN'T CHANGED MUCH SINCE THE BEGINNING OF TIME.
"AND VEXANA *UNDERSTOOD* THAT. MAGIC MADE SENSE TO HER, SO LONG AS IT WAS BLOOD AND SPIT AND SWEAT AND FLESH.
"THAT WAS *HER* MEDIUM, TOO."

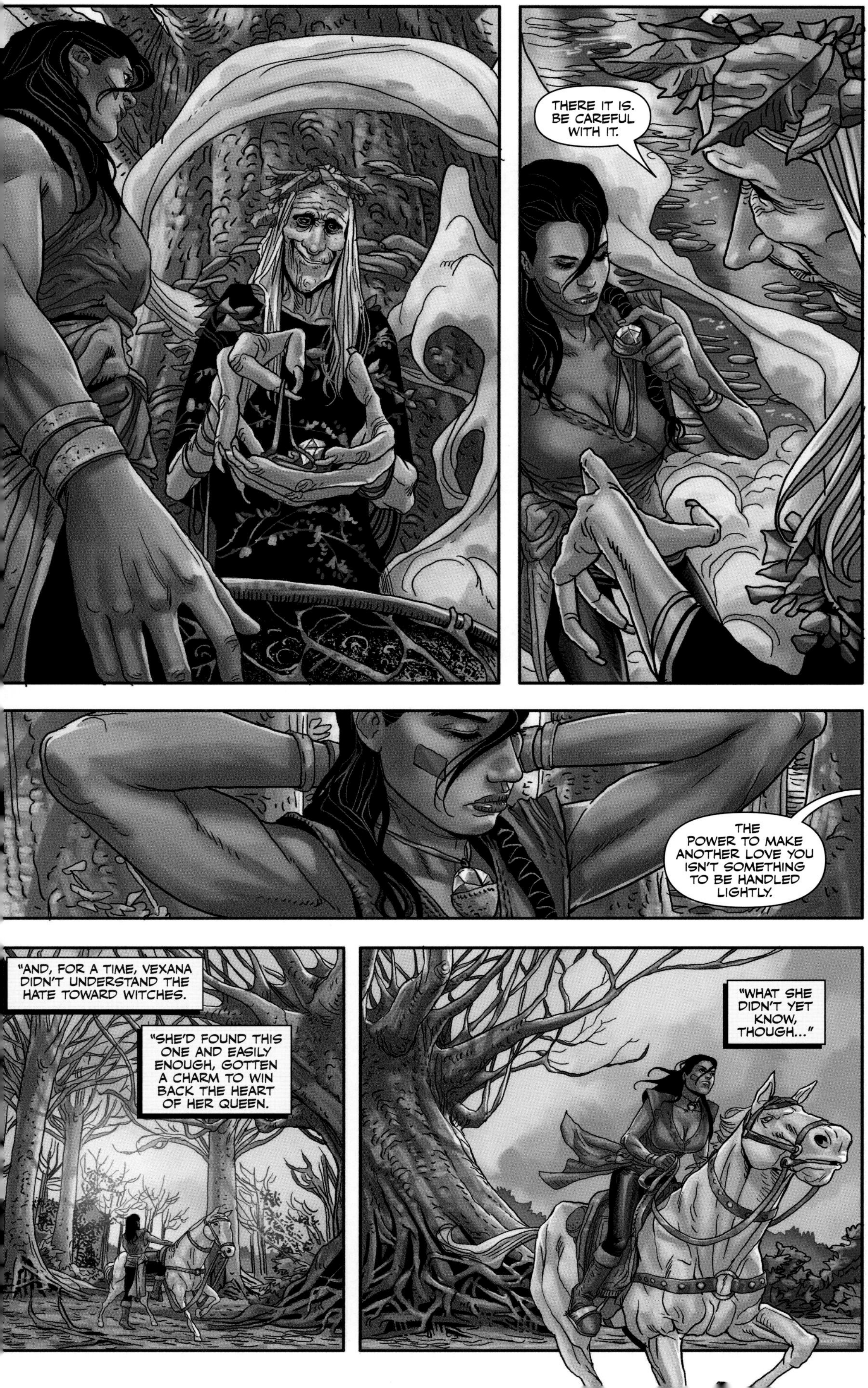
THERE IT IS. BE CAREFUL WITH IT.
THE POWER TO MAKE ANOTHER LOVE YOU ISN'T SOMETHING TO BE HANDLED LIGHTLY.
"AND, FOR A TIME, VEXANA DIDN'T UNDERSTAND THE HATE TOWARD WITCHES.
"SHE'D FOUND THIS ONE AND EASILY ENOUGH, GOTTEN A CHARM TO WIN BACK THE HEART OF HER QUEEN.
"WHAT SHE DIDN'T YET KNOW, THOUGH..."

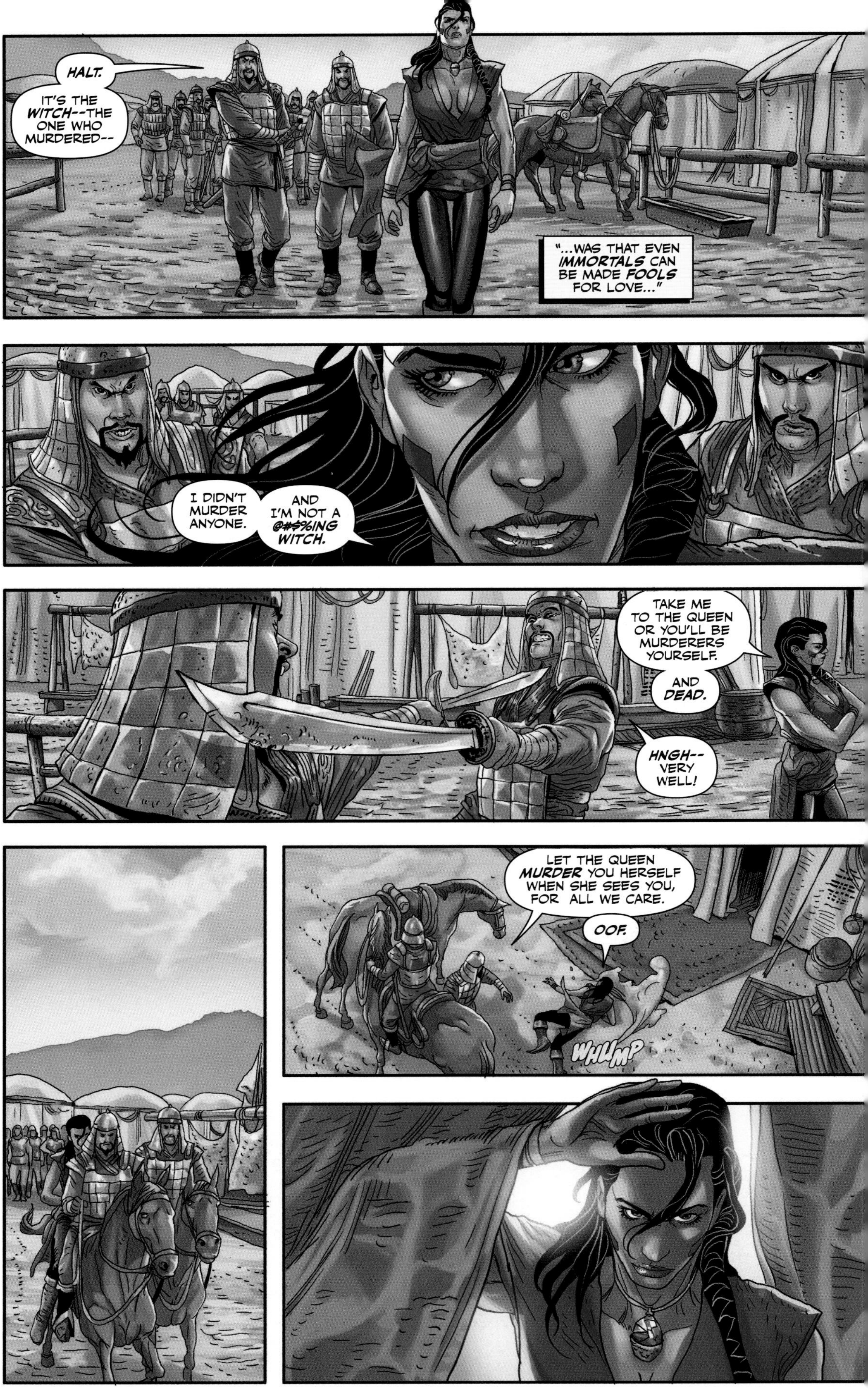
HALT.
IT'S THE WITCH--THE ONE WHO MURDERED--
"...WAS THAT EVEN IMMORTALS CAN BE MADE FOOLS FOR LOVE..."
I DIDN'T MURDER ANYONE.
AND I'M NOT A @#$%ING WITCH.
TAKE ME TO THE QUEEN OR YOU'LL BE MURDERERS YOURSELF.
AND DEAD.
HNGH--VERY WELL!
LET THE QUEEN MURDER YOU HERSELF WHEN SHE SEES YOU, FOR ALL WE CARE.
OOF.
WHUMP

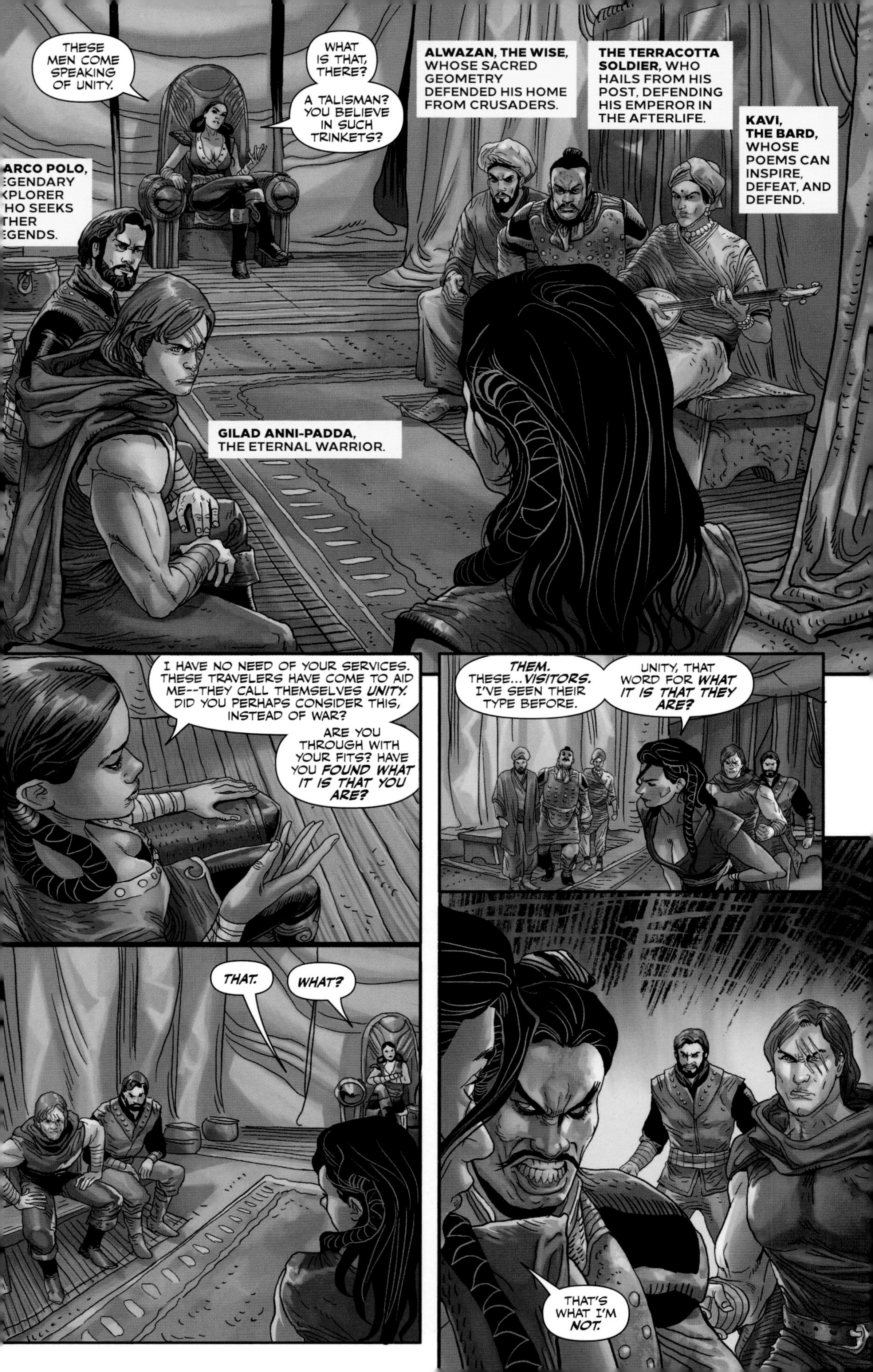

THESE MEN COME SPEAKING OF UNITY.
WHAT IS THAT, THERE?
A TALISMAN? YOU BELIEVE IN SUCH TRINKETS?
ALWAZAN, THE WISE, WHOSE SACRED GEOMETRY DEFENDED HIS HOME FROM CRUSADERS.
THE TERRACOTTA SOLDIER, WHO HAILS FROM HIS POST, DEFENDING HIS EMPEROR IN THE AFTERLIFE.
KAVI, THE BARD, WHOSE POEMS CAN INSPIRE, DEFEAT, AND DEFEND.
ARCO POLO, EGENDARY XPLORER HO SEEKS THER EGENDS.
GILAD ANNI-PADDA, THE ETERNAL WARRIOR.
I HAVE NO NEED OF YOUR SERVICES. THESE TRAVELERS HAVE COME TO AID ME--THEY CALL THEMSELVES UNITY. DID YOU PERHAPS CONSIDER THIS, INSTEAD OF WAR?
ARE YOU THROUGH WITH YOUR FITS? HAVE YOU FOUND WHAT IT IS THAT YOU ARE?
THEM. THESE...VISITORS. I'VE SEEN THEIR TYPE BEFORE.
UNITY, THAT WORD FOR WHAT IT IS THAT THEY ARE?
THAT.
WHAT?
THAT'S WHAT I'M NOT.

THE *LOHENGRIN*.

BOOOOM

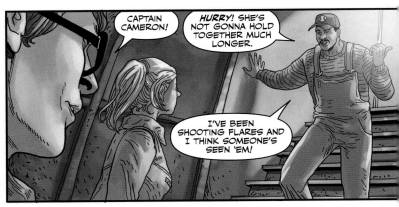

CAPTAIN CAMERON!

HURRY! SHE'S NOT GONNA HOLD TOGETHER MUCH LONGER.

I'VE BEEN SHOOTING FLARES AND I THINK SOMEONE'S SEEN 'EM!

WITH ANY LUCK, WE'LL BE RESCUED!

BOOOOOM

WHAT *WAS* THAT!?

C'MON, *SARNAI!*

NO TIME, GET IN!

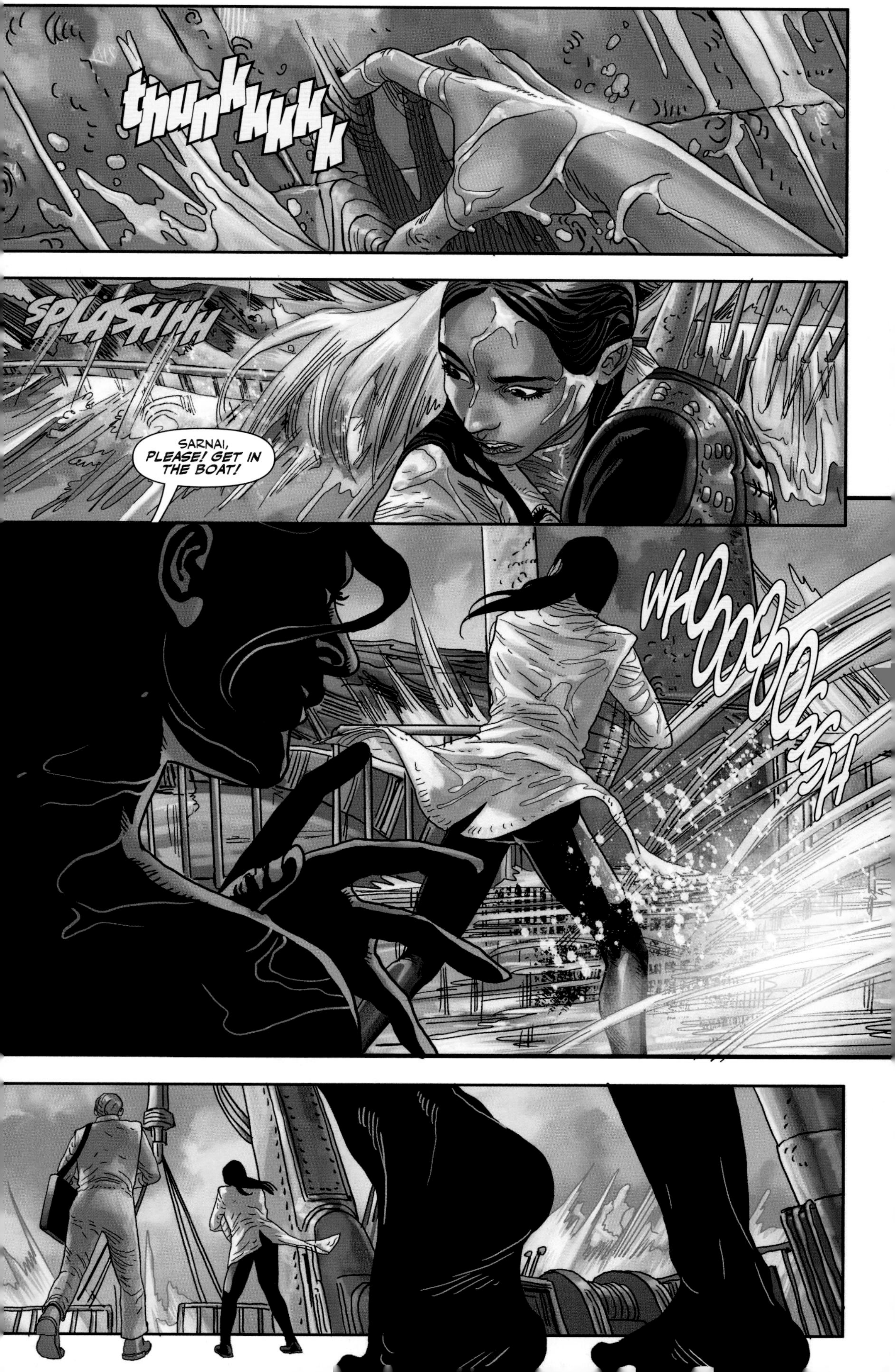
thunkkkkkk
SPLASHHH
SARNAI, PLEASE! GET IN THE BOAT!
WHOOOOOOSH

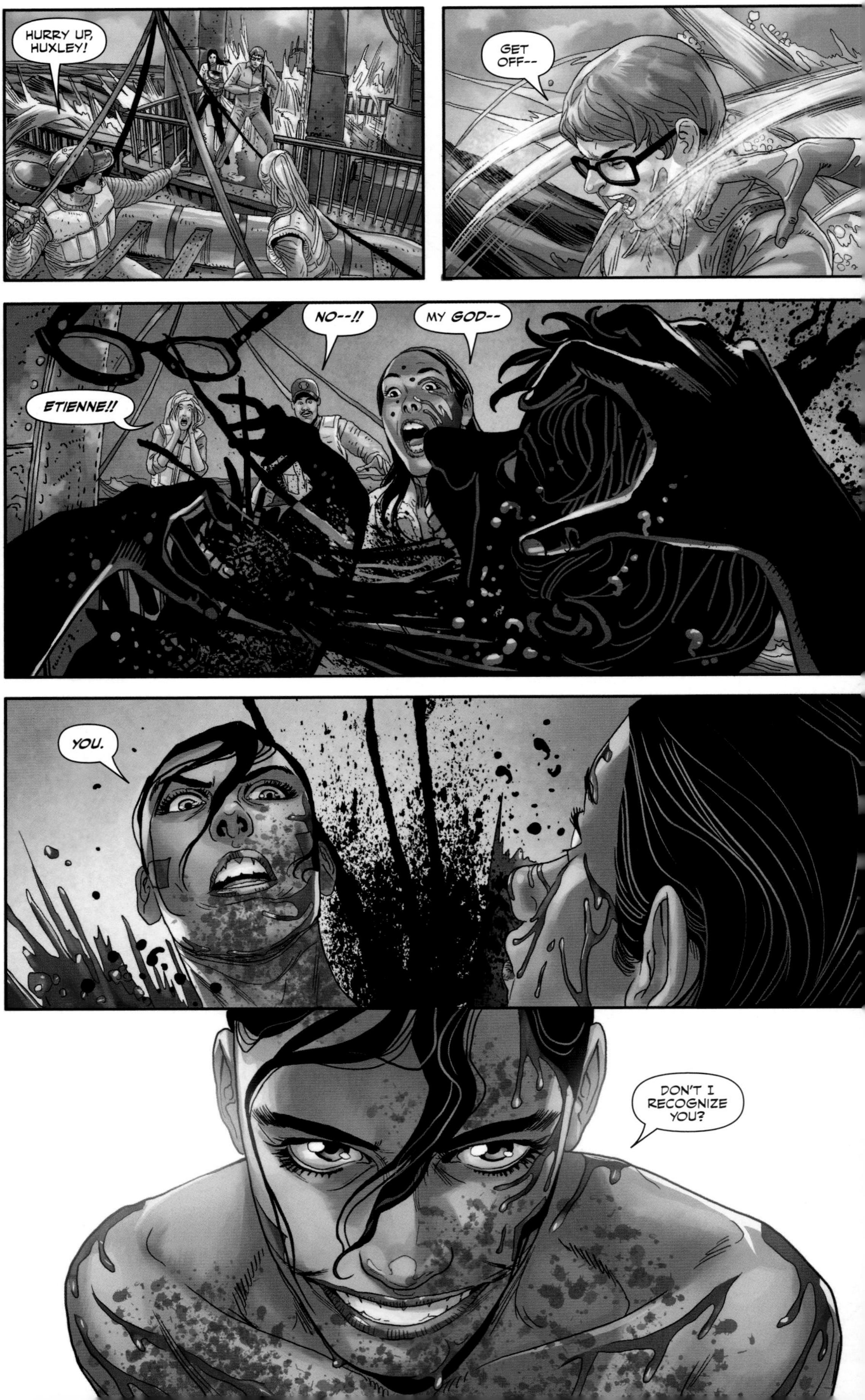
HURRY UP, HUXLEY!
GET OFF--
NO--!!
MY GOD--
ETIENNE!!
YOU.
DON'T I RECOGNIZE YOU?

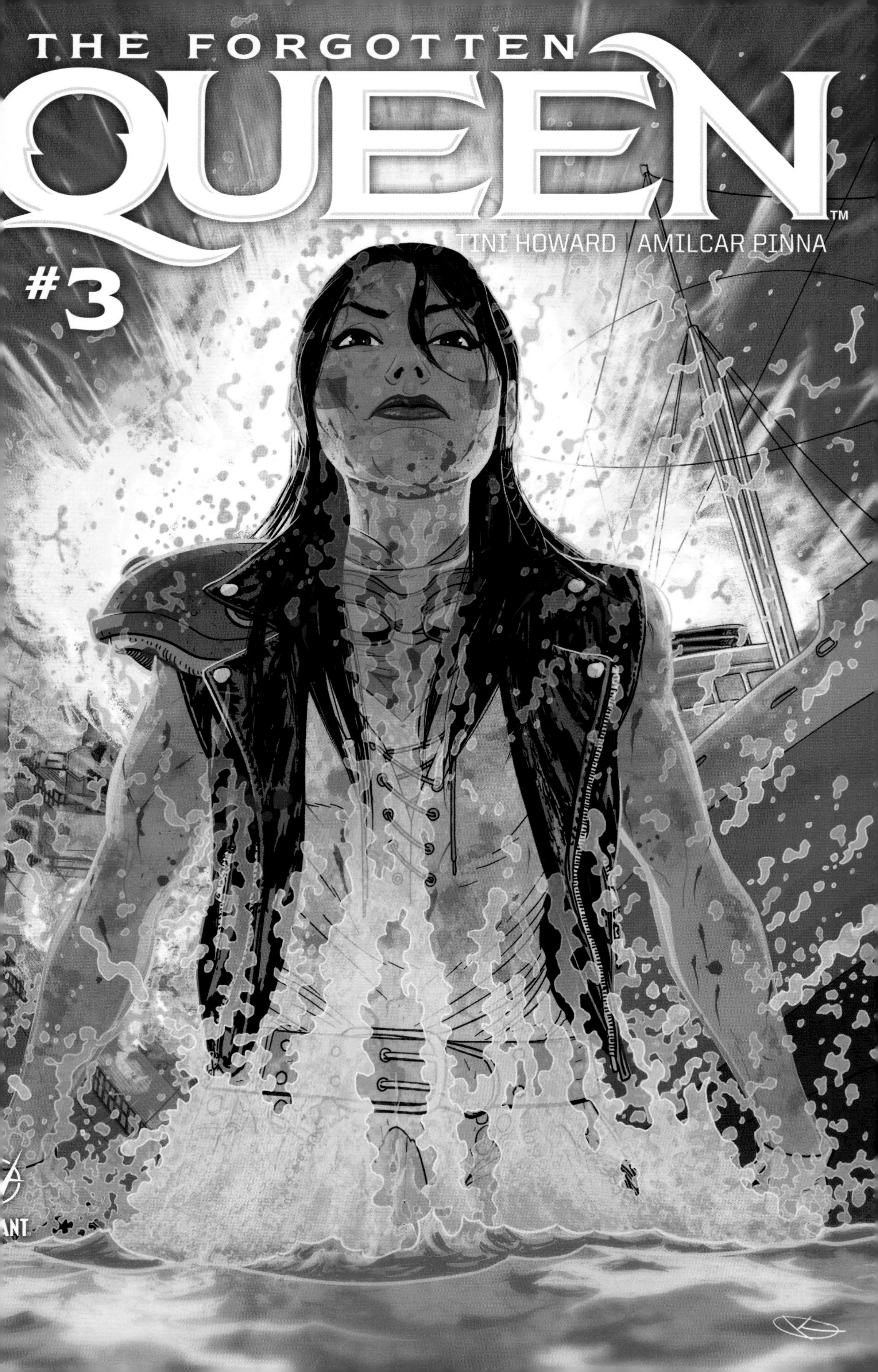
THE FORGOTTEN
QUEEN™
TINI HOWARD | AMILCAR PINNA
#3

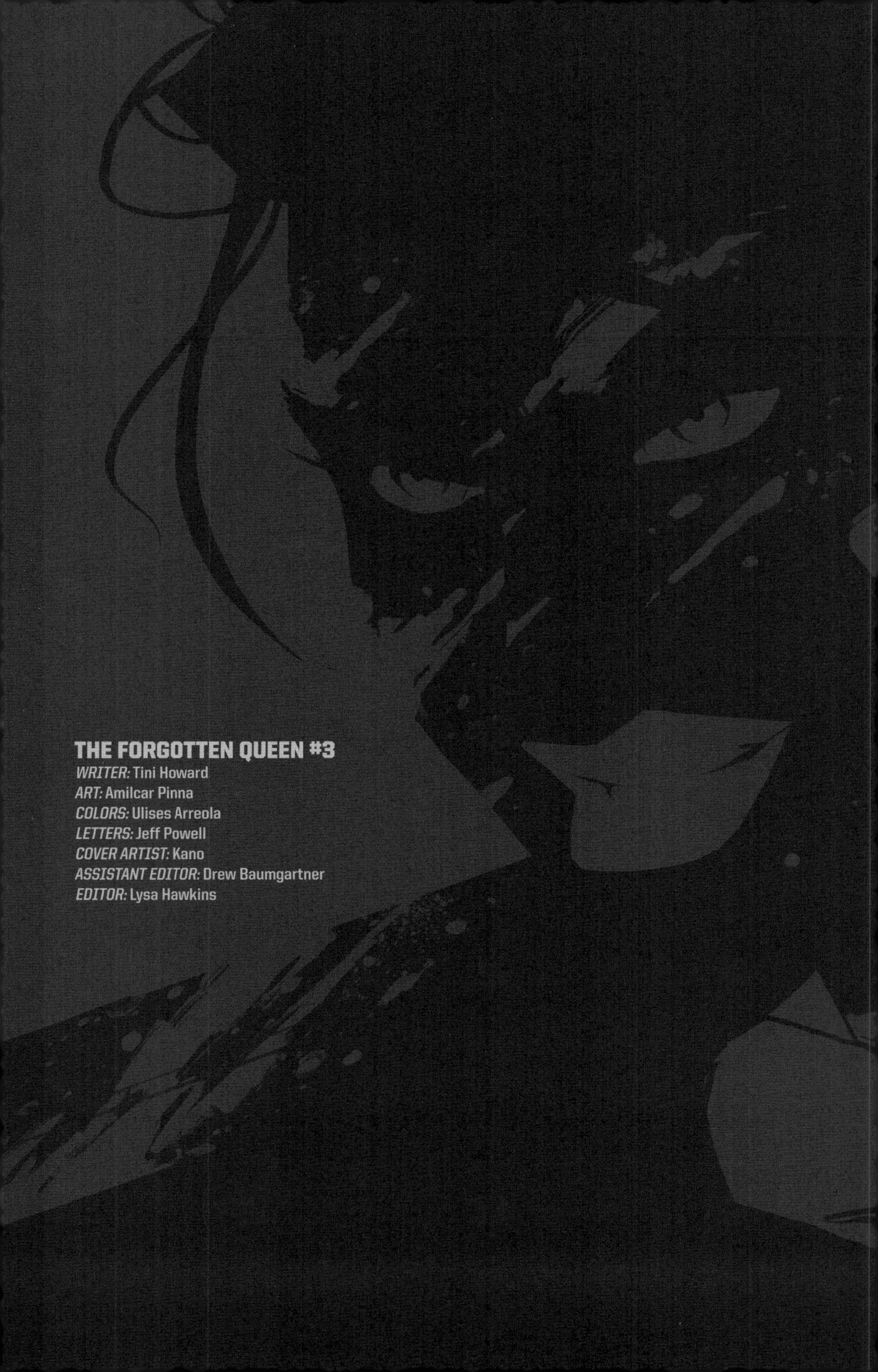

THE FORGOTTEN QUEEN #3

WRITER: Tini Howard
ART: Amilcar Pinna
COLORS: Ulises Arreola
LETTERS: Jeff Powell
COVER ARTIST: Kano
ASSISTANT EDITOR: Drew Baumgartner
EDITOR: Lysa Hawkins

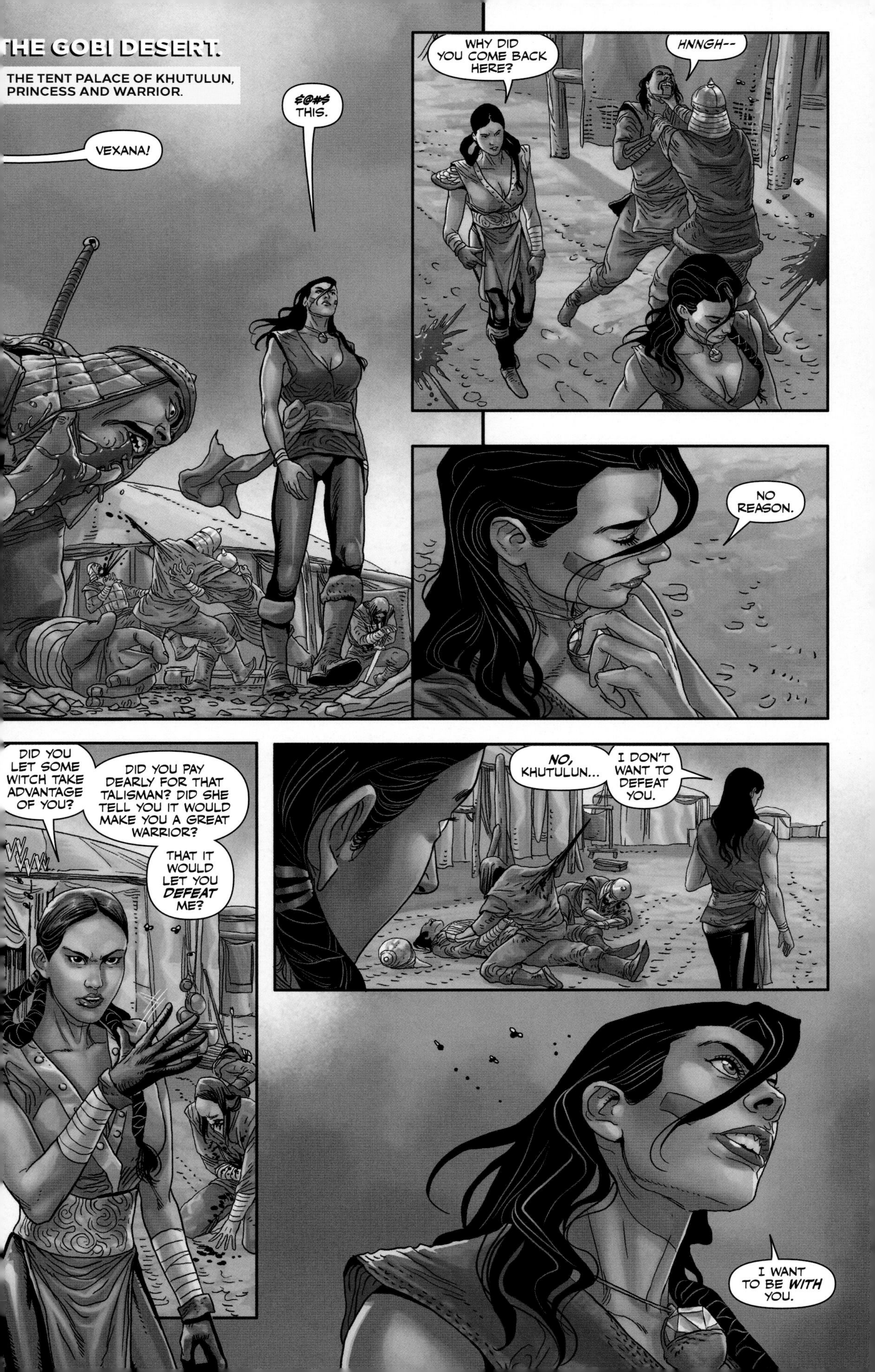
THE GOBI DESERT.
THE TENT PALACE OF KHUTULUN, PRINCESS AND WARRIOR.
VEXANA!
$@#$ THIS.
WHY DID YOU COME BACK HERE?
HNNGH--
NO REASON.
DID YOU LET SOME WITCH TAKE ADVANTAGE OF YOU?
DID YOU PAY DEARLY FOR THAT TALISMAN? DID SHE TELL YOU IT WOULD MAKE YOU A GREAT WARRIOR?
THAT IT WOULD LET YOU DEFEAT ME?
NO, KHUTULUN...
I DON'T WANT TO DEFEAT YOU.
I WANT TO BE WITH YOU.

AND WHAT? *FATHER MY CHILDREN?* FIGHT AND *DIE* FOR ME? TELL ME, VEXANA.

WHAT CAN YOU *POSSIBLY* DO FOR ME?

THESE WARRIORS PROMISE UNITY AND *PEACE.* WHERE LEADERS CAN *TRULY* EXCEL.

YEAH, AS PART OF A *TEAM.*

NEVER ON YOUR *OWN.* NEVER BY YOUR OWN *NAME.* I BARELY EVEN *HAVE* A NAME, I'LL ASK *NOTHING.*

THE *GLORY* WILL BE YOUR *OWN.*

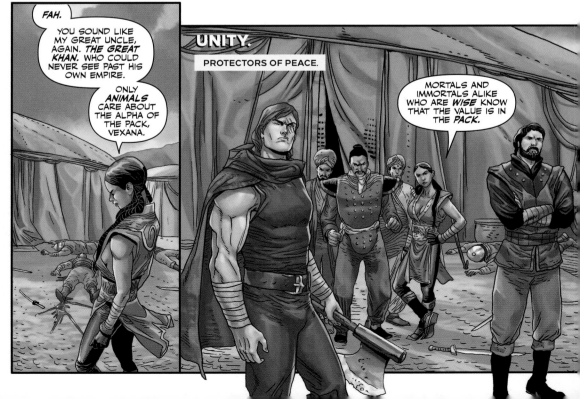

FAH.

YOU SOUND LIKE MY GREAT UNCLE, AGAIN. *THE GREAT KHAN.* WHO COULD NEVER SEE PAST HIS OWN EMPIRE.

ONLY *ANIMALS* CARE ABOUT THE ALPHA OF THE PACK, VEXANA.

UNITY.

PROTECTORS OF PEACE.

MORTALS AND IMMORTALS ALIKE WHO ARE *WISE* KNOW THAT THE VALUE IS IN THE *PACK.*

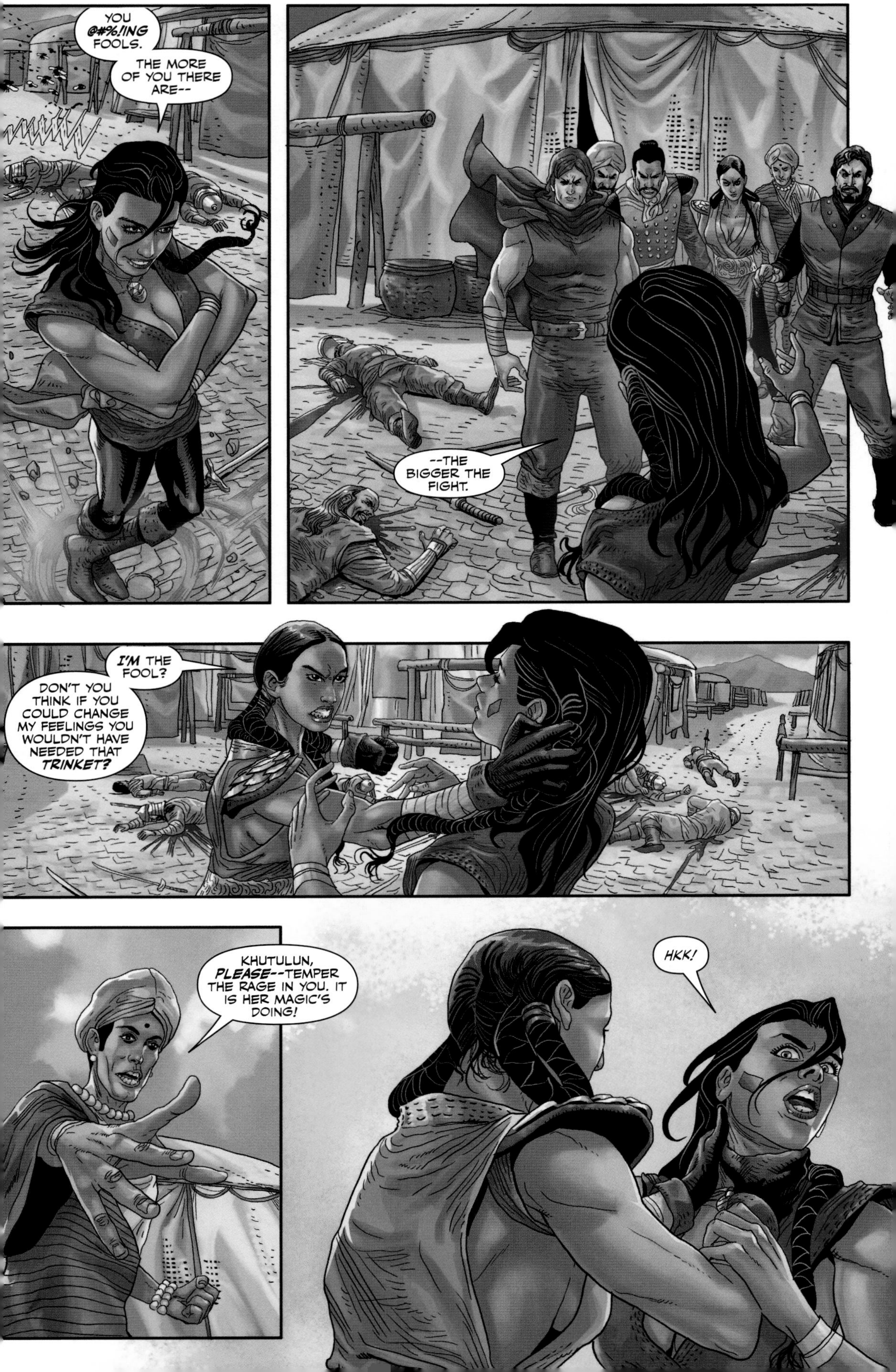
YOU @#%!ING FOOLS.
THE MORE OF YOU THERE ARE--
--THE BIGGER THE FIGHT.
I'M THE FOOL?
DON'T YOU THINK IF YOU COULD CHANGE MY FEELINGS YOU WOULDN'T HAVE NEEDED THAT TRINKET?
KHUTULUN, PLEASE--TEMPER THE RAGE IN YOU. IT IS HER MAGIC'S DOING!
HKK!

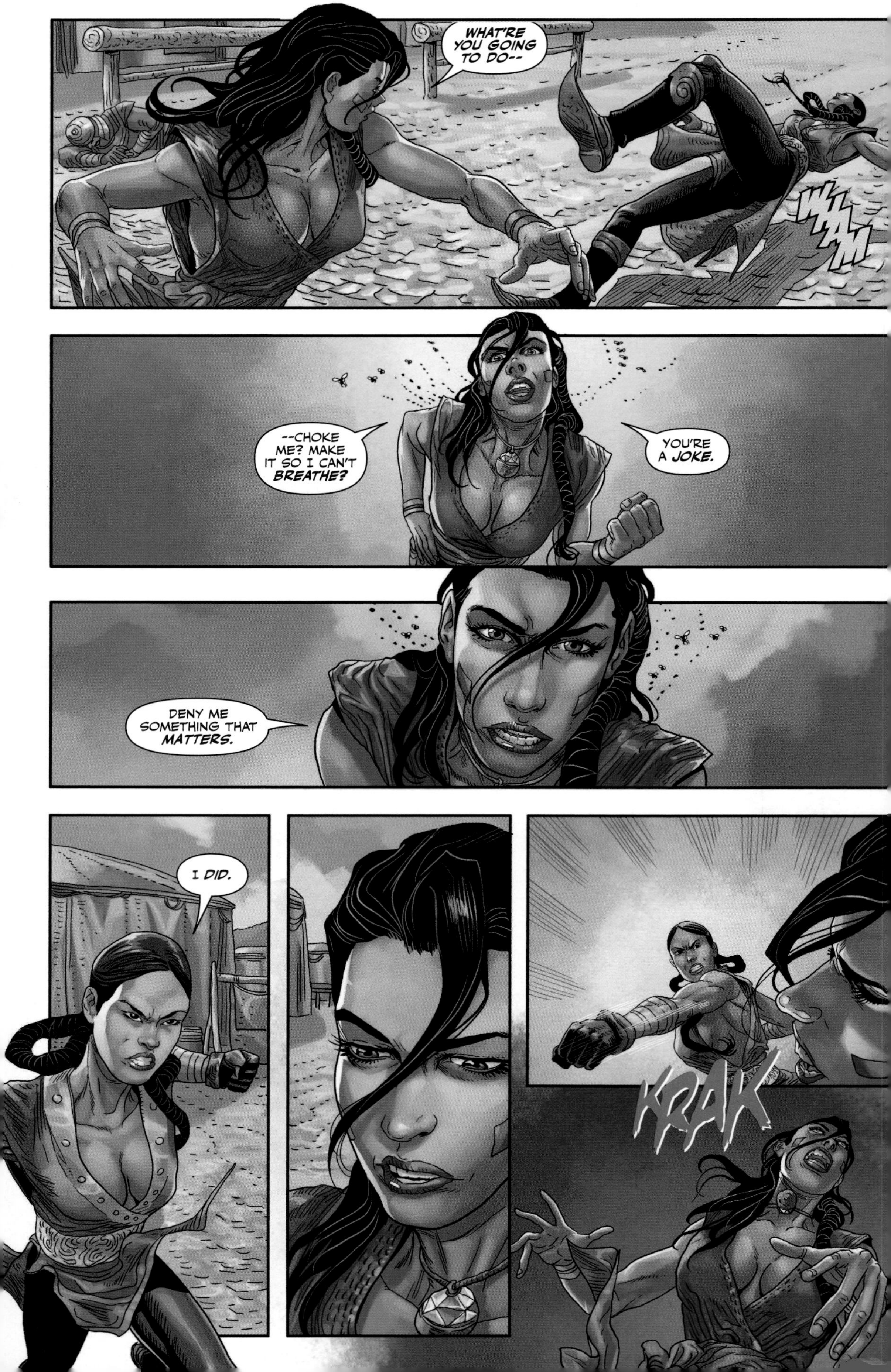
WHAT'RE YOU GOING TO DO--
WHAM
--CHOKE ME? MAKE IT SO I CAN'T BREATHE?
YOU'RE A JOKE.
DENY ME SOMETHING THAT MATTERS.
I DID.
KRAK

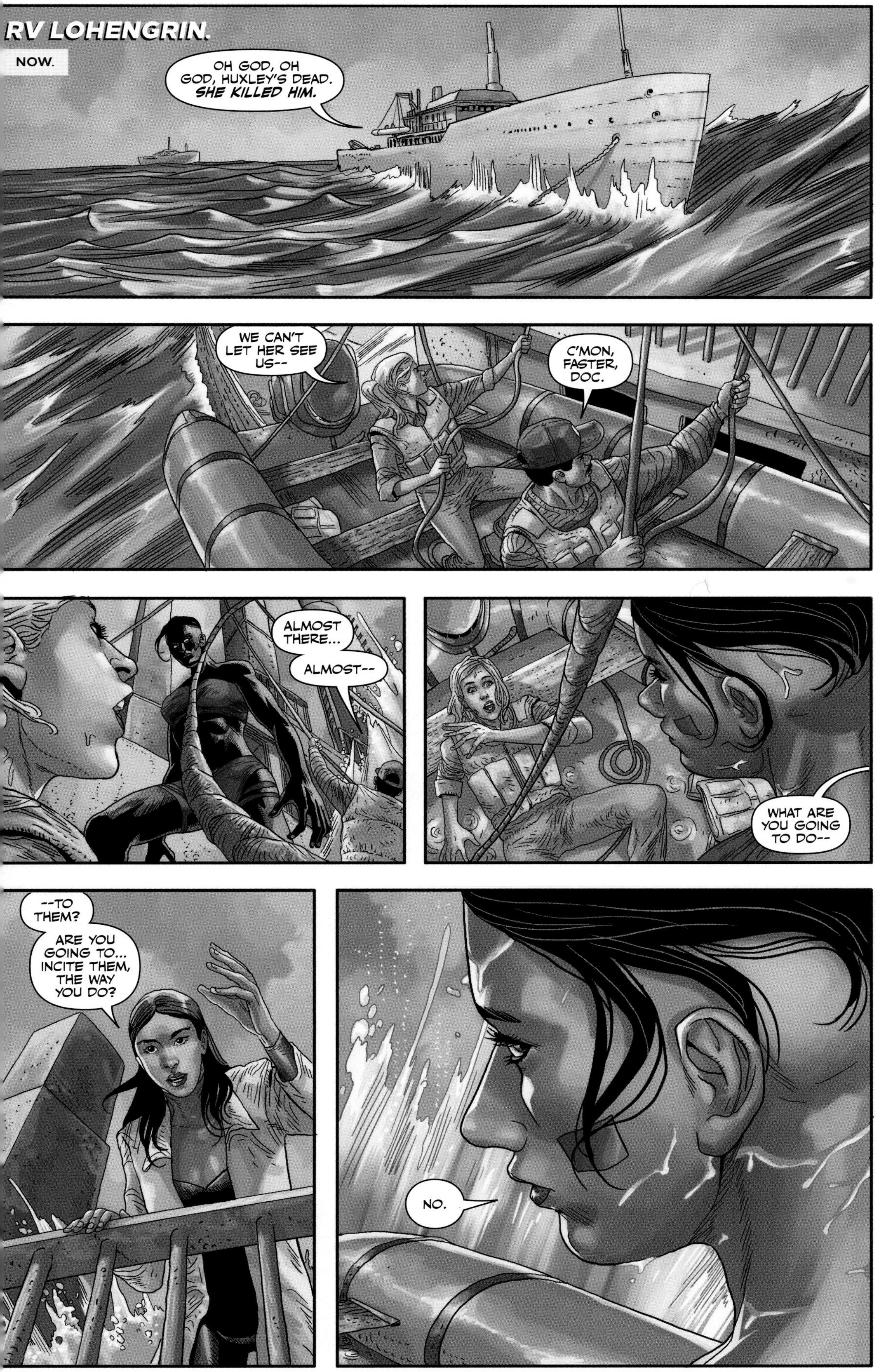
RV LOHENGRIN.
NOW.
OH GOD, OH GOD, HUXLEY'S DEAD. SHE KILLED HIM.
WE CAN'T LET HER SEE US--
C'MON, FASTER, DOC.
ALMOST THERE...
ALMOST--
WHAT ARE YOU GOING TO DO--
--TO THEM?
ARE YOU GOING TO... INCITE THEM, THE WAY YOU DO?
NO.

THEY AREN'T A THREAT.

YOU SAID I LOOKED FAMILIAR. I CAN EXPLAIN WHY--IT'S TEMÜJIN, THE KHAN. HE HAD SO MANY CHILDREN, WE CAN STILL TRACE HIS GENETICS TODAY--

WHAT?

WHAT'S THAT, 600 YEARS?

CLOSER TO 700, ACTUALLY.

THAT'S FUNNY, THAT YOU WOULD EVEN THINK TO TRACE THAT. THAT WASN'T THAT LONG AGO.

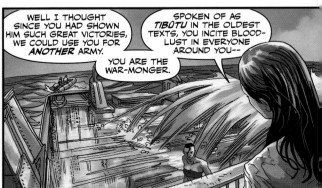

WELL I THOUGHT SINCE YOU HAD SHOWN HIM SUCH GREAT VICTORIES, WE COULD USE YOU FOR *ANOTHER* ARMY.

SPOKEN OF AS *TIBŪTU* IN THE OLDEST TEXTS, YOU INCITE BLOOD-LUST IN EVERYONE AROUND YOU--

YOU ARE THE WAR-MONGER.

≥TCH≤ NOT EVERYONE.

AND YOU DON'T WANT MY HELP.

WHERE ARE YOU GOING?

THE SHIP IS SINKING!

GETTING DRESSED.

I'VE GOT A STORY FOR YOU.

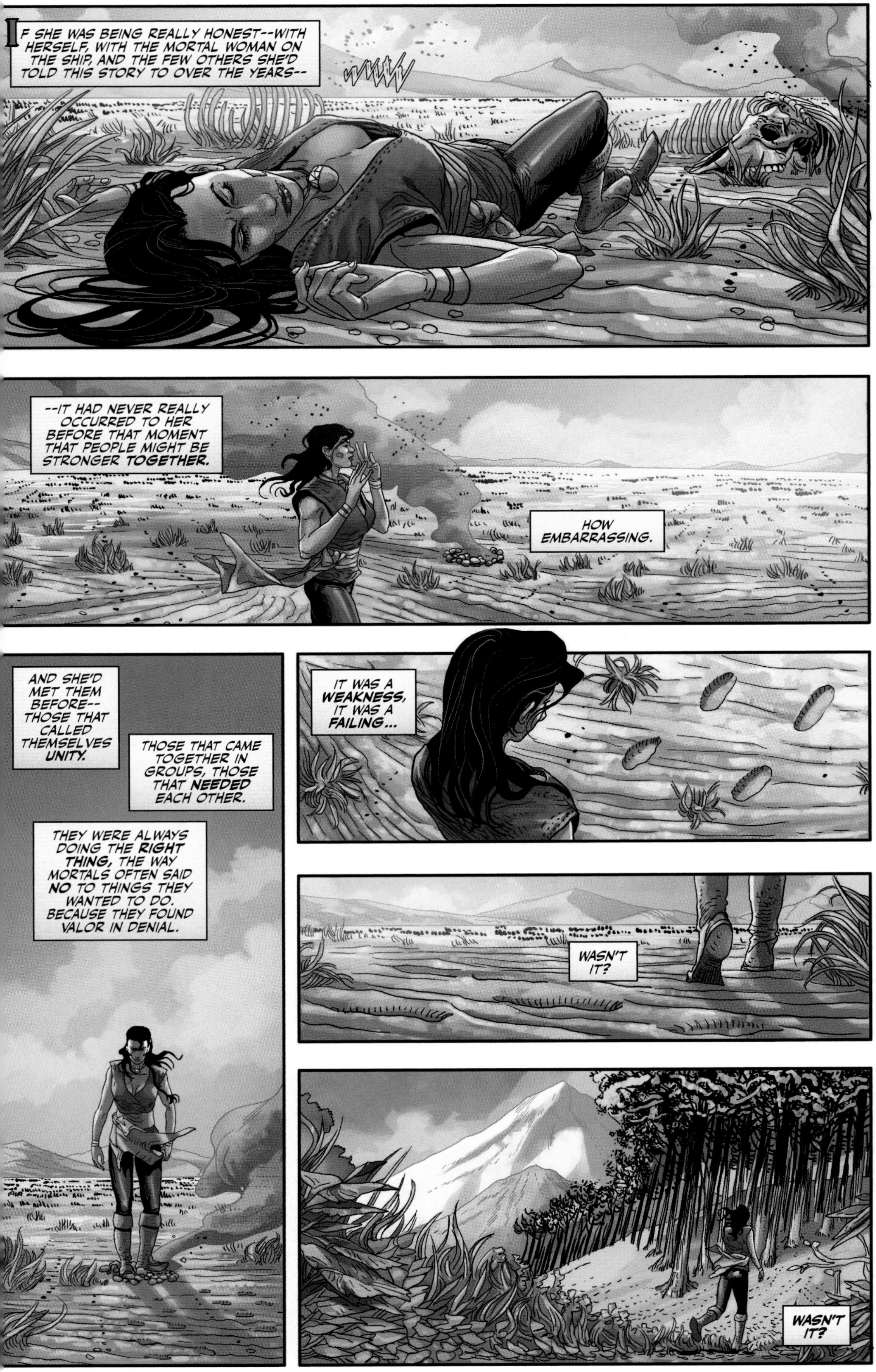
IF SHE WAS BEING REALLY HONEST--WITH HERSELF, WITH THE MORTAL WOMAN ON THE SHIP, AND THE FEW OTHERS SHE'D TOLD THIS STORY TO OVER THE YEARS--
--IT HAD NEVER REALLY OCCURRED TO HER BEFORE THAT MOMENT THAT PEOPLE MIGHT BE STRONGER TOGETHER.
HOW EMBARRASSING.
AND SHE'D MET THEM BEFORE-- THOSE THAT CALLED THEMSELVES UNITY.
THOSE THAT CAME TOGETHER IN GROUPS, THOSE THAT NEEDED EACH OTHER.
THEY WERE ALWAYS DOING THE RIGHT THING, THE WAY MORTALS OFTEN SAID NO TO THINGS THEY WANTED TO DO. BECAUSE THEY FOUND VALOR IN DENIAL.
IT WAS A WEAKNESS, IT WAS A FAILING...
WASN'T IT?
WASN'T IT?

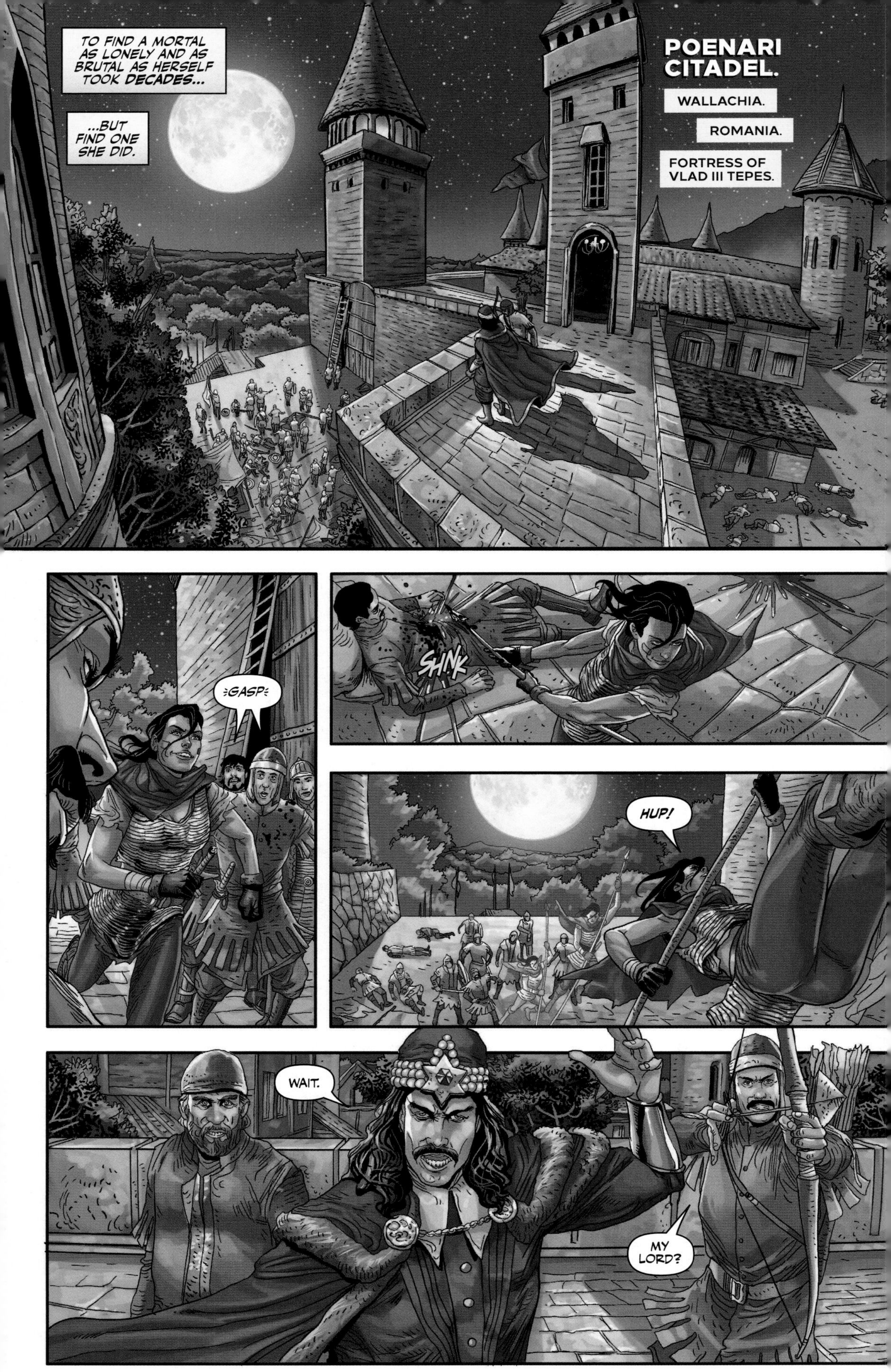
TO FIND A MORTAL AS LONELY AND AS BRUTAL AS HERSELF TOOK DECADES...
...BUT FIND ONE SHE DID.
POENARI CITADEL.
WALLACHIA.
ROMANIA.
FORTRESS OF VLAD III TEPES.
GASP
SHINK
HUP!
WAIT.
MY LORD?

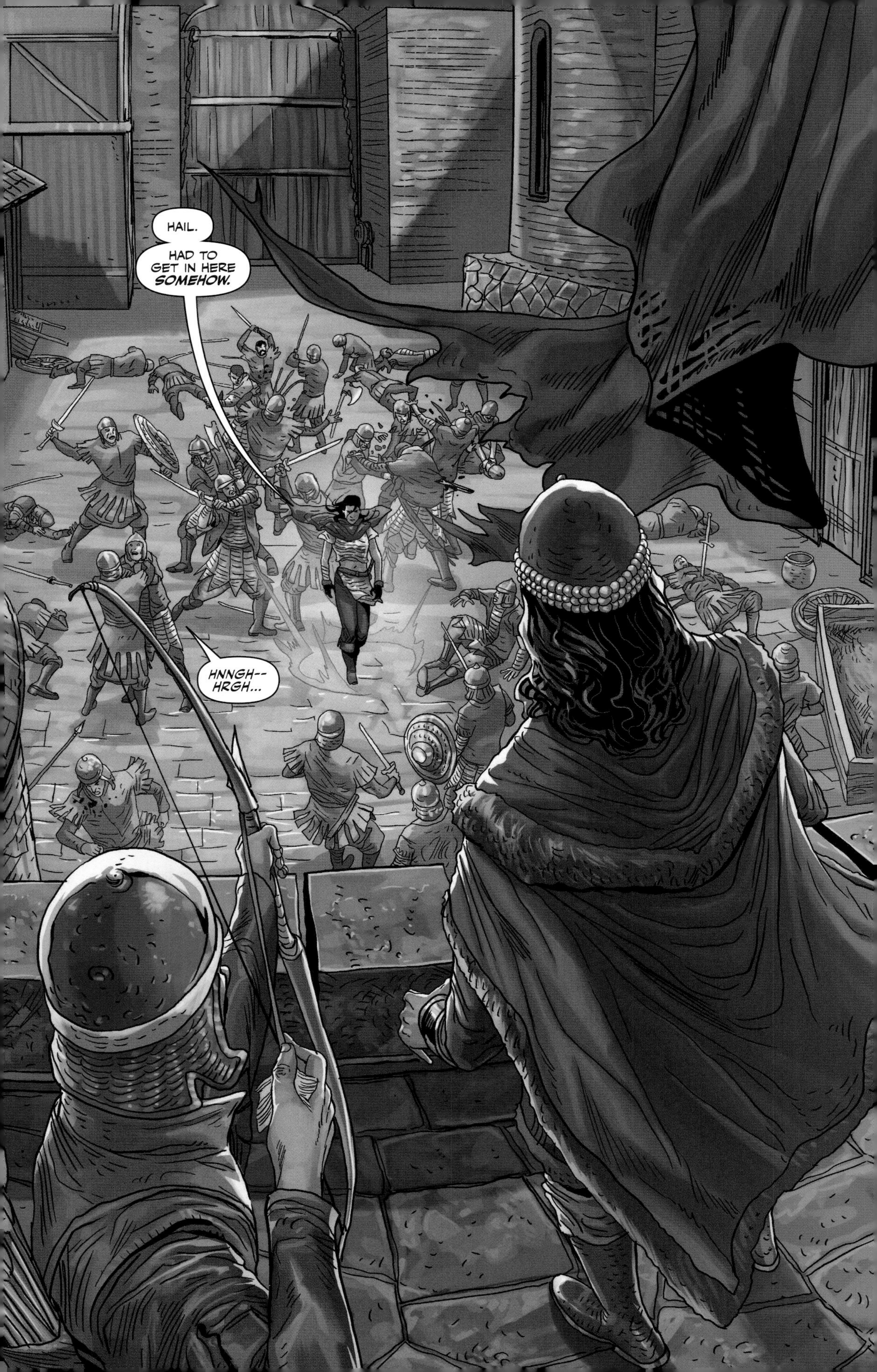
HAIL.
HAD TO GET IN HERE *SOMEHOW.*
HNNGH-- HRGH...

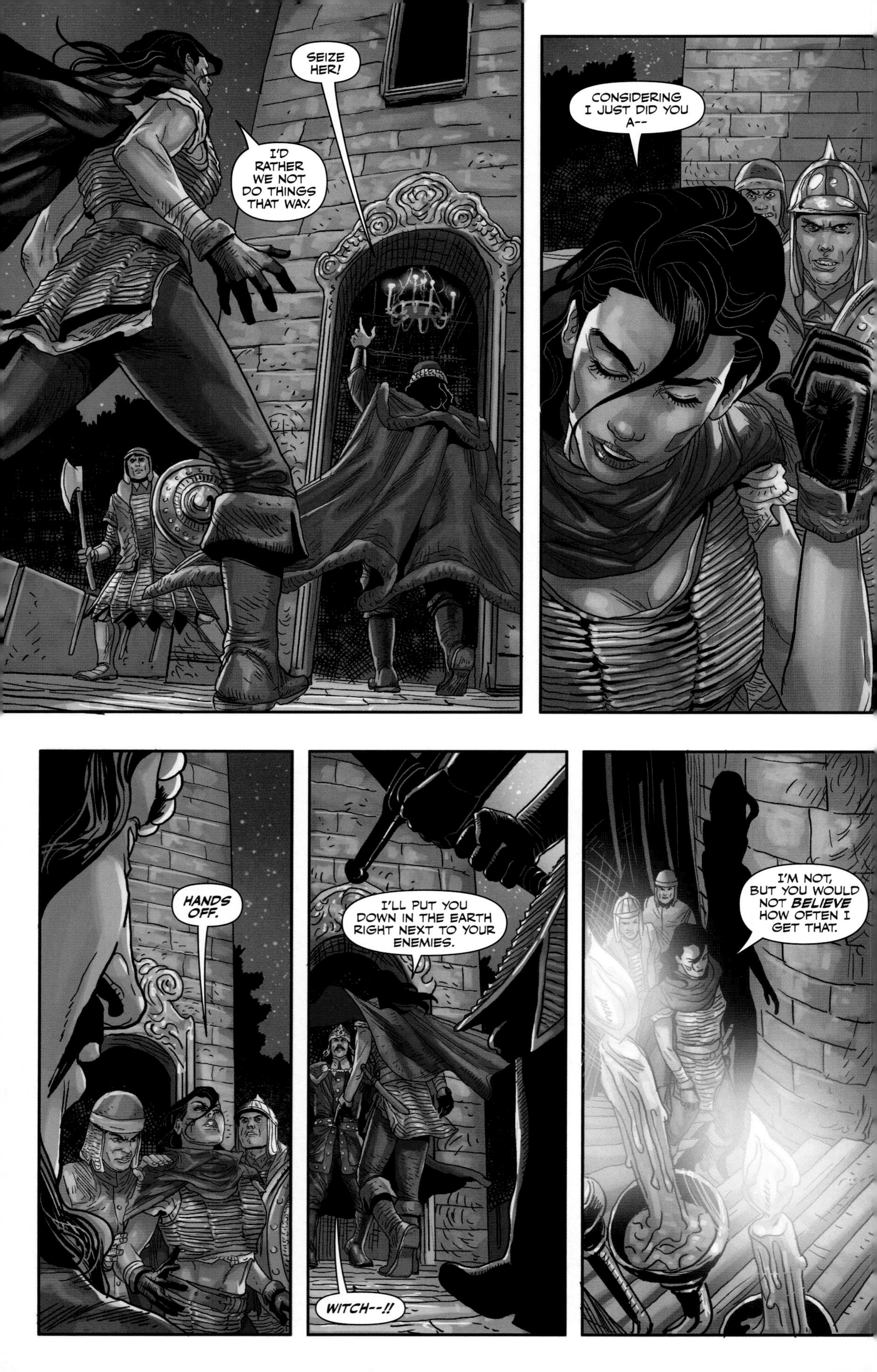
SEIZE HER!
I'D RATHER WE NOT DO THINGS THAT WAY.
CONSIDERING I JUST DID YOU A--
HANDS OFF.
I'LL PUT YOU DOWN IN THE EARTH RIGHT NEXT TO YOUR ENEMIES.
WITCH--!!
I'M NOT, BUT YOU WOULD NOT BELIEVE HOW OFTEN I GET THAT.

I AM VLAD DRACULA. I AM ATTEMPTING TO MAKE ORDER OUT OF CHAOS, FOLLOWING THE DEATH OF MY ELDERS.

MY PEOPLE CALL FOR ME TO PROTECT THEM FROM EXTERIOR THREATS, AND I CANNOT EVEN PROTECT THEM FROM NEIGHBORING LORDS.

MY OWN BROTHER-IN-LAW RADU RIDES WITH THE TURKS. HE PLOTS AGAINST ME. I KNOW IT.

PLEASE, EAT.

NO, THANK YOU.

IS IT TRUE, THAT YOU ARE IMMORTAL?

I UNDERSTAND THE VALUE OF A LIE TO FRIGHTEN SUBJECTS.

IT ISN'T A LIE. I AM IMMORTAL.

THEN YOU DO NOT EAT.

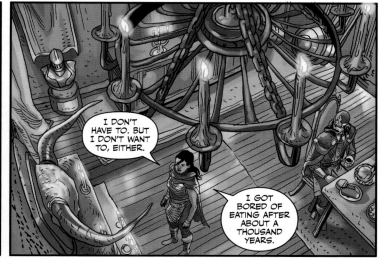

I DON'T HAVE TO. BUT I DON'T WANT TO, EITHER.

I GOT BORED OF EATING AFTER ABOUT A THOUSAND YEARS.

SO WHAT DO YOU WANT THEN, DEMON?

YOU OFFER ME THE POWER OF BLOODLUST. YOU MUST WANT SOMETHING IN RETURN.

SO LONELY HAD SHE BEEN, SO DESPERATE FOR COMPANIONSHIP WHO ACCEPTED HER FOR WHAT SHE WAS...

NOTHING.

IT HADN'T OCCURRED TO HER TO ASK FOR ANYTHING AT ALL.

I DON'T WANT ANYTHING. I JUST WANT TO SHARE WHAT I CAN DO WITH POWERFUL MORTALS. TO DRIVE YOUR MEN INTO BLOODLUST AGAINST THEIR FOES--

OH.

YOU MIS-UNDERSTAND.

I DON'T WANT YOU TO USE YOUR POWER ON MY MEN.

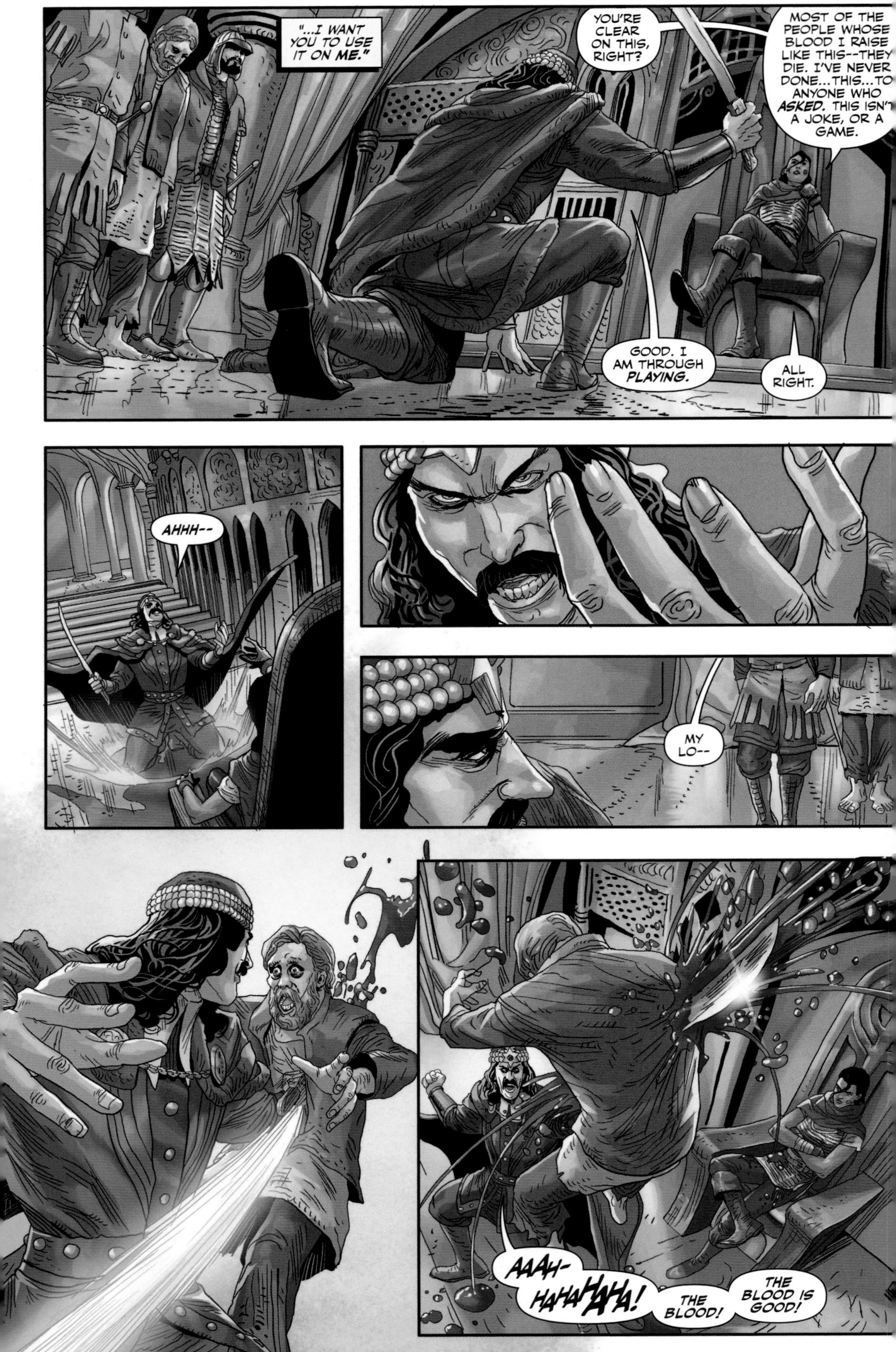
"...I WANT YOU TO USE IT ON ME."
YOU'RE CLEAR ON THIS, RIGHT?
MOST OF THE PEOPLE WHOSE BLOOD I RAISE LIKE THIS--THEY DIE. I'VE NEVER DONE...THIS...TO ANYONE WHO ASKED. THIS ISN'T A JOKE, OR A GAME.
GOOD. I AM THROUGH PLAYING.
ALL RIGHT.
AHHH--
MY LO--
AAAH-HAHAHAHA!
THE BLOOD!
THE BLOOD IS GOOD!

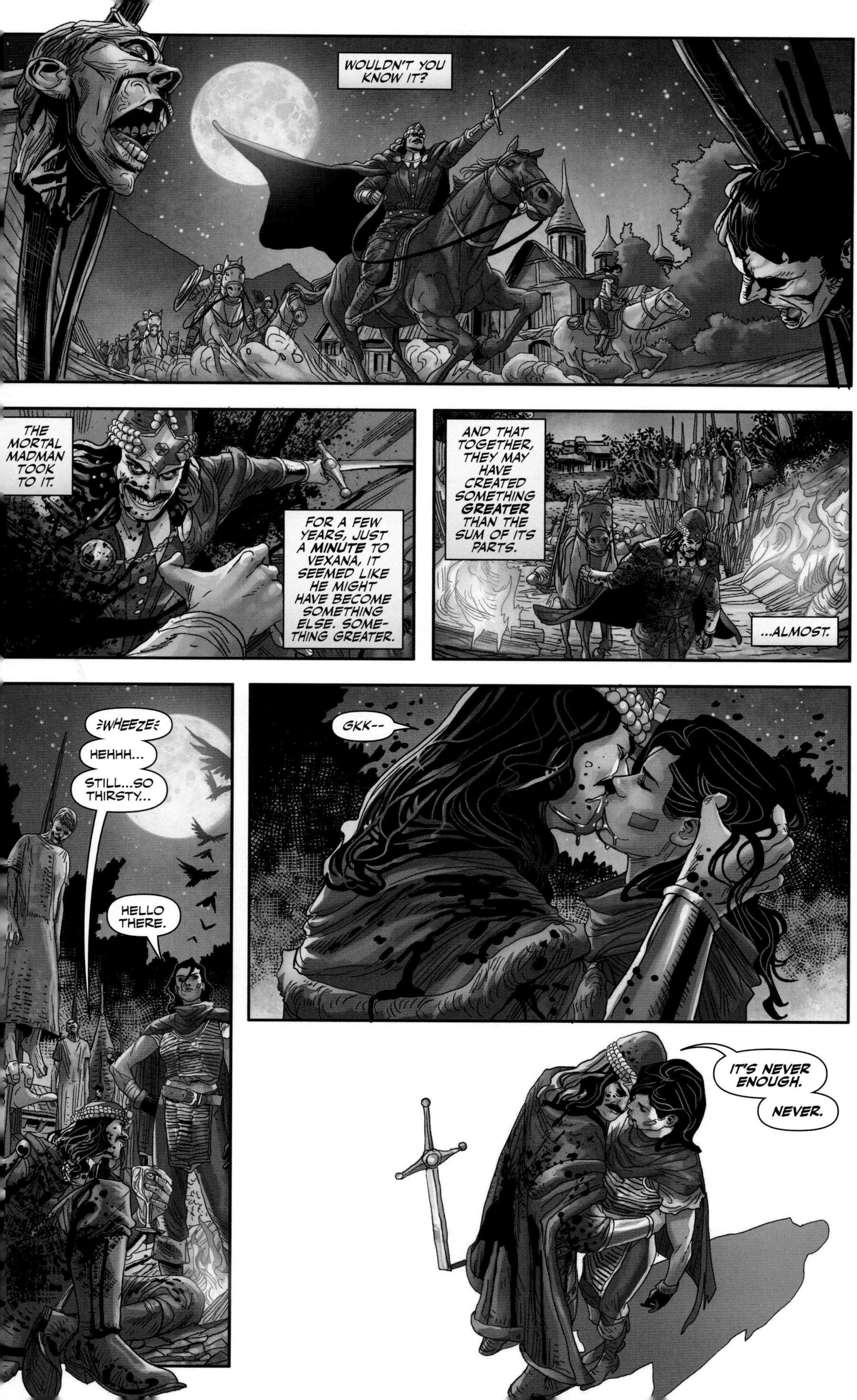
WOULDN'T YOU KNOW IT?
THE MORTAL MADMAN TOOK TO IT.
FOR A FEW YEARS, JUST A MINUTE TO VEXANA, IT SEEMED LIKE HE MIGHT HAVE BECOME SOMETHING ELSE. SOMETHING GREATER.
AND THAT TOGETHER, THEY MAY HAVE CREATED SOMETHING GREATER THAN THE SUM OF ITS PARTS.
...ALMOST.
WHEEZE
HEHHH...
STILL...SO THIRSTY...
HELLO THERE.
GKK--
IT'S NEVER ENOUGH.
NEVER.

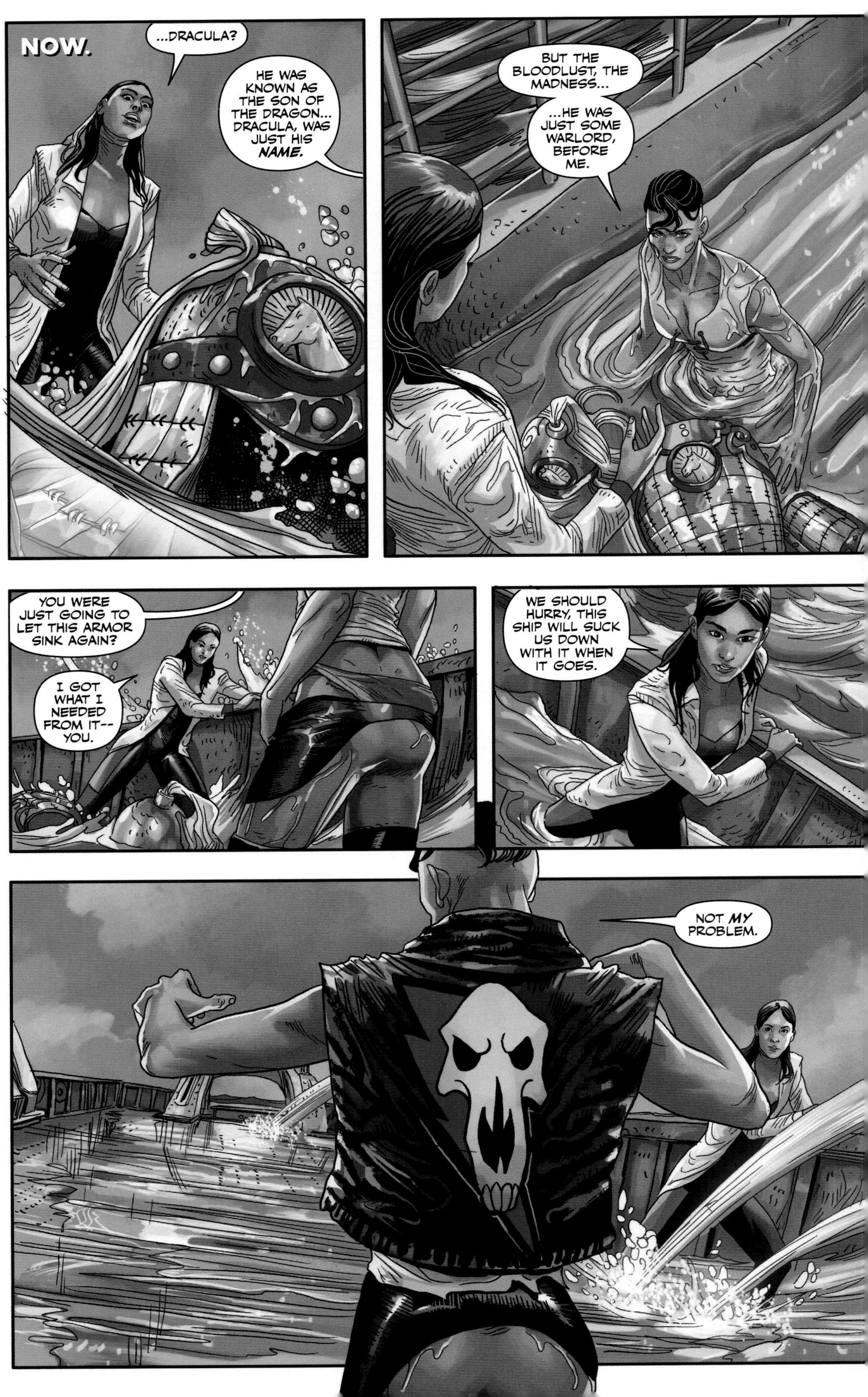
NOW.
...DRACULA?
HE WAS KNOWN AS THE SON OF THE DRAGON... DRACULA, WAS JUST HIS *NAME.*
BUT THE BLOODLUST, THE MADNESS...
...HE WAS JUST SOME WARLORD, BEFORE ME.
YOU WERE JUST GOING TO LET THIS ARMOR SINK AGAIN?
I GOT WHAT I NEEDED FROM IT-- YOU.
WE SHOULD HURRY, THIS SHIP WILL SUCK US DOWN WITH IT WHEN IT GOES.
NOT *MY* PROBLEM.

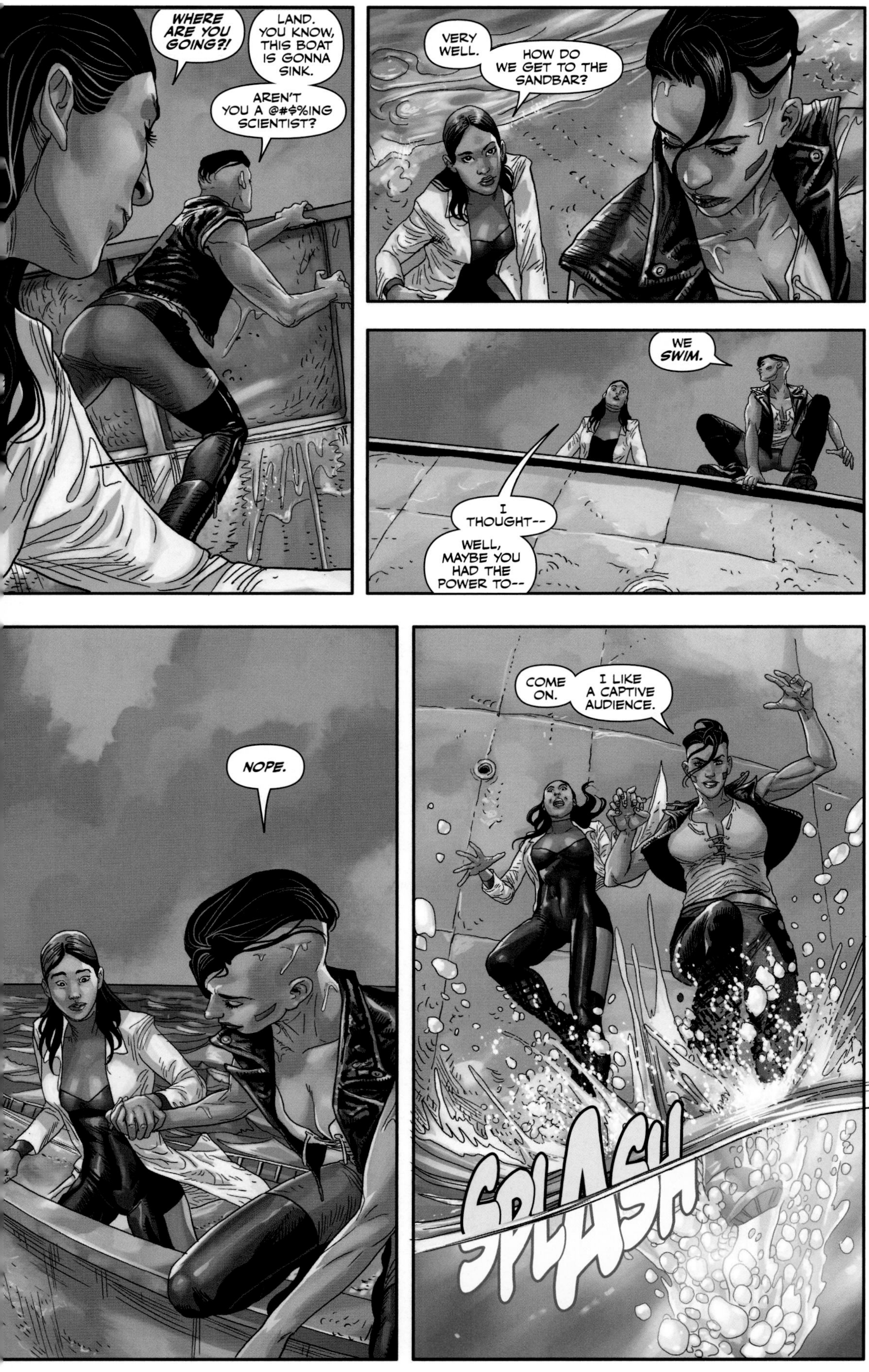
WHERE ARE YOU GOING?!
LAND. YOU KNOW, THIS BOAT IS GONNA SINK.
AREN'T YOU A @#$%ING SCIENTIST?
VERY WELL.
HOW DO WE GET TO THE SANDBAR?
WE SWIM.
I THOUGHT--
WELL, MAYBE YOU HAD THE POWER TO--
NOPE.
COME ON.
I LIKE A CAPTIVE AUDIENCE.
SPLASH

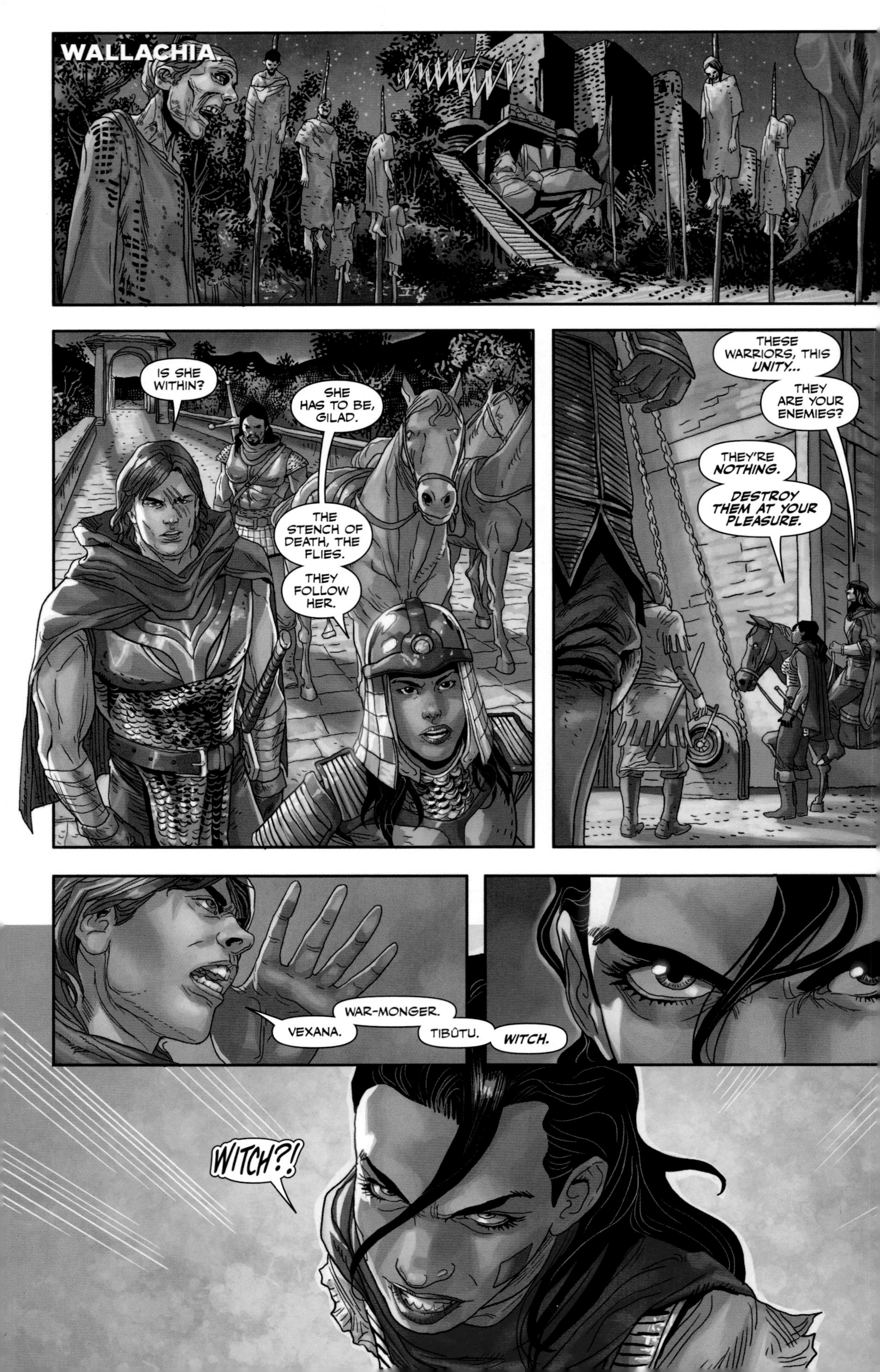
WALLACHIA.
IS SHE WITHIN?
SHE HAS TO BE, GILAD.
THE STENCH OF DEATH, THE FLIES.
THEY FOLLOW HER.
THESE WARRIORS, THIS UNITY...
THEY ARE YOUR ENEMIES?
THEY'RE NOTHING.
DESTROY THEM AT YOUR PLEASURE.
VEXANA.
WAR-MONGER.
TIBÛTU.
WITCH.
WITCH?!

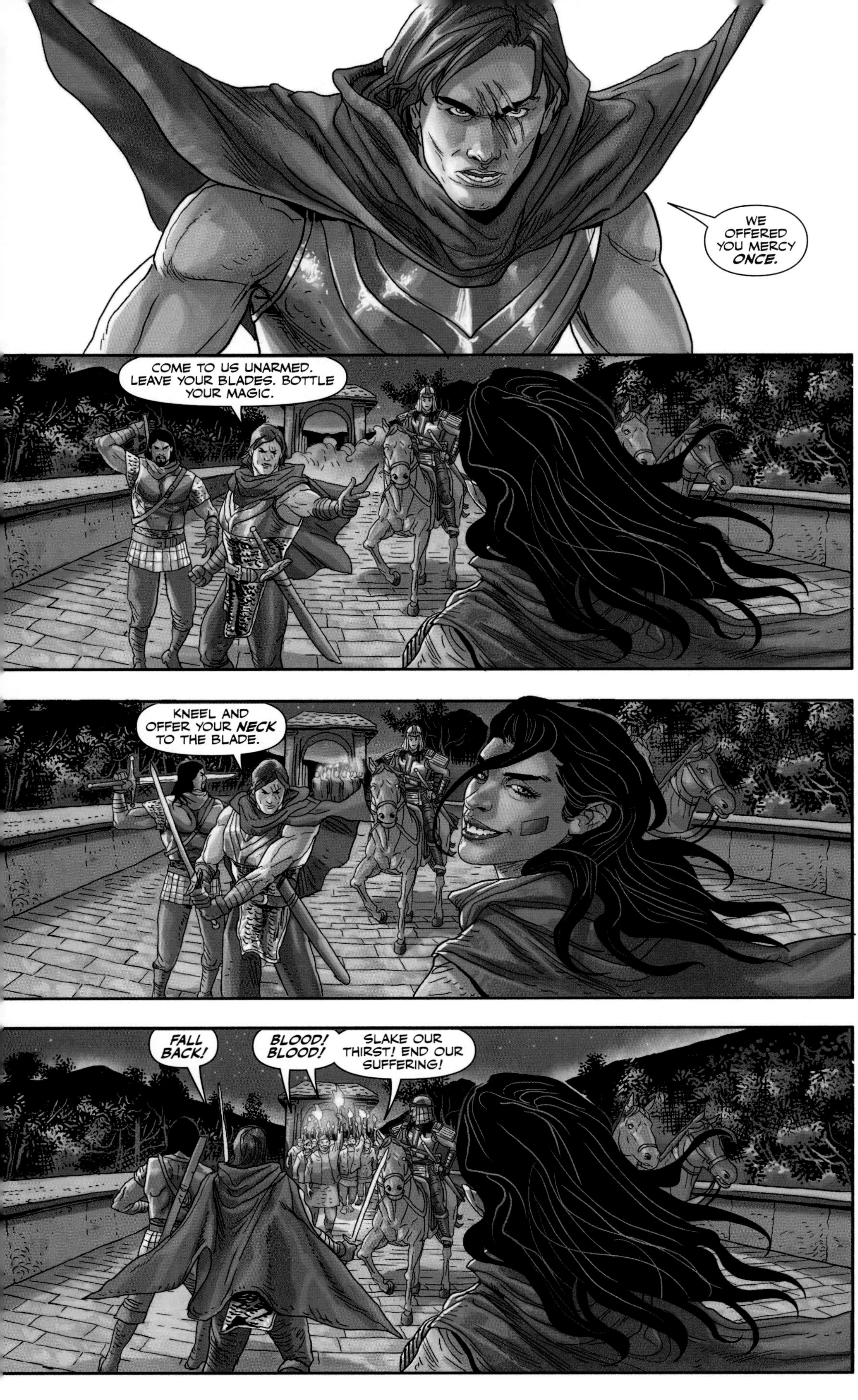
WE OFFERED YOU MERCY ONCE.
COME TO US UNARMED. LEAVE YOUR BLADES. BOTTLE YOUR MAGIC.
KNEEL AND OFFER YOUR NECK TO THE BLADE.
FALL BACK!
BLOOD! BLOOD!
SLAKE OUR THIRST! END OUR SUFFERING!

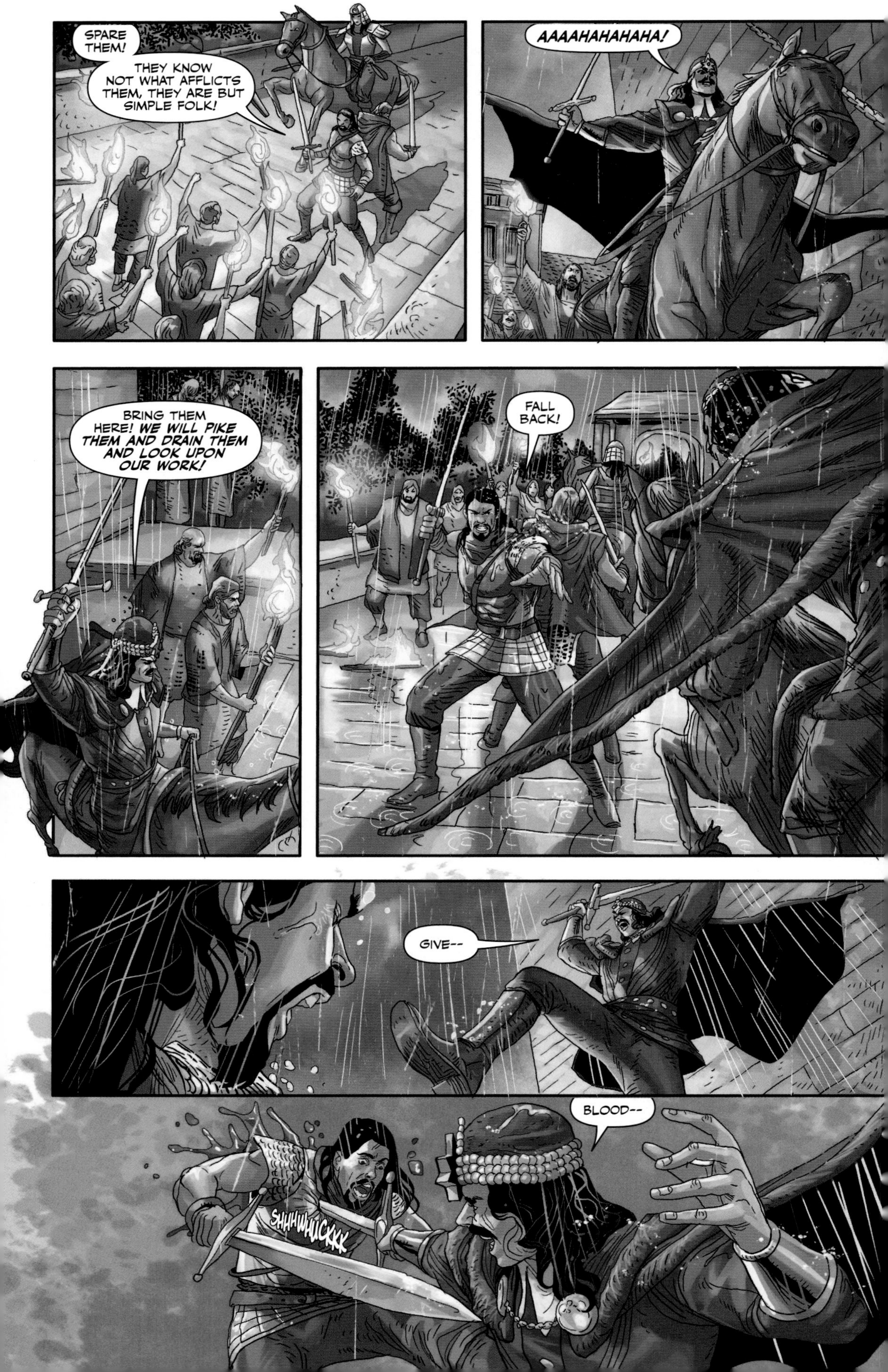
SPARE THEM!
THEY KNOW NOT WHAT AFFLICTS THEM, THEY ARE BUT SIMPLE FOLK!
AAAAHAHAHAHA!
BRING THEM HERE! WE WILL PIKE THEM AND DRAIN THEM AND LOOK UPON OUR WORK!
FALL BACK!
GIVE--
BLOOD--
SHHHWHUCKKK

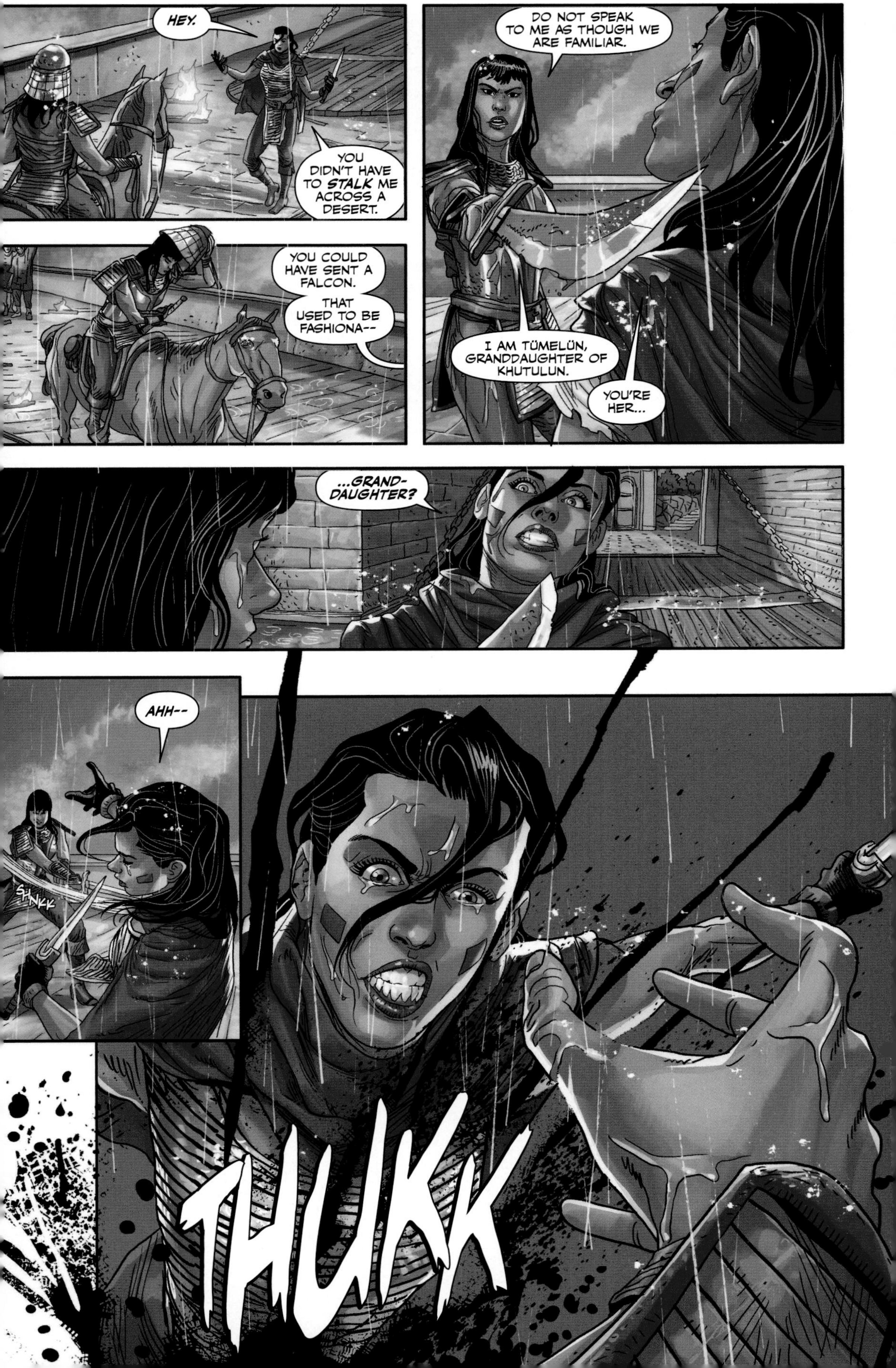
HEY.
YOU DIDN'T HAVE TO STALK ME ACROSS A DESERT.
YOU COULD HAVE SENT A FALCON.
THAT USED TO BE FASHIONA--
DO NOT SPEAK TO ME AS THOUGH WE ARE FAMILIAR.
I AM TÜMELÜN, GRANDDAUGHTER OF KHUTULUN.
YOU'RE HER...
...GRAND-DAUGHTER?
AHH--
SHNKK
THUKK

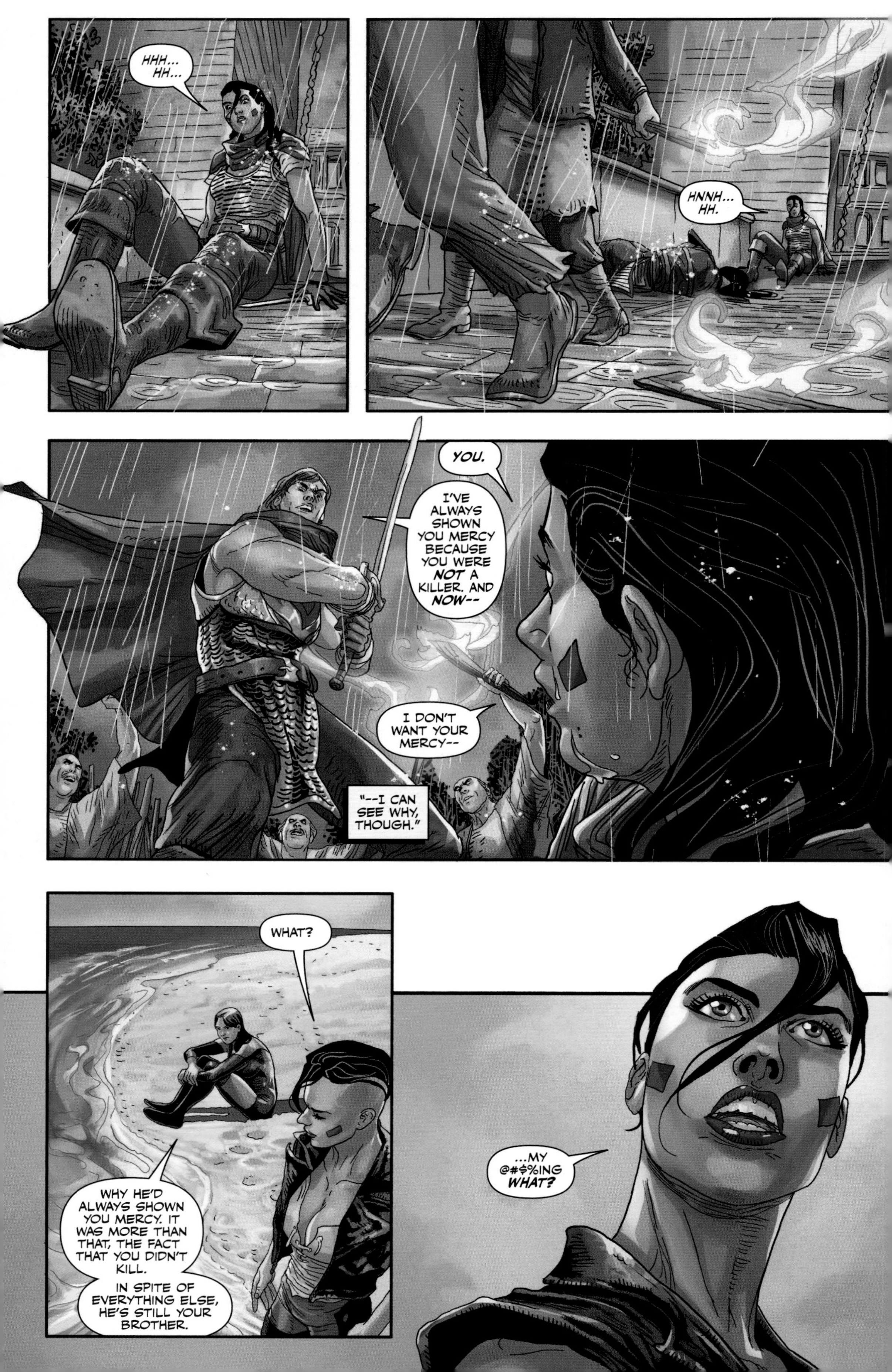
HHH... HH...
HNNH... HH.
YOU.
I'VE ALWAYS SHOWN YOU MERCY BECAUSE YOU WERE NOT A KILLER. AND NOW--
I DON'T WANT YOUR MERCY--
"--I CAN SEE WHY, THOUGH."
WHAT?
WHY HE'D ALWAYS SHOWN YOU MERCY. IT WAS MORE THAN THAT, THE FACT THAT YOU DIDN'T KILL.
IN SPITE OF EVERYTHING ELSE, HE'S STILL YOUR BROTHER.
...MY @#$%ING WHAT?

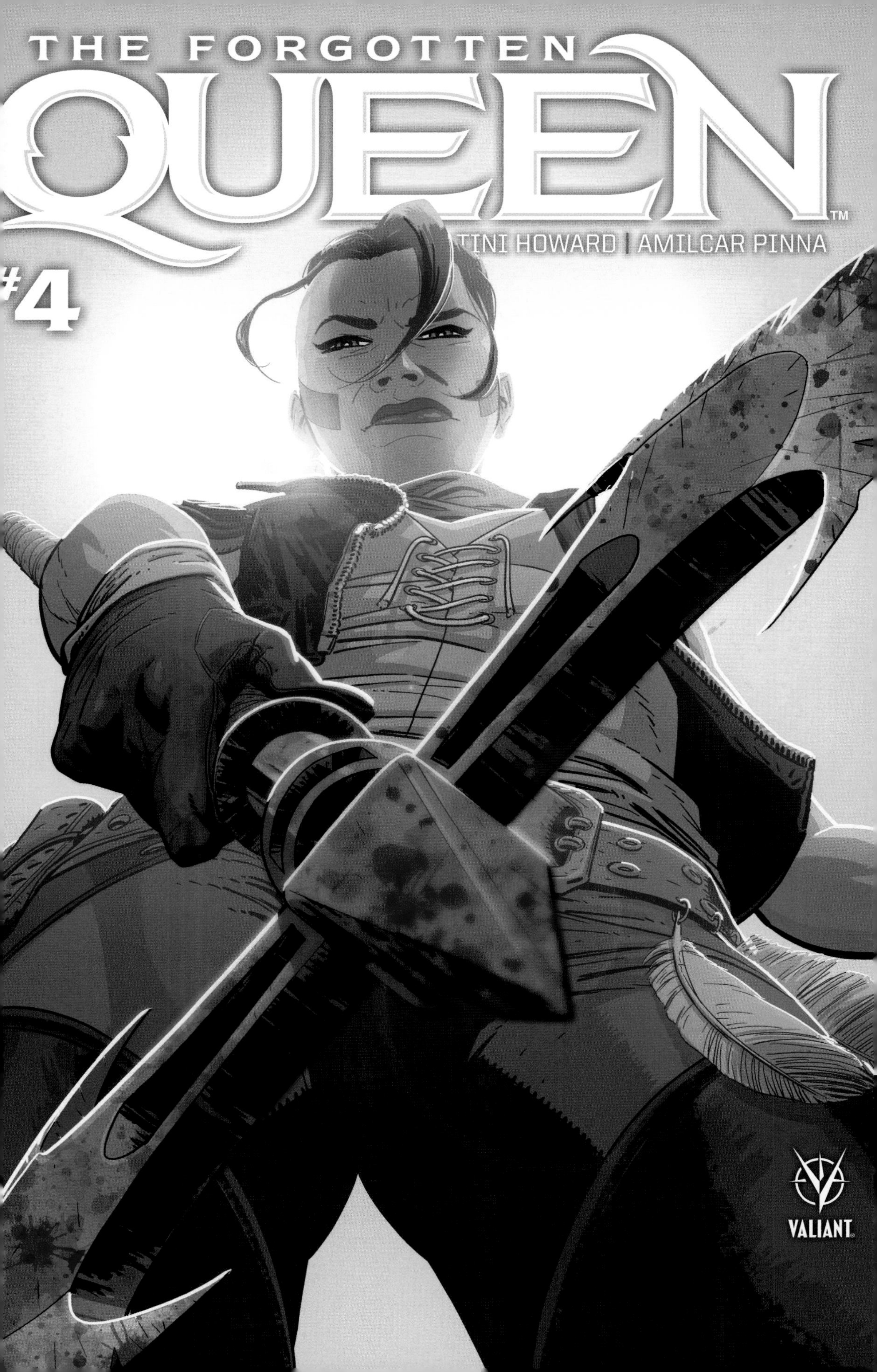
THE FORGOTTEN
QUEEN™
TINI HOWARD | AMILCAR PINNA
#4
VALIANT

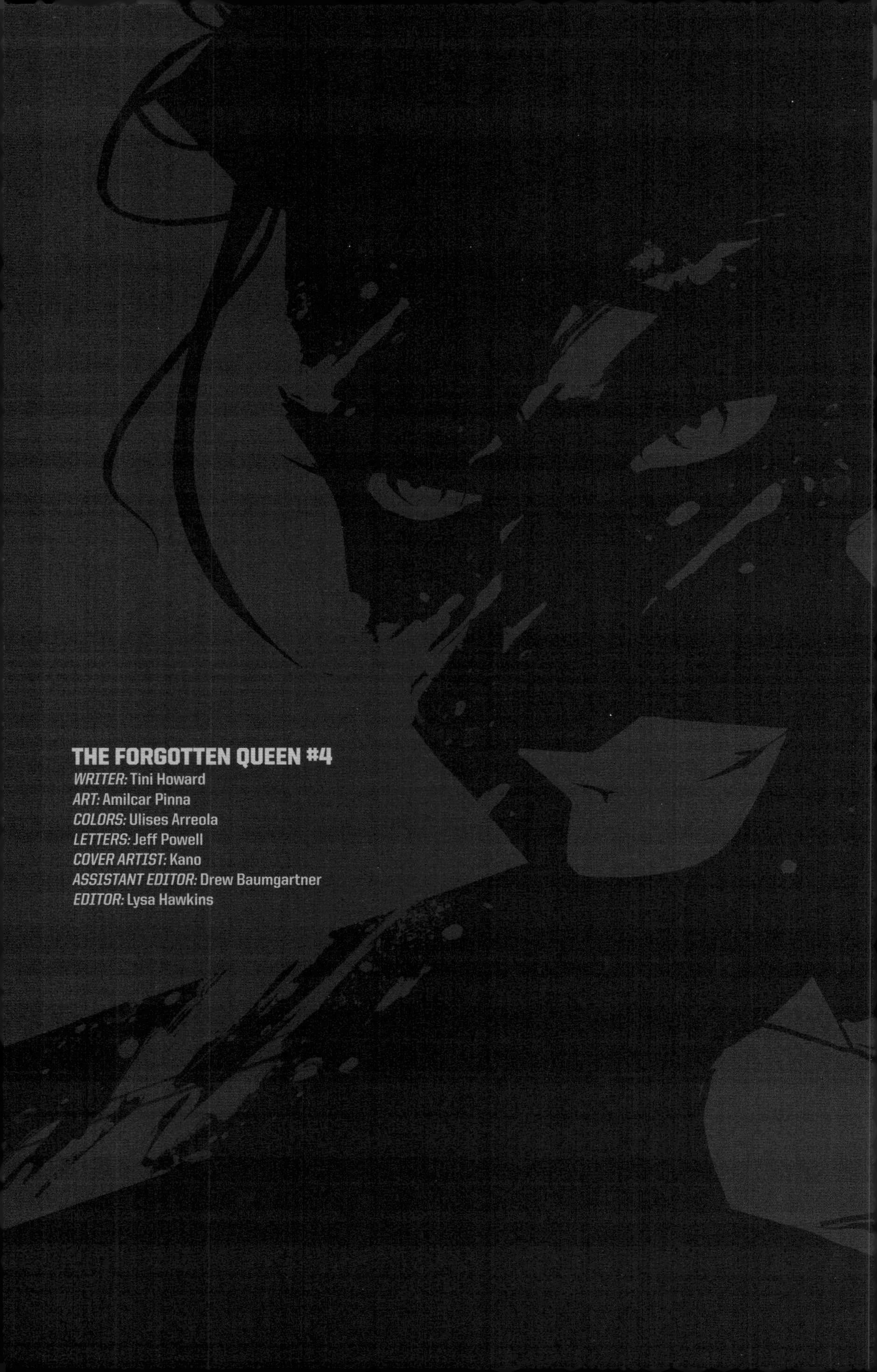

THE FORGOTTEN QUEEN #4

WRITER: Tini Howard
ART: Amilcar Pinna
COLORS: Ulises Arreola
LETTERS: Jeff Powell
COVER ARTIST: Kano
ASSISTANT EDITOR: Drew Baumgartner
EDITOR: Lysa Hawkins

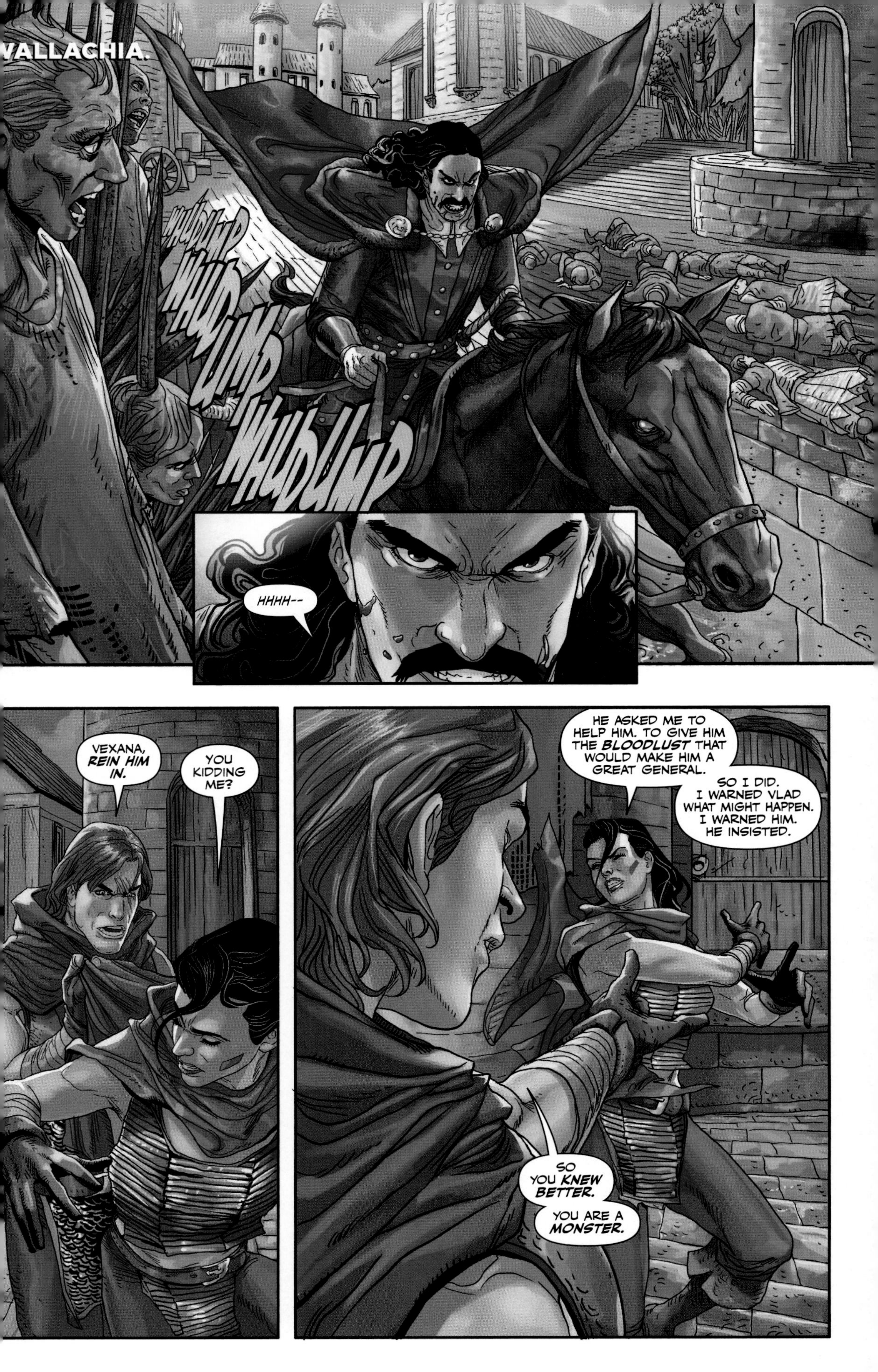
WALLACHIA.
WHUDUMP
WHUDUMP
WHUDUMP
WHUDUMP
HHHH--
VEXANA, REIN HIM IN.
YOU KIDDING ME?
HE ASKED ME TO HELP HIM. TO GIVE HIM THE BLOODLUST THAT WOULD MAKE HIM A GREAT GENERAL.
SO I DID. I WARNED VLAD WHAT MIGHT HAPPEN. I WARNED HIM. HE INSISTED.
SO YOU KNEW BETTER.
YOU ARE A MONSTER.

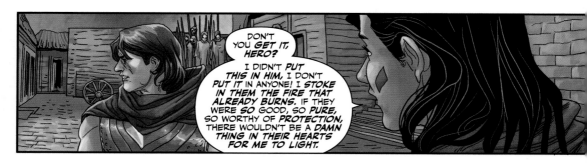

DON'T YOU *GET IT*, HERO?

I DIDN'T *PUT THIS IN HIM*, I DON'T *PUT IT IN ANYONE!* I *STOKE* IN THEM THE FIRE THAT *ALREADY BURNS.* IF THEY WERE *SO GOOD,* SO *PURE,* SO WORTHY OF *PROTECTION,* THERE WOULDN'T BE A *DAMN* THING IN THEIR HEARTS FOR ME TO LIGHT.

REIN TEPES IN, OR I'LL BE FORCED TO.

TCH. I DON'T WANT THAT.

LET'S CUT HIM OFF, HE'S HEADED SOUTH.

YAH!

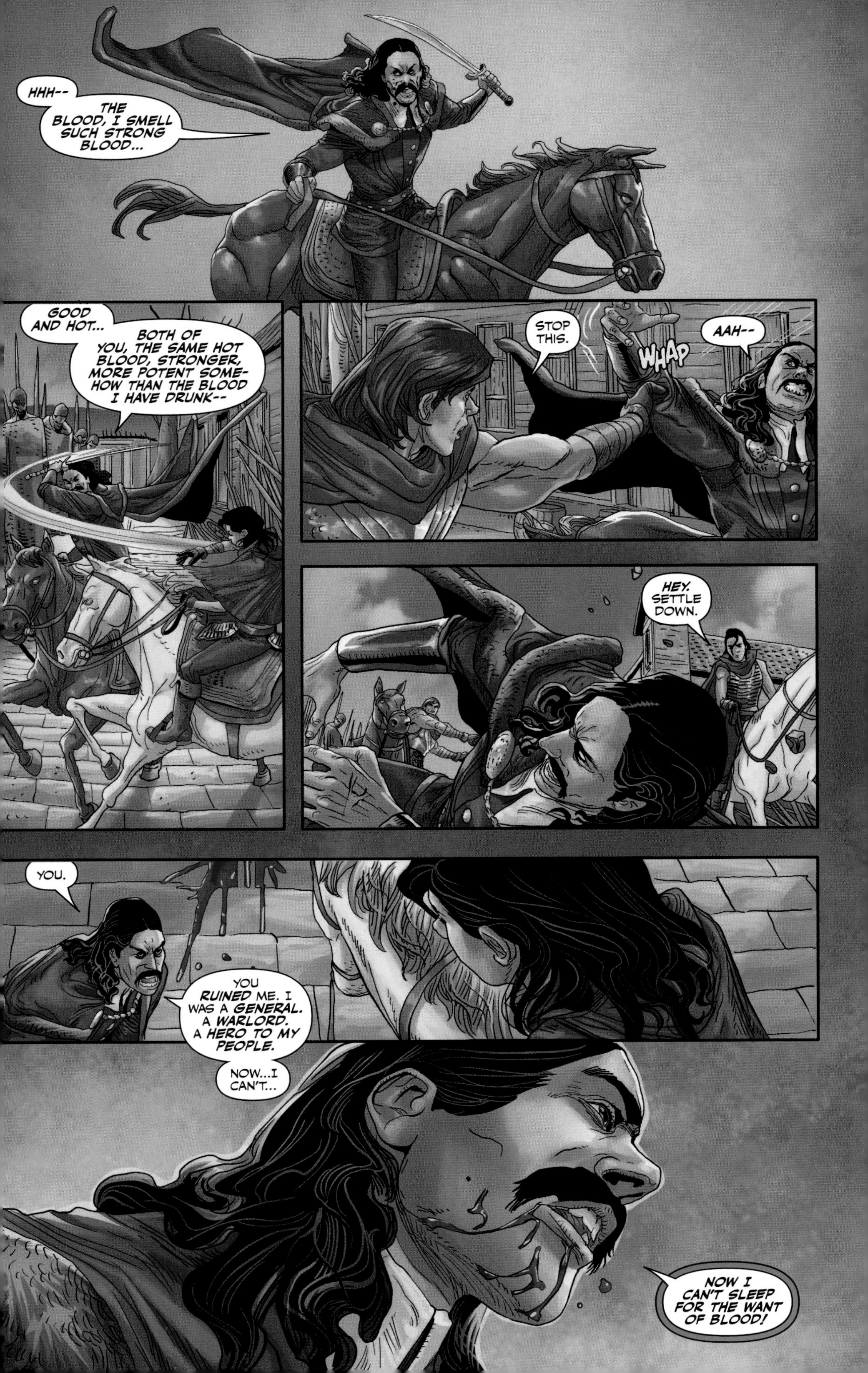
HHH--
THE BLOOD, I SMELL SUCH STRONG BLOOD...
GOOD AND HOT...
BOTH OF YOU, THE SAME HOT BLOOD, STRONGER, MORE POTENT SOMEHOW THAN THE BLOOD I HAVE DRUNK--
STOP THIS.
WHAP
AAH--
HEY. SETTLE DOWN.
YOU.
YOU RUINED ME. I WAS A GENERAL. A WARLORD. A HERO TO MY PEOPLE.
NOW...I CAN'T...
NOW I CAN'T SLEEP FOR THE WANT OF BLOOD!

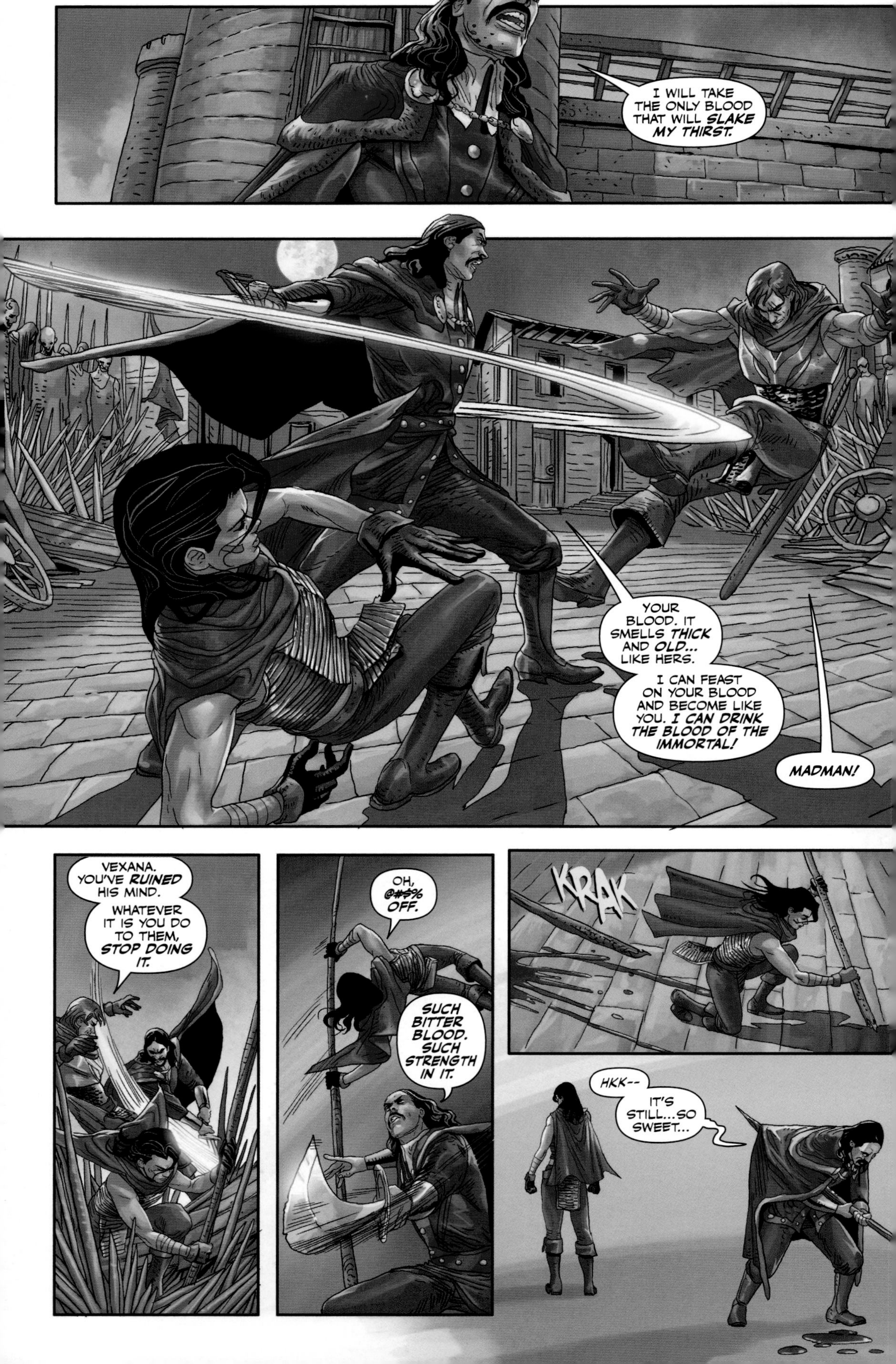
I WILL TAKE THE ONLY BLOOD THAT WILL SLAKE MY THIRST.
YOUR BLOOD. IT SMELLS THICK AND OLD... LIKE HERS.
I CAN FEAST ON YOUR BLOOD AND BECOME LIKE YOU. I CAN DRINK THE BLOOD OF THE IMMORTAL!
MADMAN!
VEXANA. YOU'VE RUINED HIS MIND.
WHATEVER IT IS YOU DO TO THEM, STOP DOING IT.
OH, @#$% OFF.
SUCH BITTER BLOOD. SUCH STRENGTH IN IT.
KRAK
HKK--
IT'S STILL...SO SWEET...

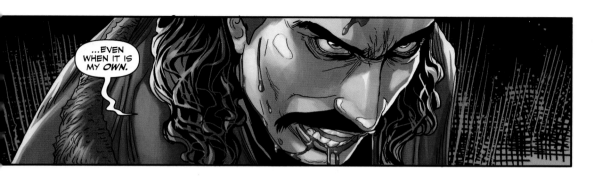

...EVEN WHEN IT IS MY *OWN.*

"FROM THERE, HONESTLY, THINGS GO BLURRY FOR A WHILE.

ENOUGH FROM YOU.

"FOR ALL HIS TALK OF *MERCY,* HE SURE FORGOT IT WHEN WE THREW THE @#$% DOWN.

"OR MAYBE I JUST REALLY *GOT TO HIM.*"

"THAT'S *FAMILY,* I SUPPOSE."

"YEAH, ABOUT THAT..."

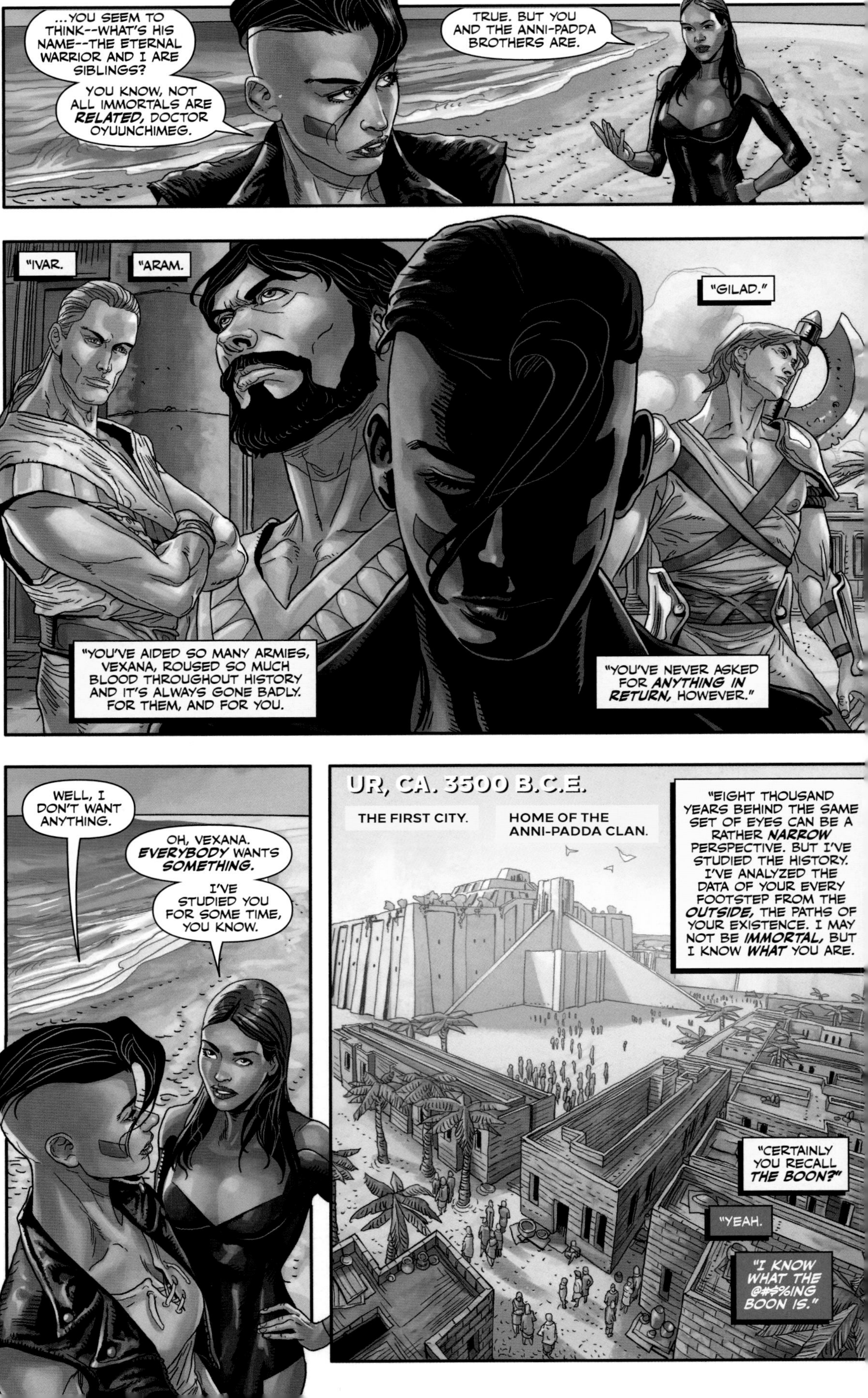
...YOU SEEM TO THINK--WHAT'S HIS NAME--THE ETERNAL WARRIOR AND I ARE SIBLINGS?
YOU KNOW, NOT ALL IMMORTALS ARE RELATED, DOCTOR OYUUNCHIMEG.
TRUE. BUT YOU AND THE ANNI-PADDA BROTHERS ARE.
"IVAR.
"ARAM.
"GILAD."
"YOU'VE AIDED SO MANY ARMIES, VEXANA, ROUSED SO MUCH BLOOD THROUGHOUT HISTORY AND IT'S ALWAYS GONE BADLY. FOR THEM, AND FOR YOU.
"YOU'VE NEVER ASKED FOR ANYTHING IN RETURN, HOWEVER."
WELL, I DON'T WANT ANYTHING.
OH, VEXANA. EVERYBODY WANTS SOMETHING.
I'VE STUDIED YOU FOR SOME TIME, YOU KNOW.
UR, CA. 3500 B.C.E.
THE FIRST CITY.
HOME OF THE ANNI-PADDA CLAN.
"EIGHT THOUSAND YEARS BEHIND THE SAME SET OF EYES CAN BE A RATHER NARROW PERSPECTIVE. BUT I'VE STUDIED THE HISTORY. I'VE ANALYZED THE DATA OF YOUR EVERY FOOTSTEP FROM THE OUTSIDE, THE PATHS OF YOUR EXISTENCE. I MAY NOT BE IMMORTAL, BUT I KNOW WHAT YOU ARE.
"CERTAINLY YOU RECALL THE BOON?"
"YEAH.
"I KNOW WHAT THE @#$%ING BOON IS."

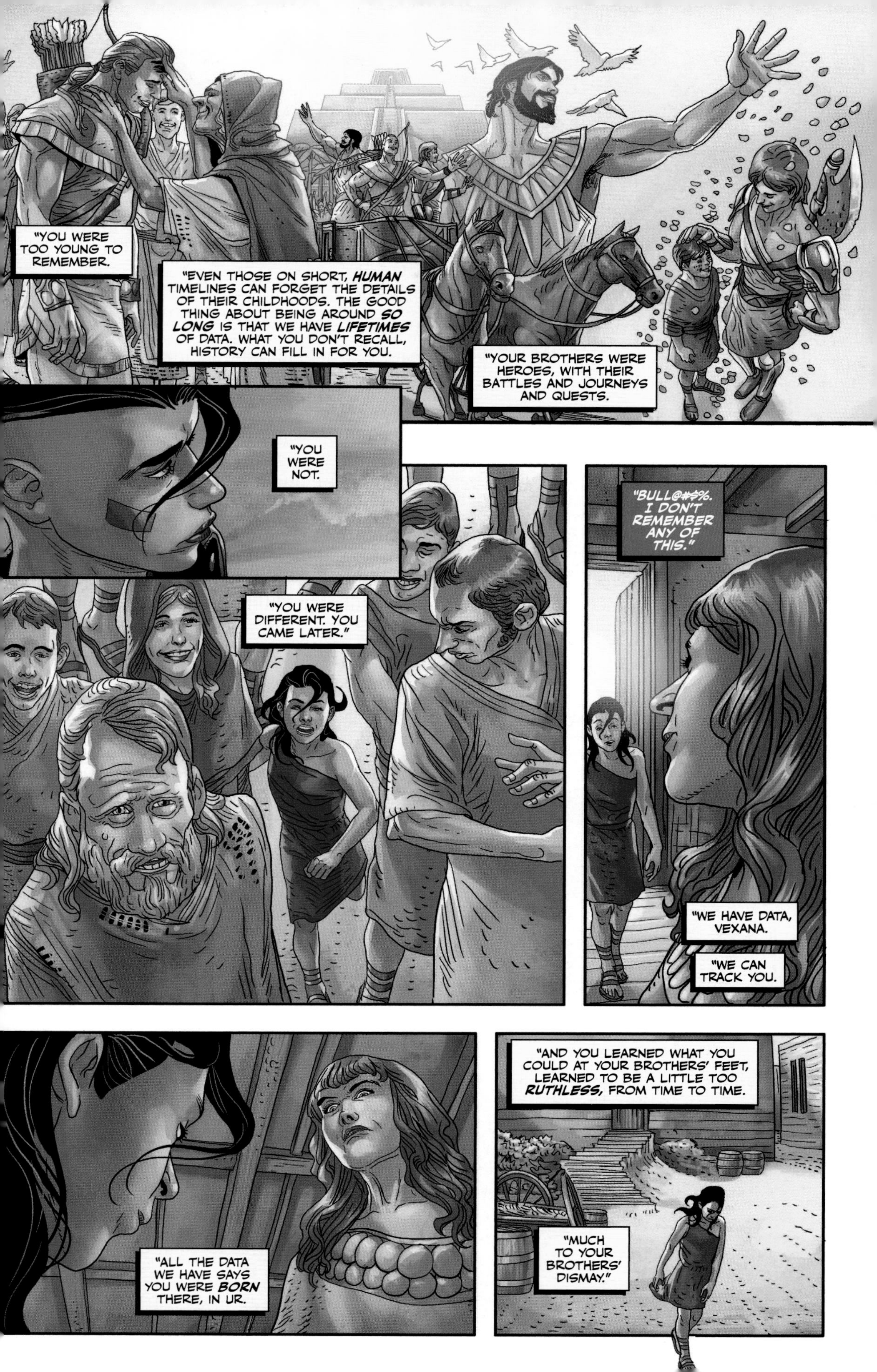
"YOU WERE TOO YOUNG TO REMEMBER.
"EVEN THOSE ON SHORT, HUMAN TIMELINES CAN FORGET THE DETAILS OF THEIR CHILDHOODS. THE GOOD THING ABOUT BEING AROUND SO LONG IS THAT WE HAVE LIFETIMES OF DATA. WHAT YOU DON'T RECALL, HISTORY CAN FILL IN FOR YOU.
"YOUR BROTHERS WERE HEROES, WITH THEIR BATTLES AND JOURNEYS AND QUESTS.
"YOU WERE NOT.
"YOU WERE DIFFERENT. YOU CAME LATER."
"BULL@#$%. I DON'T REMEMBER ANY OF THIS."
"WE HAVE DATA, VEXANA.
"WE CAN TRACK YOU.
"ALL THE DATA WE HAVE SAYS YOU WERE BORN THERE, IN UR.
"AND YOU LEARNED WHAT YOU COULD AT YOUR BROTHERS' FEET, LEARNED TO BE A LITTLE TOO RUTHLESS, FROM TIME TO TIME.
"MUCH TO YOUR BROTHERS' DISMAY."

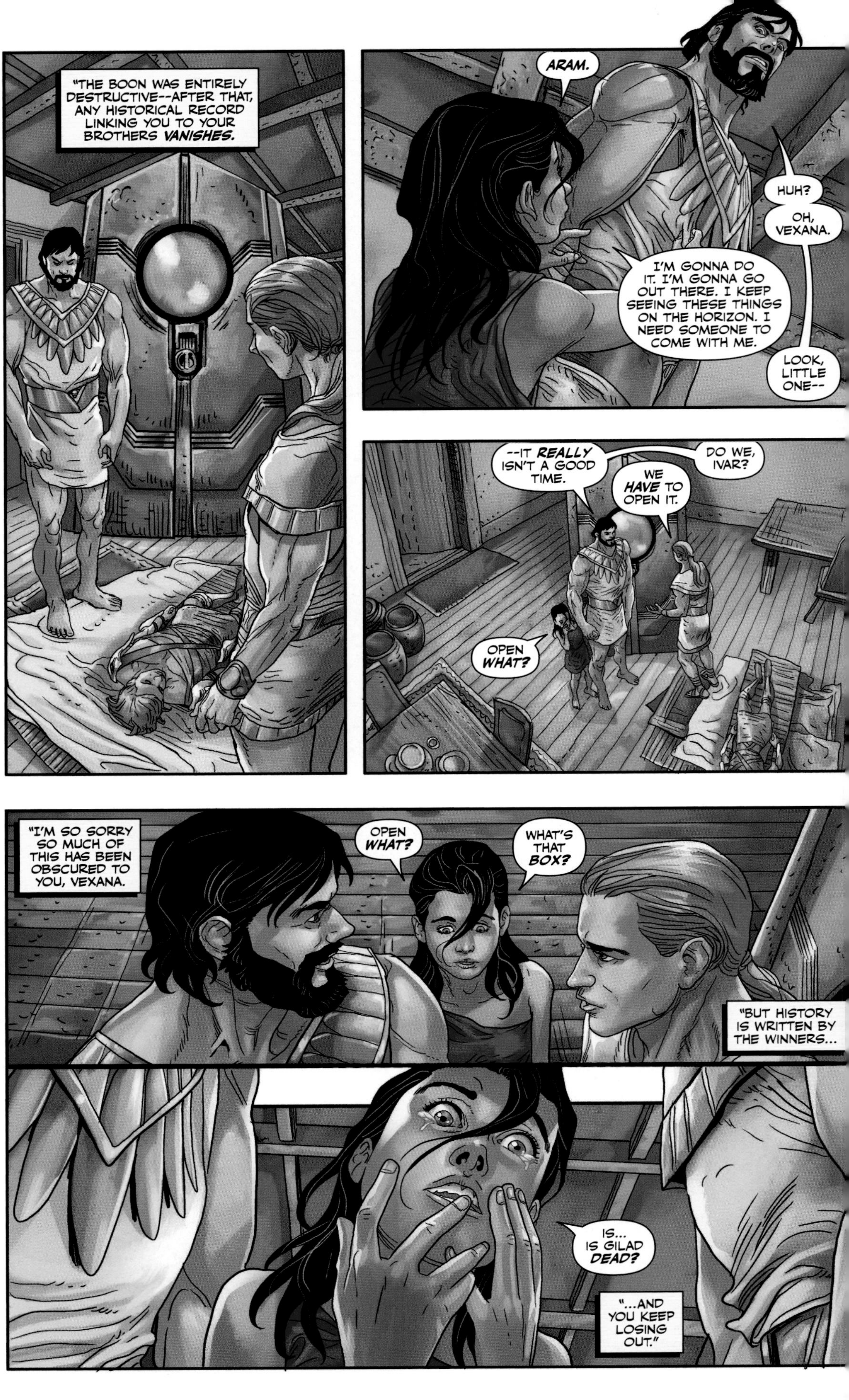
"THE BOON WAS ENTIRELY DESTRUCTIVE--AFTER THAT, ANY HISTORICAL RECORD LINKING YOU TO YOUR BROTHERS VANISHES.
ARAM.
HUH?
OH, VEXANA.
I'M GONNA DO IT. I'M GONNA GO OUT THERE. I KEEP SEEING THESE THINGS ON THE HORIZON. I NEED SOMEONE TO COME WITH ME.
LOOK, LITTLE ONE--
--IT REALLY ISN'T A GOOD TIME.
WE HAVE TO OPEN IT.
DO WE, IVAR?
OPEN WHAT?
"I'M SO SORRY SO MUCH OF THIS HAS BEEN OBSCURED TO YOU, VEXANA.
OPEN WHAT?
WHAT'S THAT BOX?
"BUT HISTORY IS WRITTEN BY THE WINNERS...
IS... IS GILAD DEAD?
"...AND YOU KEEP LOSING OUT."

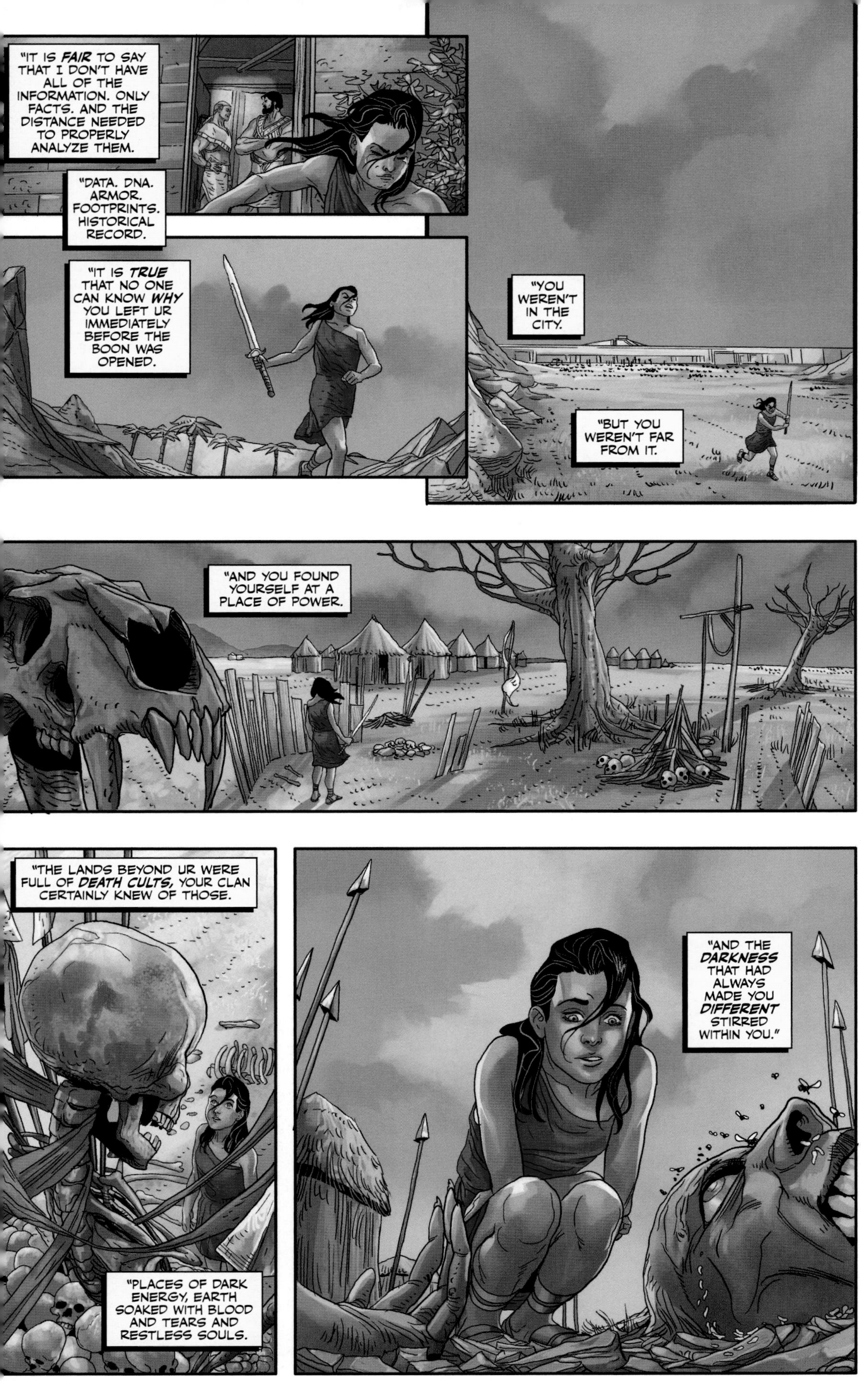
"IT IS FAIR TO SAY THAT I DON'T HAVE ALL OF THE INFORMATION. ONLY FACTS. AND THE DISTANCE NEEDED TO PROPERLY ANALYZE THEM.
"DATA. DNA. ARMOR. FOOTPRINTS. HISTORICAL RECORD.
"IT IS TRUE THAT NO ONE CAN KNOW WHY YOU LEFT UR IMMEDIATELY BEFORE THE BOON WAS OPENED.
"YOU WEREN'T IN THE CITY.
"BUT YOU WEREN'T FAR FROM IT.
"AND YOU FOUND YOURSELF AT A PLACE OF POWER.
"THE LANDS BEYOND UR WERE FULL OF DEATH CULTS, YOUR CLAN CERTAINLY KNEW OF THOSE.
"PLACES OF DARK ENERGY, EARTH SOAKED WITH BLOOD AND TEARS AND RESTLESS SOULS.
"AND THE DARKNESS THAT HAD ALWAYS MADE YOU DIFFERENT STIRRED WITHIN YOU."

I REMEMBER THAT PLACE.

"OUT WHERE THOSE DEATH CULTS HAD KILLED SO MANY PEOPLE THE GROUND FELT *SOAKED* WITH HEAVY DEATH ENERGY. LIKE A BUNCH OF GHOSTS, ANGRY, JUST *WAITING* FOR SOMETHING TO DO. SOMEWHERE TO GO. A MOMENT TO STRIKE.

"I WAS SO *ANGRY* AT MY BROTHERS. AND THIS PLACE FELT SO *WRONG.*

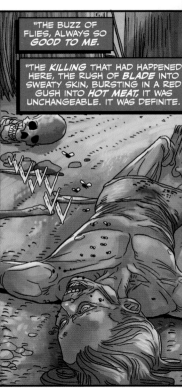

"THE BUZZ OF FLIES, ALWAYS SO *GOOD TO ME.*

"THE *KILLING* THAT HAD HAPPENED HERE, THE RUSH OF *BLADE* INTO SWEATY SKIN, BURSTING IN A RED GUSH INTO *HOT MEAT,* IT WAS UNCHANGEABLE. IT WAS DEFINITE.

"AND I THOUGHT:

"I WANT TO *CHANGE* THINGS LIKE THAT, TOO.

"AND THEN SOMETHING HAPPENED."

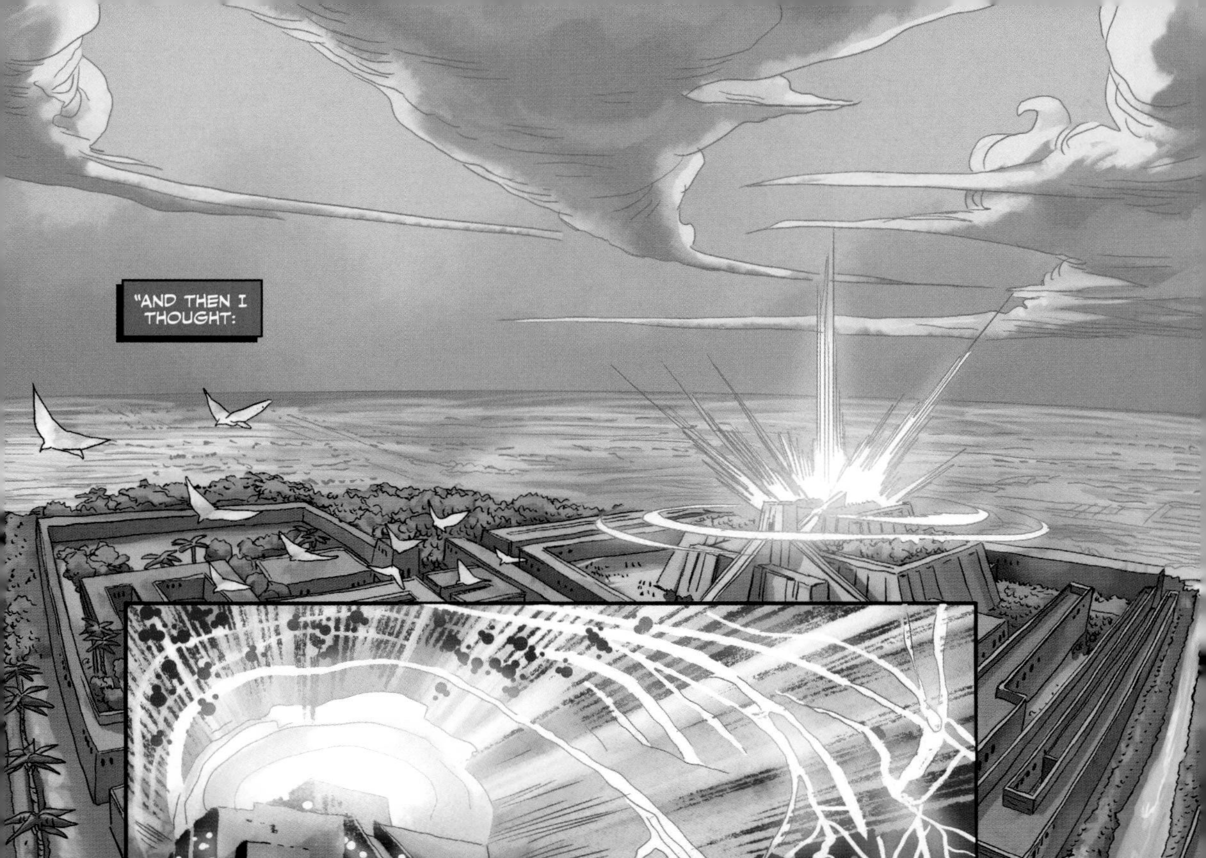
"AND THEN I THOUGHT:
"DID I MAKE THAT HAPPEN?

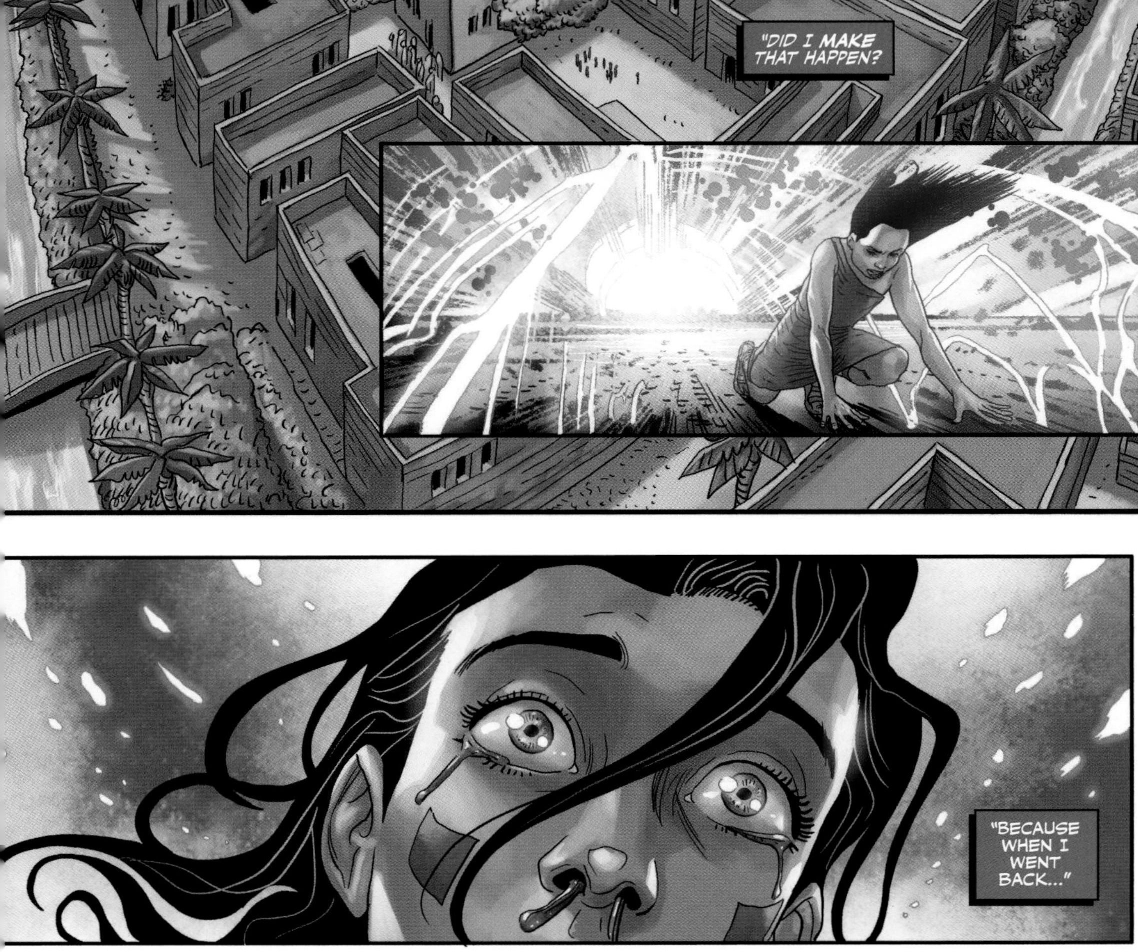
"BECAUSE WHEN I WENT BACK..."

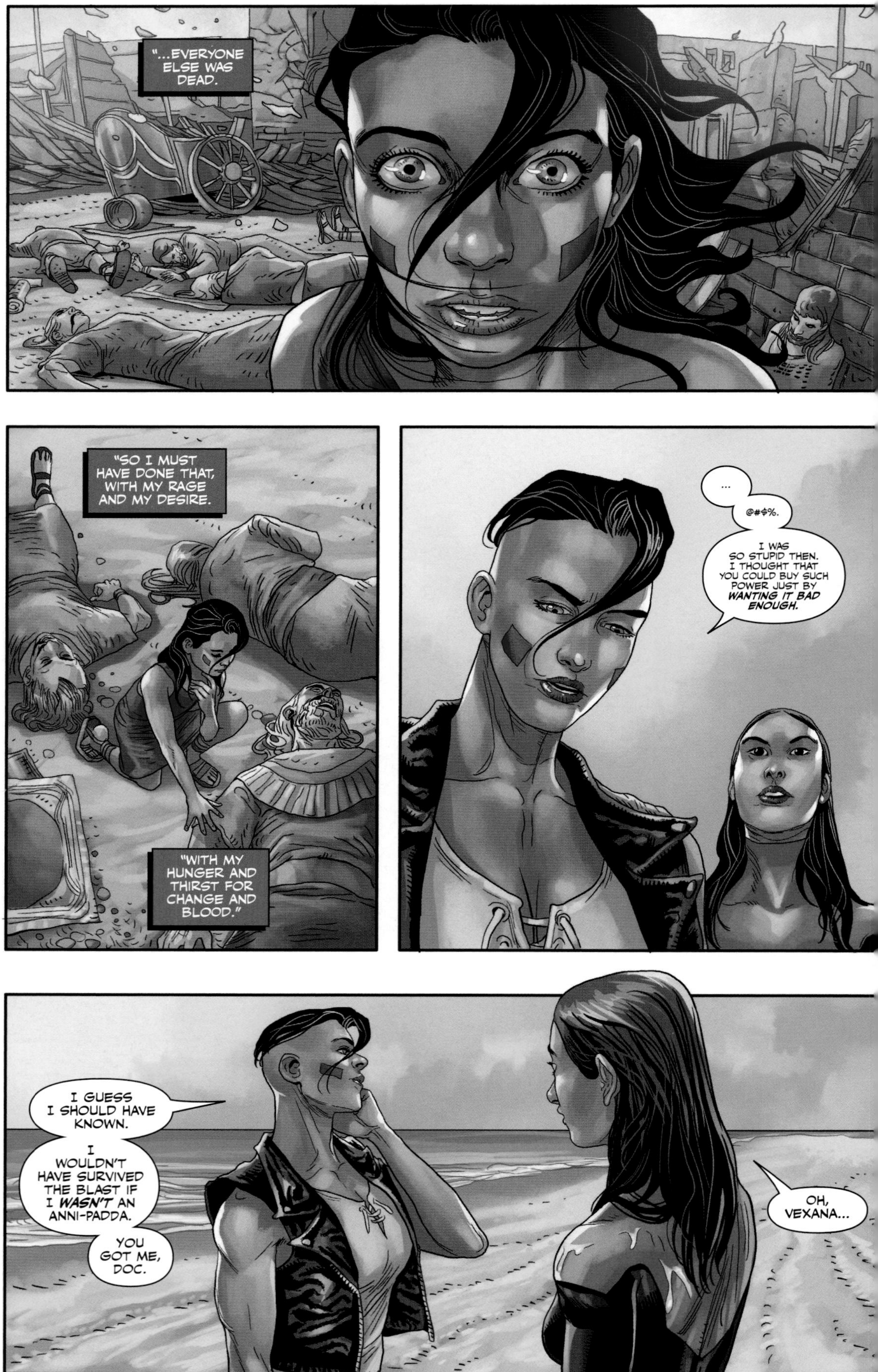
"...EVERYONE ELSE WAS DEAD.
"SO I MUST HAVE DONE THAT, WITH MY RAGE AND MY DESIRE.
"WITH MY HUNGER AND THIRST FOR CHANGE AND BLOOD."
...
@#$%.
I WAS SO STUPID THEN. I THOUGHT THAT YOU COULD BUY SUCH POWER JUST BY WANTING IT BAD ENOUGH.
I GUESS I SHOULD HAVE KNOWN.
I WOULDN'T HAVE SURVIVED THE BLAST IF I WASN'T AN ANNI-PADDA.
YOU GOT ME, DOC.
OH, VEXANA...

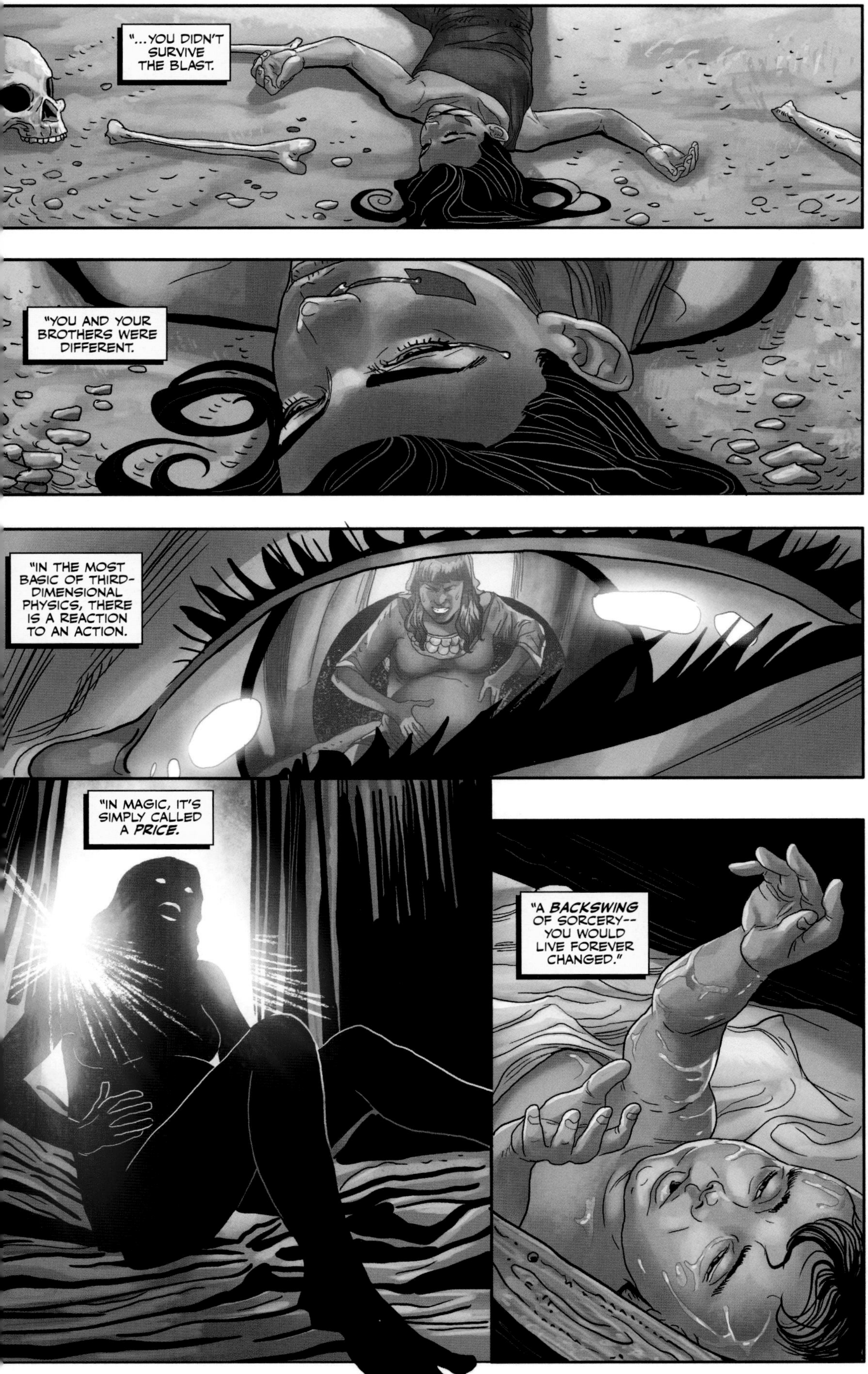
"...YOU DIDN'T SURVIVE THE BLAST.
"YOU AND YOUR BROTHERS WERE DIFFERENT.
"IN THE MOST BASIC OF THIRD-DIMENSIONAL PHYSICS, THERE IS A REACTION TO AN ACTION.
"IN MAGIC, IT'S SIMPLY CALLED A *PRICE.*
"A *BACKSWING* OF SORCERY--YOU WOULD LIVE FOREVER CHANGED."

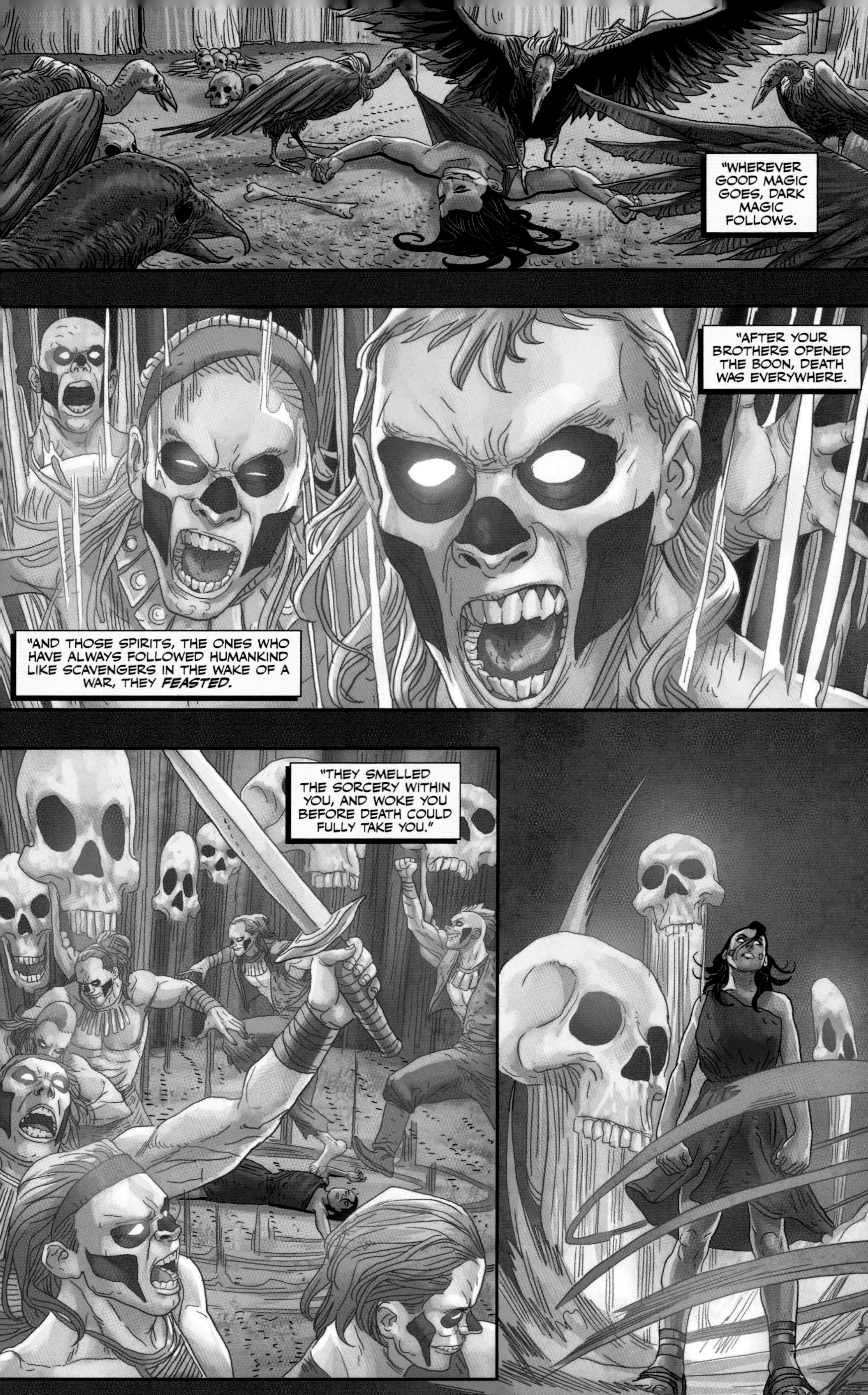
"WHEREVER GOOD MAGIC GOES, DARK MAGIC FOLLOWS.
"AFTER YOUR BROTHERS OPENED THE BOON, DEATH WAS EVERYWHERE.
"AND THOSE SPIRITS, THE ONES WHO HAVE ALWAYS FOLLOWED HUMANKIND LIKE SCAVENGERS IN THE WAKE OF A WAR, THEY *FEASTED*.
"THEY SMELLED THE SORCERY WITHIN YOU, AND WOKE YOU BEFORE DEATH COULD FULLY TAKE YOU."

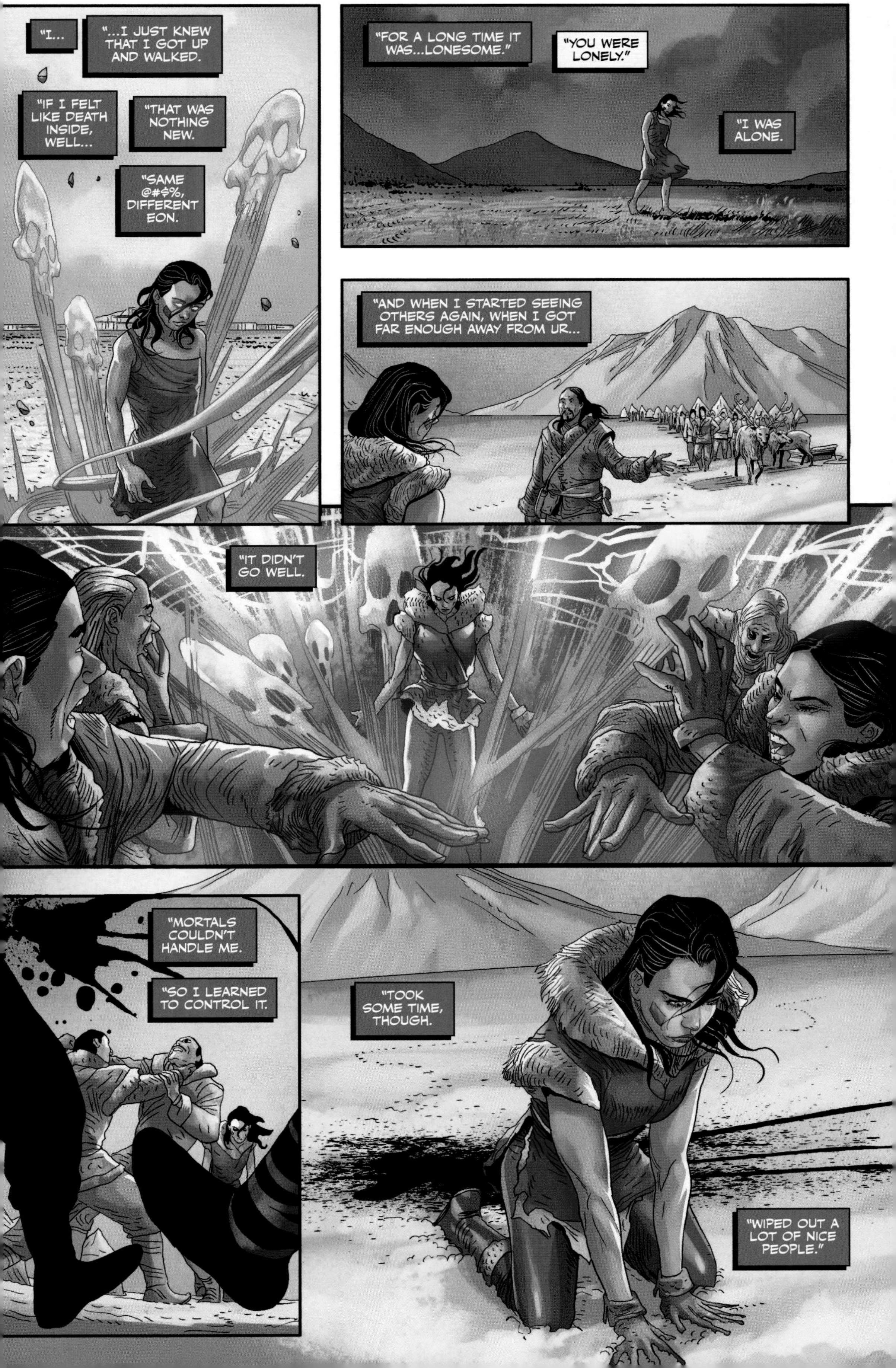
"I...
"...I JUST KNEW THAT I GOT UP AND WALKED.
"IF I FELT LIKE DEATH INSIDE, WELL...
"THAT WAS NOTHING NEW.
"SAME @#$%, DIFFERENT EON.
"FOR A LONG TIME IT WAS...LONESOME."
"YOU WERE LONELY."
"I WAS ALONE.
"AND WHEN I STARTED SEEING OTHERS AGAIN, WHEN I GOT FAR ENOUGH AWAY FROM UR...
"IT DIDN'T GO WELL.
"MORTALS COULDN'T HANDLE ME.
"SO I LEARNED TO CONTROL IT.
"TOOK SOME TIME, THOUGH.
"WIPED OUT A LOT OF NICE PEOPLE."

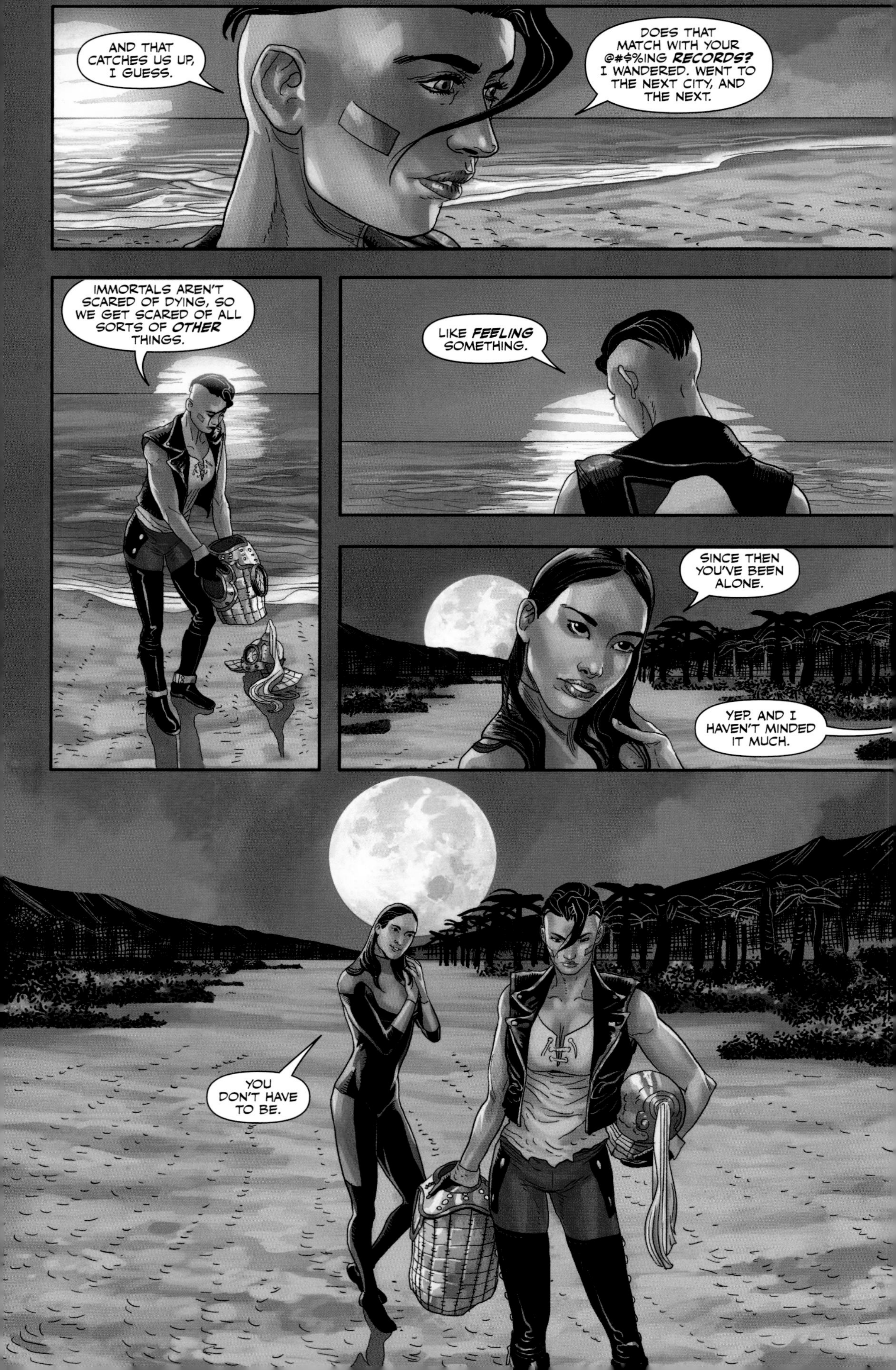
AND THAT CATCHES US UP, I GUESS.
DOES THAT MATCH WITH YOUR @#$%ING *RECORDS?* I WANDERED. WENT TO THE NEXT CITY, AND THE NEXT.
IMMORTALS AREN'T SCARED OF DYING, SO WE GET SCARED OF ALL SORTS OF *OTHER* THINGS.
LIKE *FEELING* SOMETHING.
SINCE THEN YOU'VE BEEN ALONE.
YEP. AND I HAVEN'T MINDED IT MUCH.
YOU DON'T HAVE TO BE.

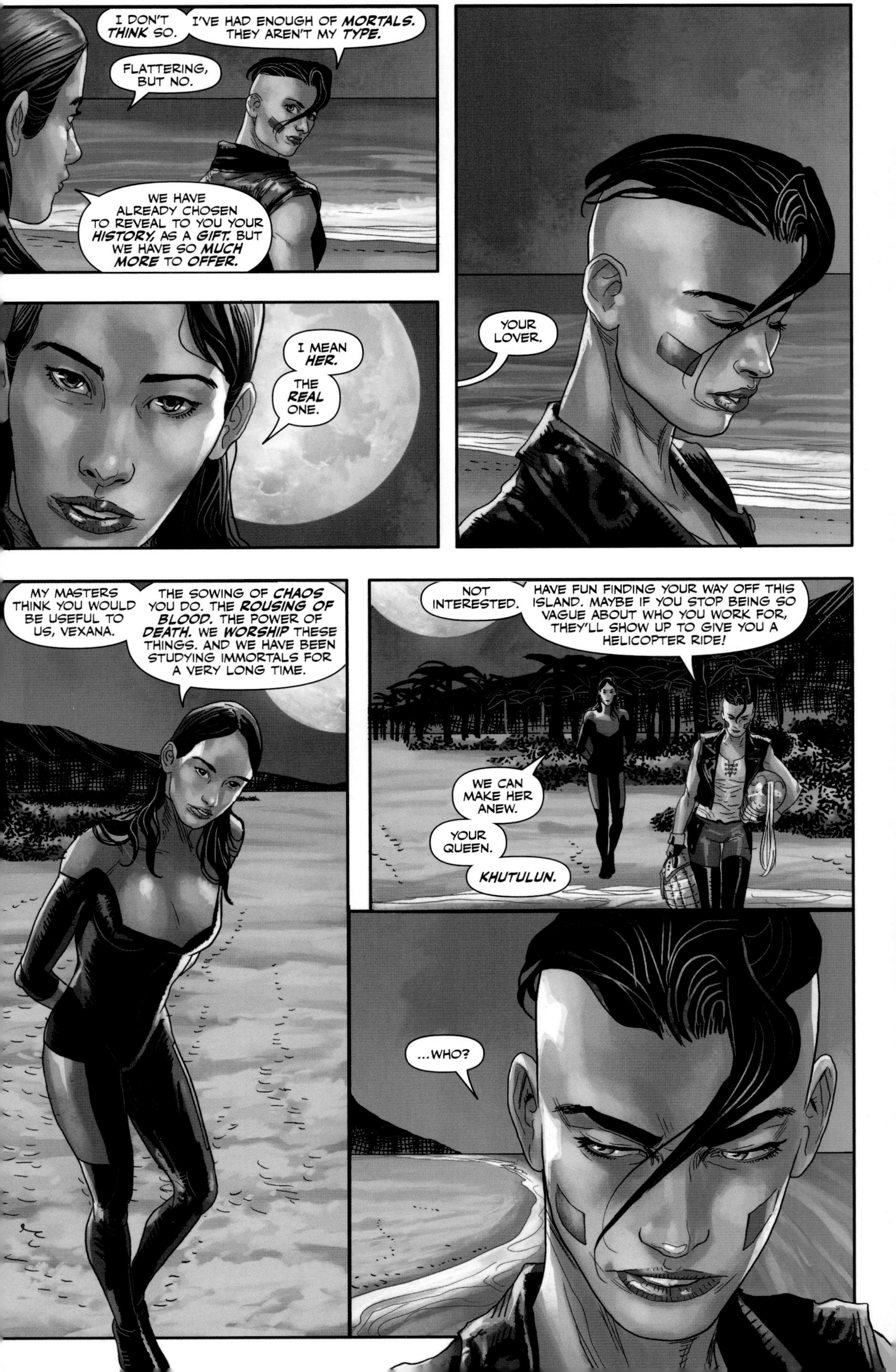
I DON'T THINK SO.
I'VE HAD ENOUGH OF MORTALS. THEY AREN'T MY TYPE.
FLATTERING, BUT NO.
WE HAVE ALREADY CHOSEN TO REVEAL TO YOU YOUR HISTORY, AS A GIFT. BUT WE HAVE SO MUCH MORE TO OFFER.
YOUR LOVER.
I MEAN HER.
THE REAL ONE.
MY MASTERS THINK YOU WOULD BE USEFUL TO US, VEXANA.
THE SOWING OF CHAOS YOU DO. THE ROUSING OF BLOOD. THE POWER OF DEATH. WE WORSHIP THESE THINGS. AND WE HAVE BEEN STUDYING IMMORTALS FOR A VERY LONG TIME.
NOT INTERESTED.
HAVE FUN FINDING YOUR WAY OFF THIS ISLAND. MAYBE IF YOU STOP BEING SO VAGUE ABOUT WHO YOU WORK FOR, THEY'LL SHOW UP TO GIVE YOU A HELICOPTER RIDE!
WE CAN MAKE HER ANEW.
YOUR QUEEN.
KHUTULUN.
...WHO?

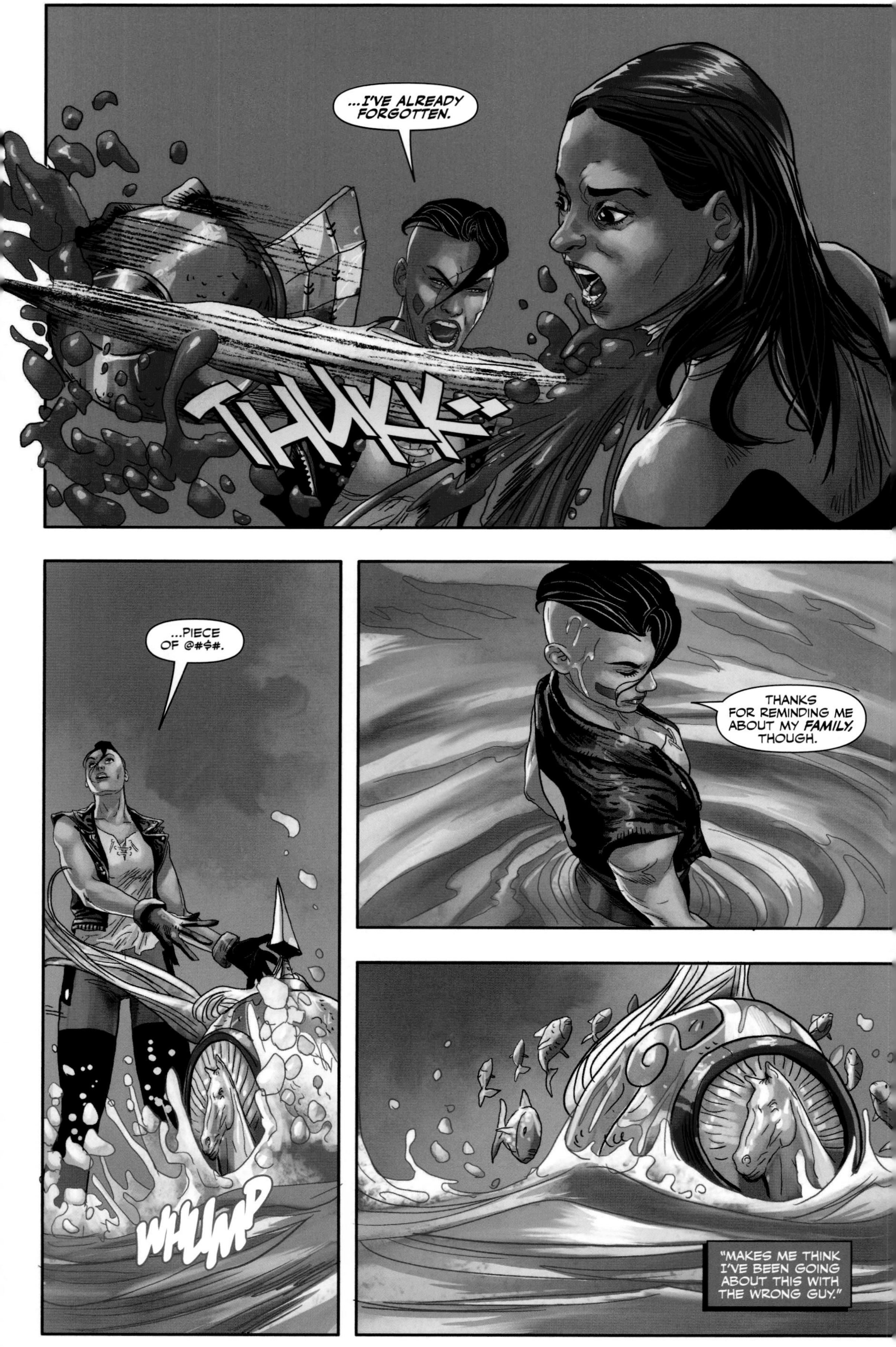
...I'VE ALREADY FORGOTTEN.
THUKK--
...PIECE OF @#$#.
WHUMP
THANKS FOR REMINDING ME ABOUT MY *FAMILY,* THOUGH.
"MAKES ME THINK I'VE BEEN GOING ABOUT THIS WITH THE WRONG GUY."

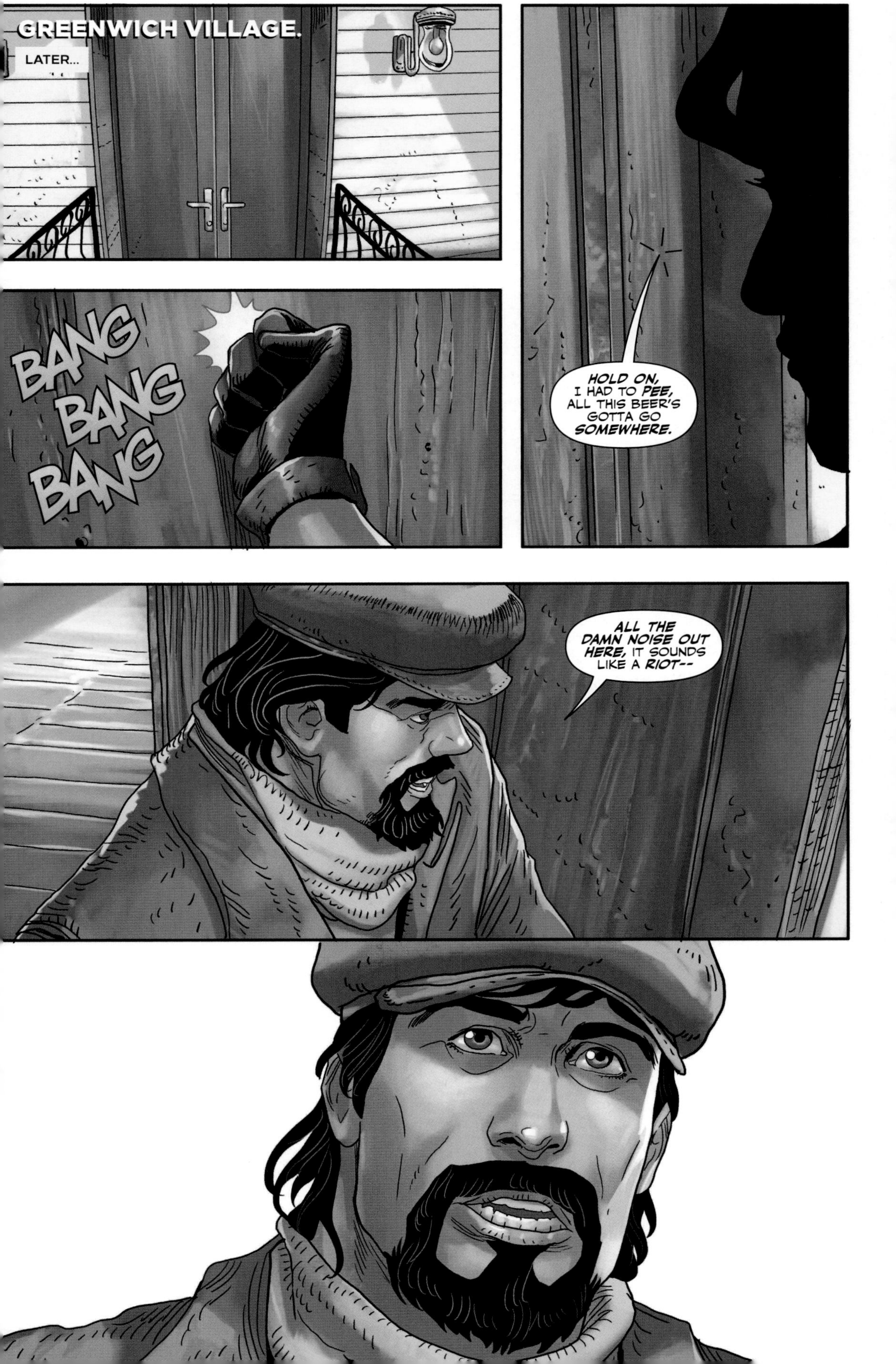
GREENWICH VILLAGE.
LATER...
BANG BANG BANG
HOLD ON, I HAD TO PEE, ALL THIS BEER'S GOTTA GO SOMEWHERE.
ALL THE DAMN NOISE OUT HERE, IT SOUNDS LIKE A RIOT--

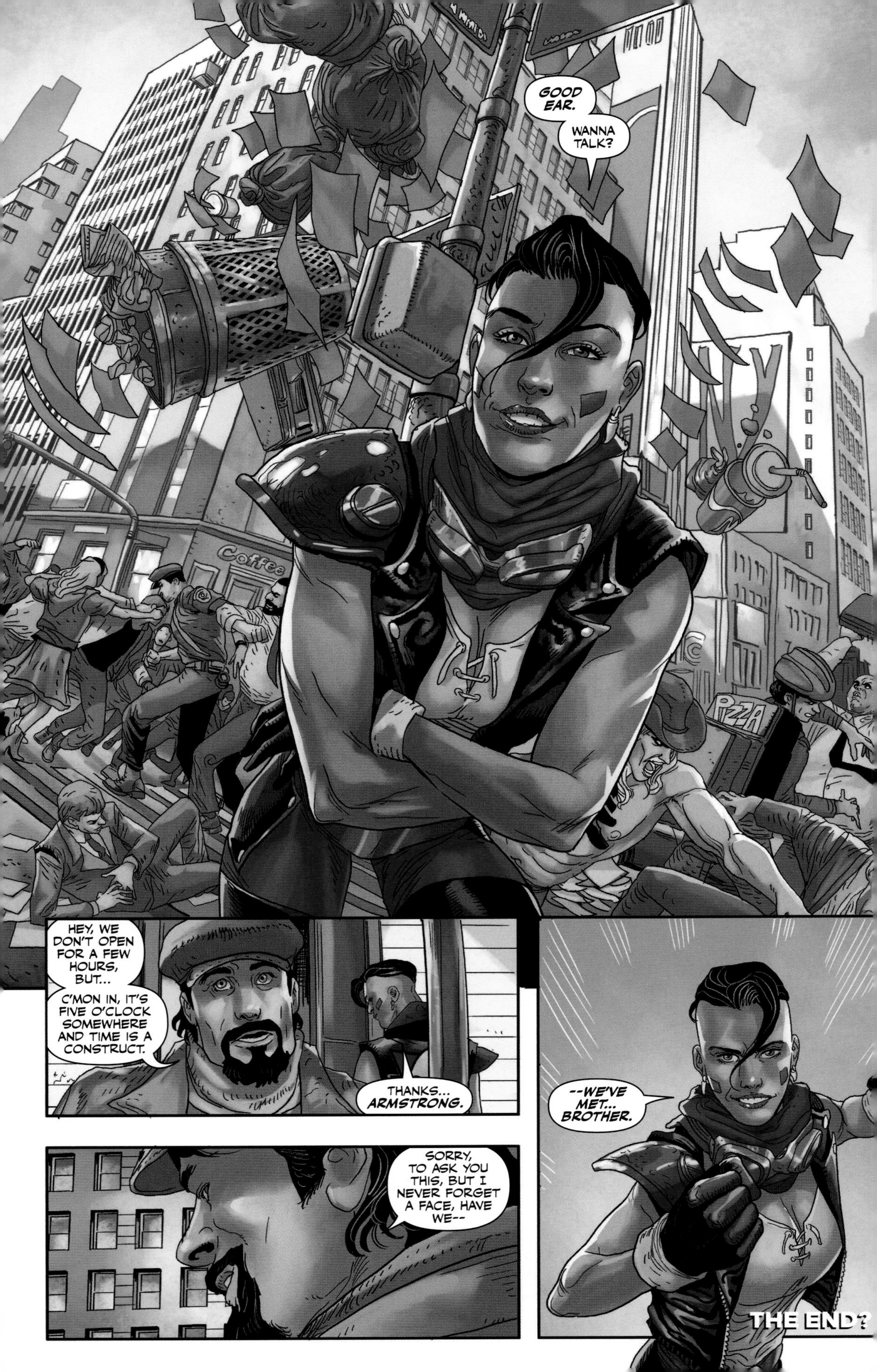
GOOD EAR.
WANNA TALK?
Coffee
PIZZA
HEY, WE DON'T OPEN FOR A FEW HOURS, BUT...
C'MON IN, IT'S FIVE O'CLOCK SOMEWHERE AND TIME IS A CONSTRUCT.
THANKS... ARMSTRONG.
SORRY, TO ASK YOU THIS, BUT I NEVER FORGET A FACE, HAVE WE--
--WE'VE MET... BROTHER.
THE END?

GALLERY

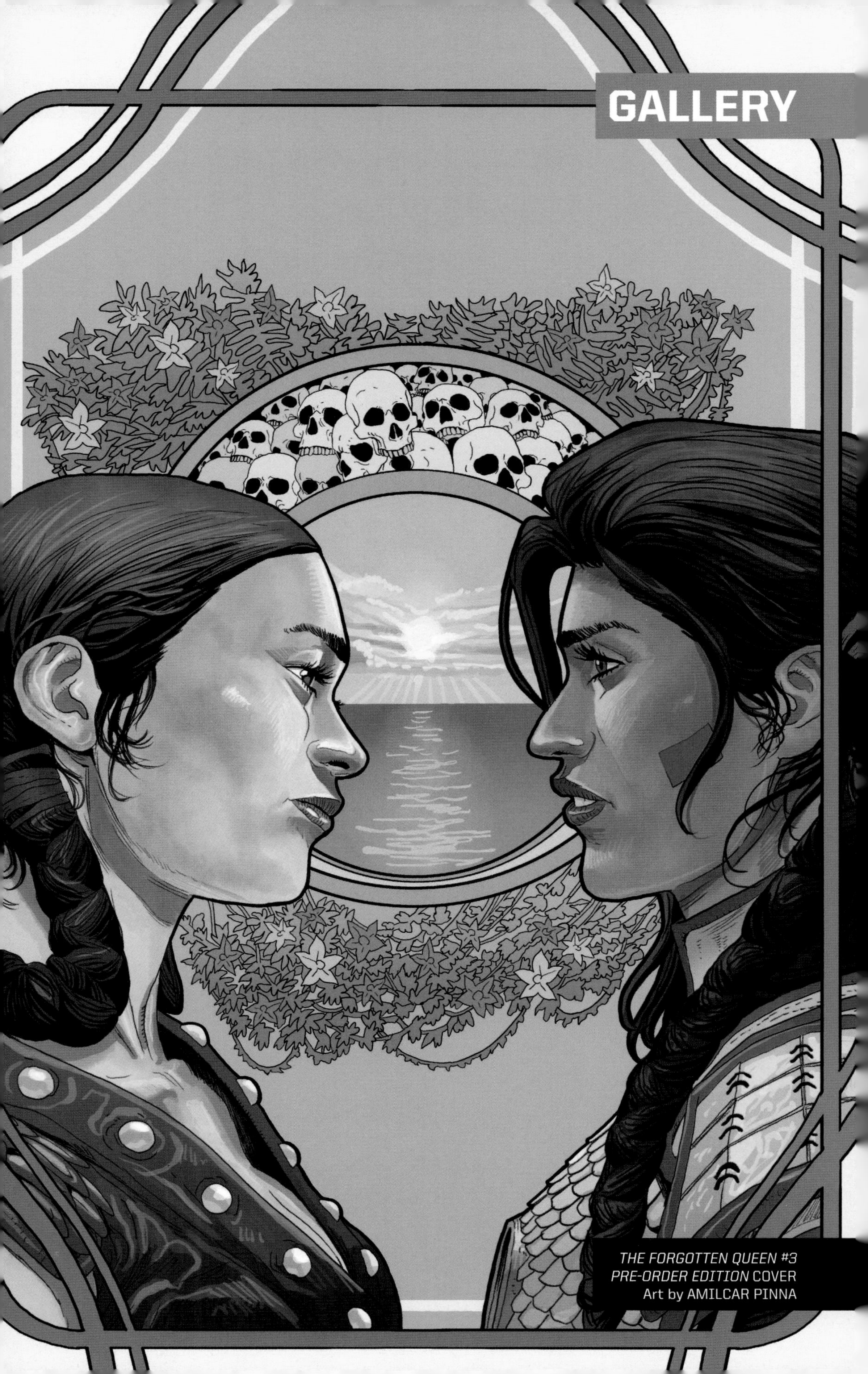

THE FORGOTTEN QUEEN #3
PRE-ORDER EDITION COVER
Art by AMILCAR PINNA

VEXANA CHARACTER DESIGN PROCESS

BY **AMILCAR PINNA**

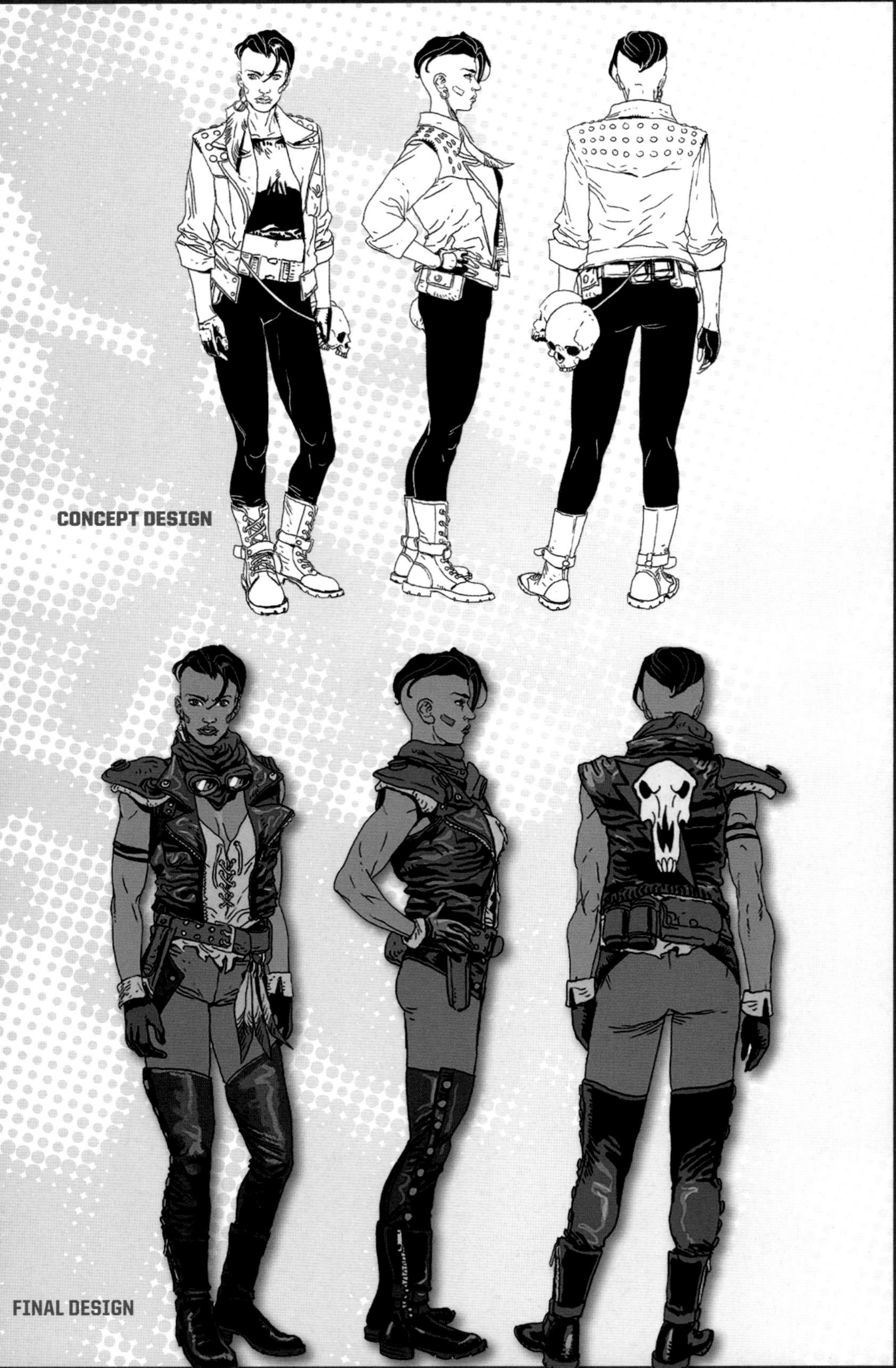

CONCEPT DESIGN
FINAL DESIGN

Originally presented in *THE FORGOTTEN QUEEN #1 PRE-ORDER EDITION.*

SWAMP WITCH CHARACTER DESIGN
WITH SERIES WRITER **TINI HOWARD**

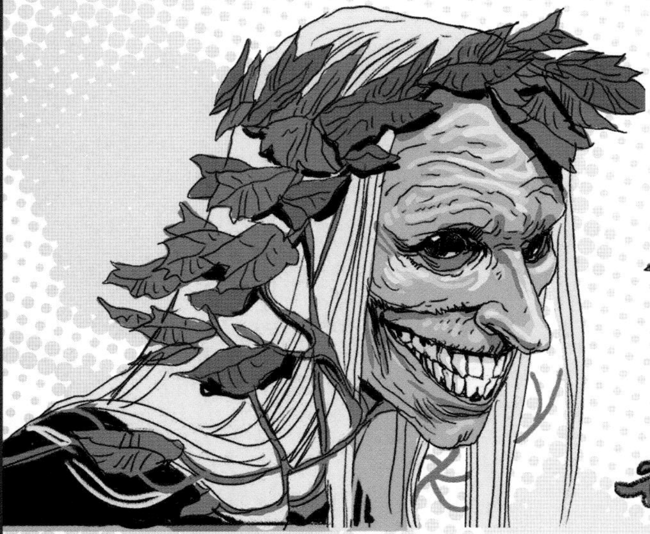

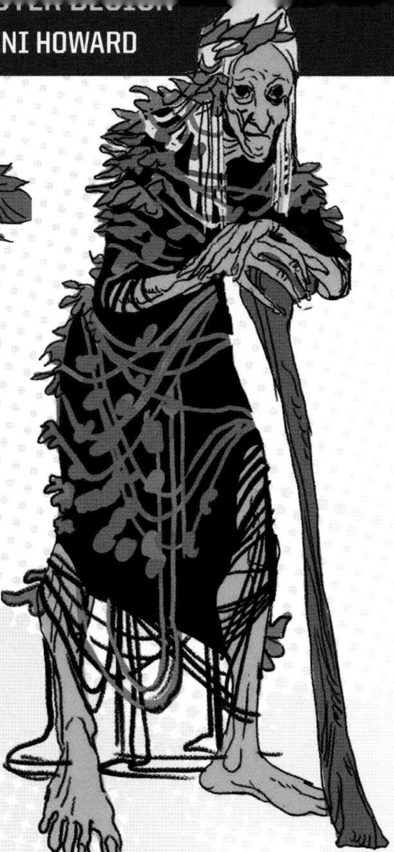

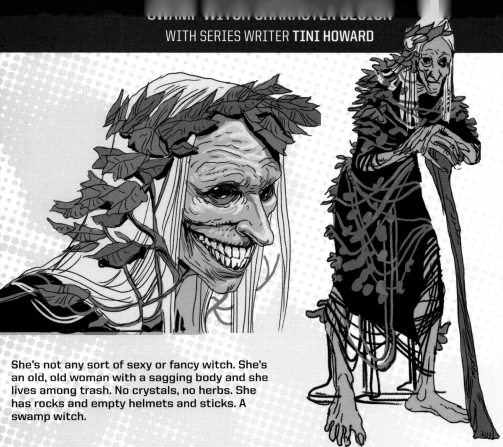

She's not any sort of sexy or fancy witch. She's an old, old woman with a sagging body and she lives among trash. No crystals, no herbs. She has rocks and empty helmets and sticks. A swamp witch.

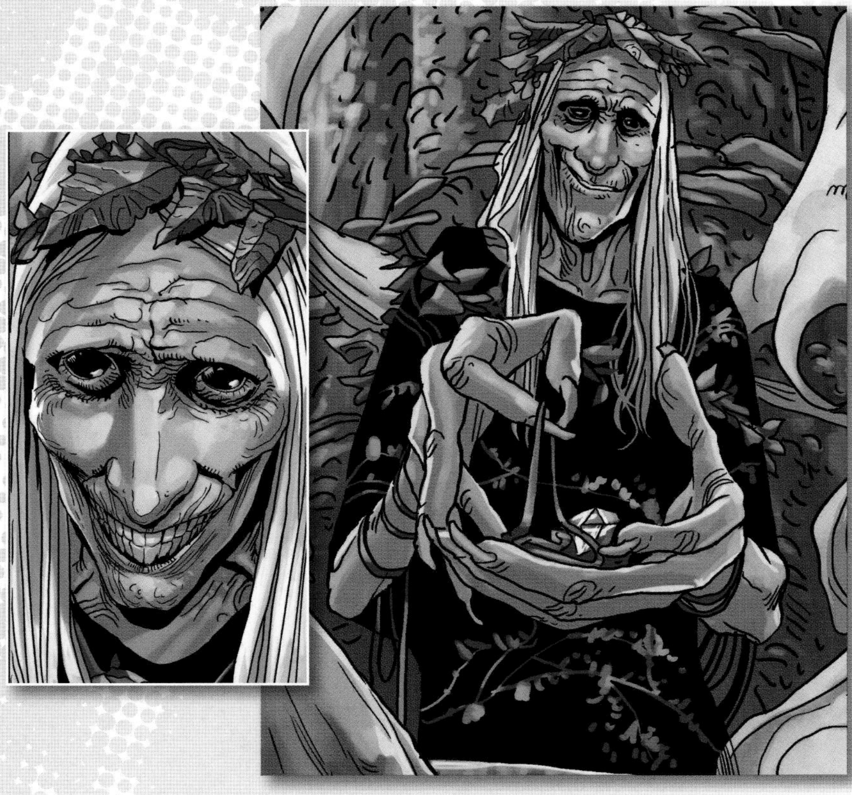

CHARACTER DESIGN BY **AMILCAR PINNA**
COLORS BY **ULISES ARREOLA**

Originally presented in *THE FORGOTTEN QUEEN #2 PRE-ORDER EDITION.*

VLAD III TEPES CHARACTER DESIGN

WITH SERIES WRITER **TINI HOWARD**

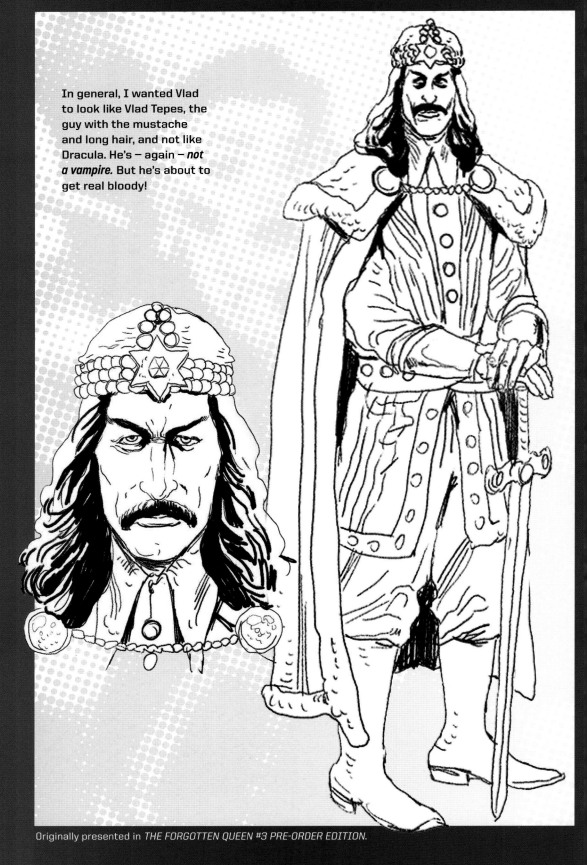

In general, I wanted Vlad to look like Vlad Tepes, the guy with the mustache and long hair, and not like Dracula. He's – again – ***not a vampire.*** But he's about to get real bloody!

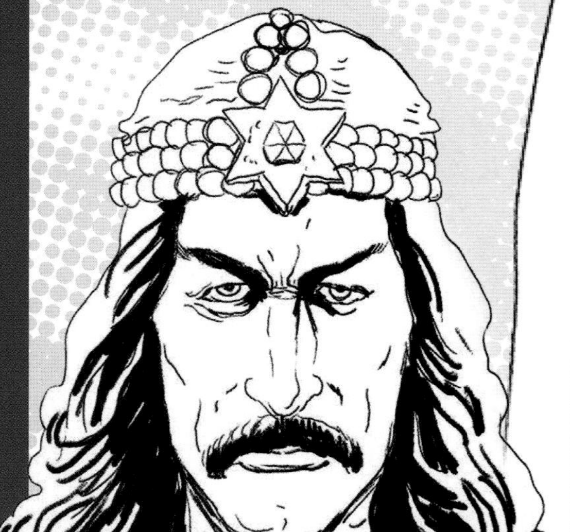

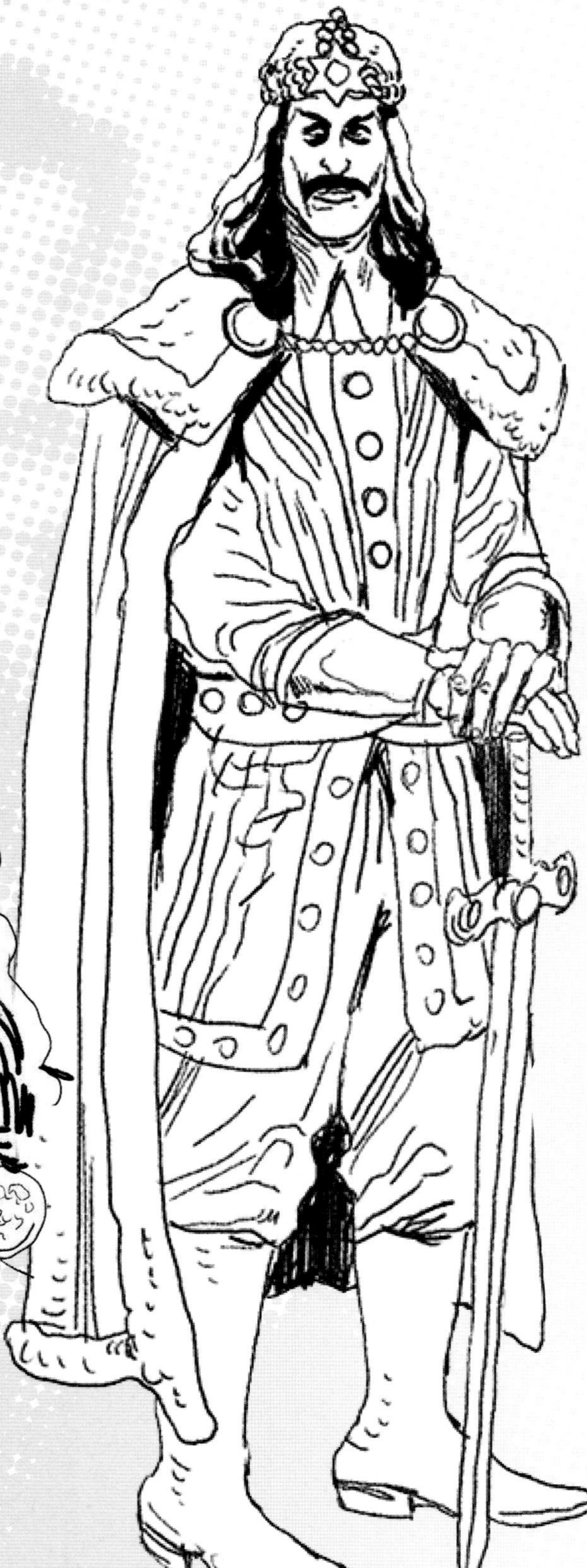

Originally presented in *THE FORGOTTEN QUEEN #3 PRE-ORDER EDITION.*

ANNI-PADDA CLAN CHARACTER STUDIES

WITH SERIES ARTIST **AMILCAR PINNA**

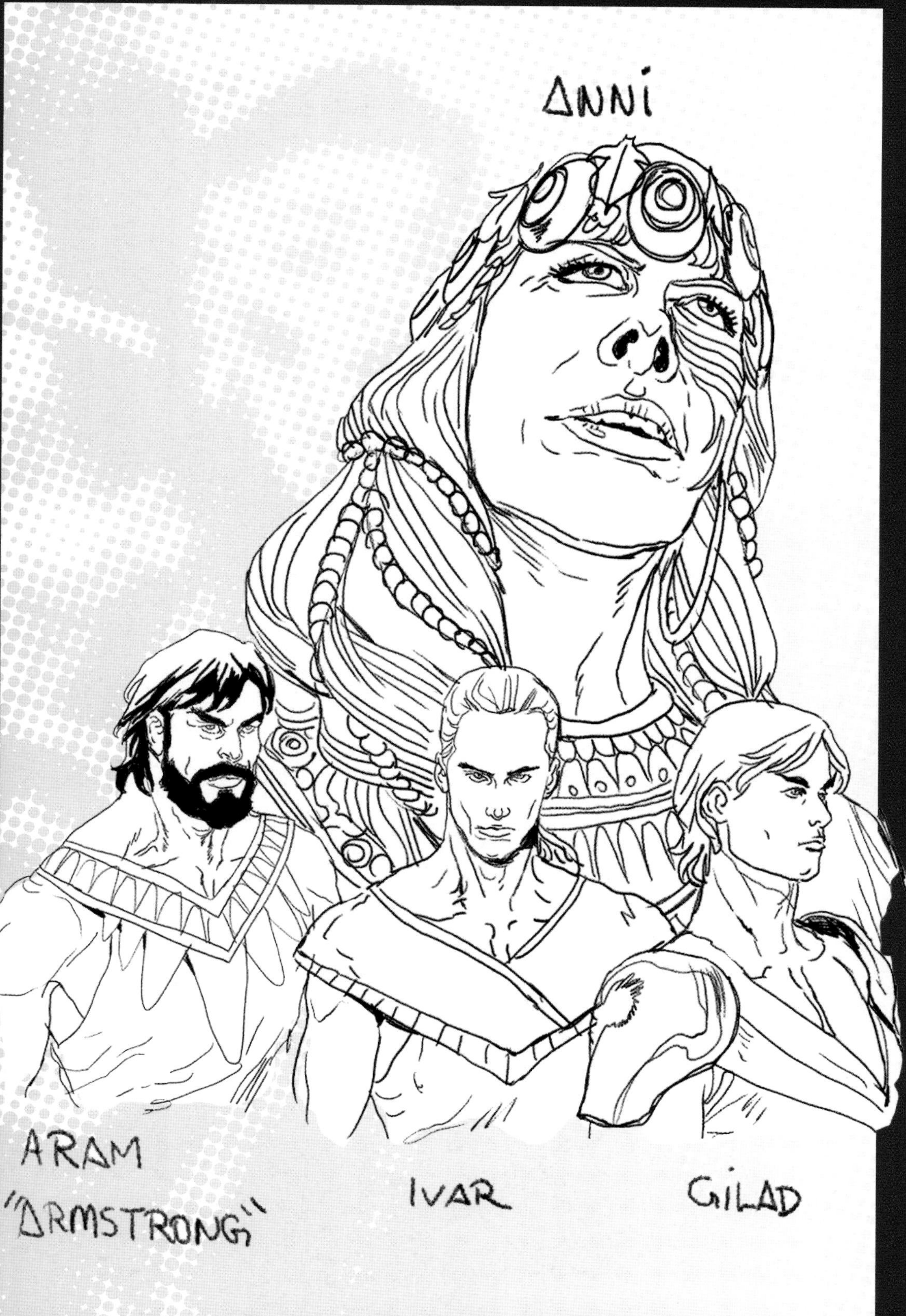
ANNI
ARAM
"ARMSTRONG"
IVAR
GILAD

CHARACTER DESIGNS BY **AMILCAR PINNA** Originally presented in *THE FORGOTTEN QUEEN #4 PRE-ORDER EDITION.*

SETTING THE SCENE WITH SERIES WRITER TINI HOWARD

So, for this page, Vexana is basically... unleashing herself? She's just experienced the first thing in her life that's any sort of emotional burn; she's never been close enough to anyone before. So she's mad and cutting loose.

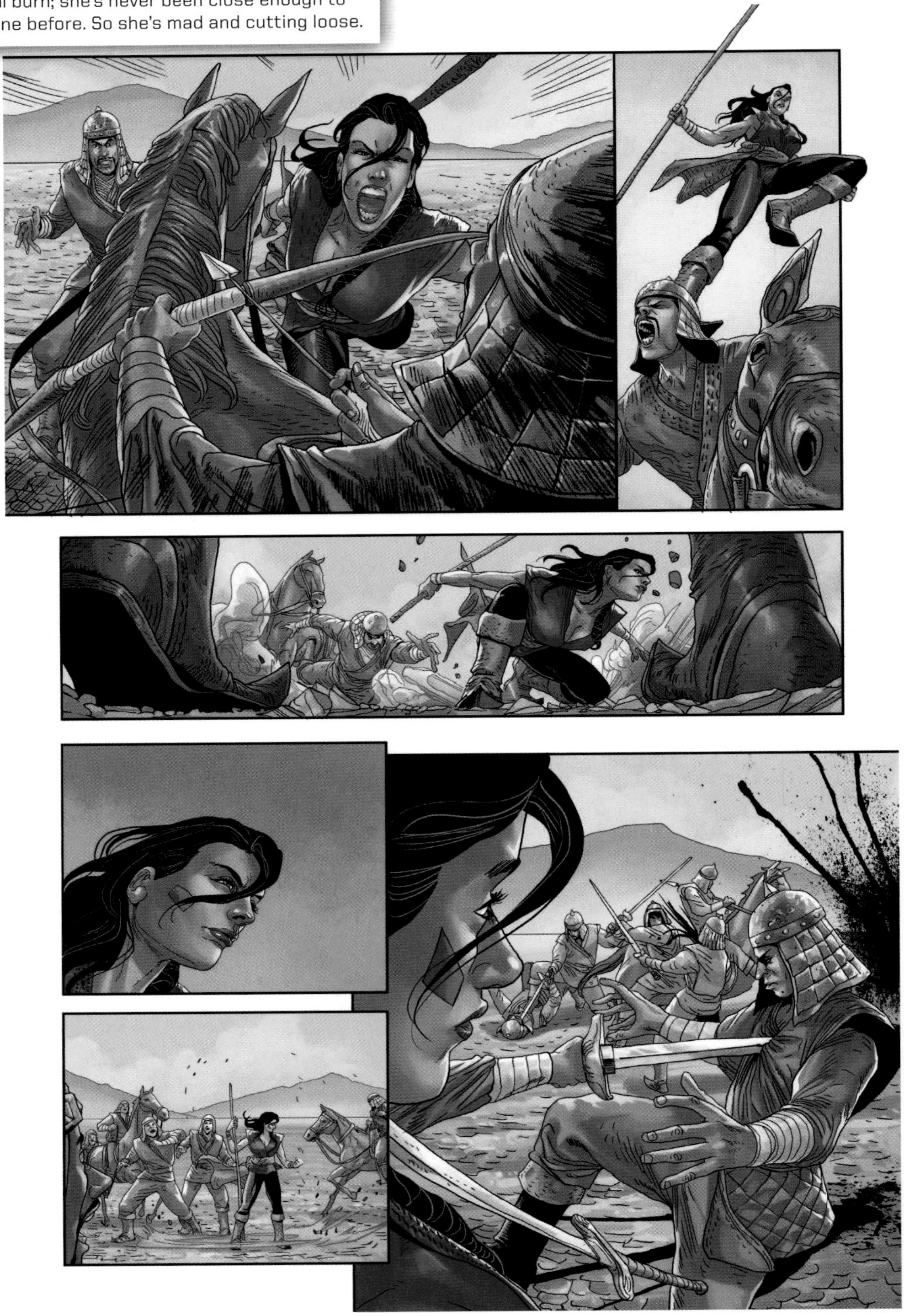

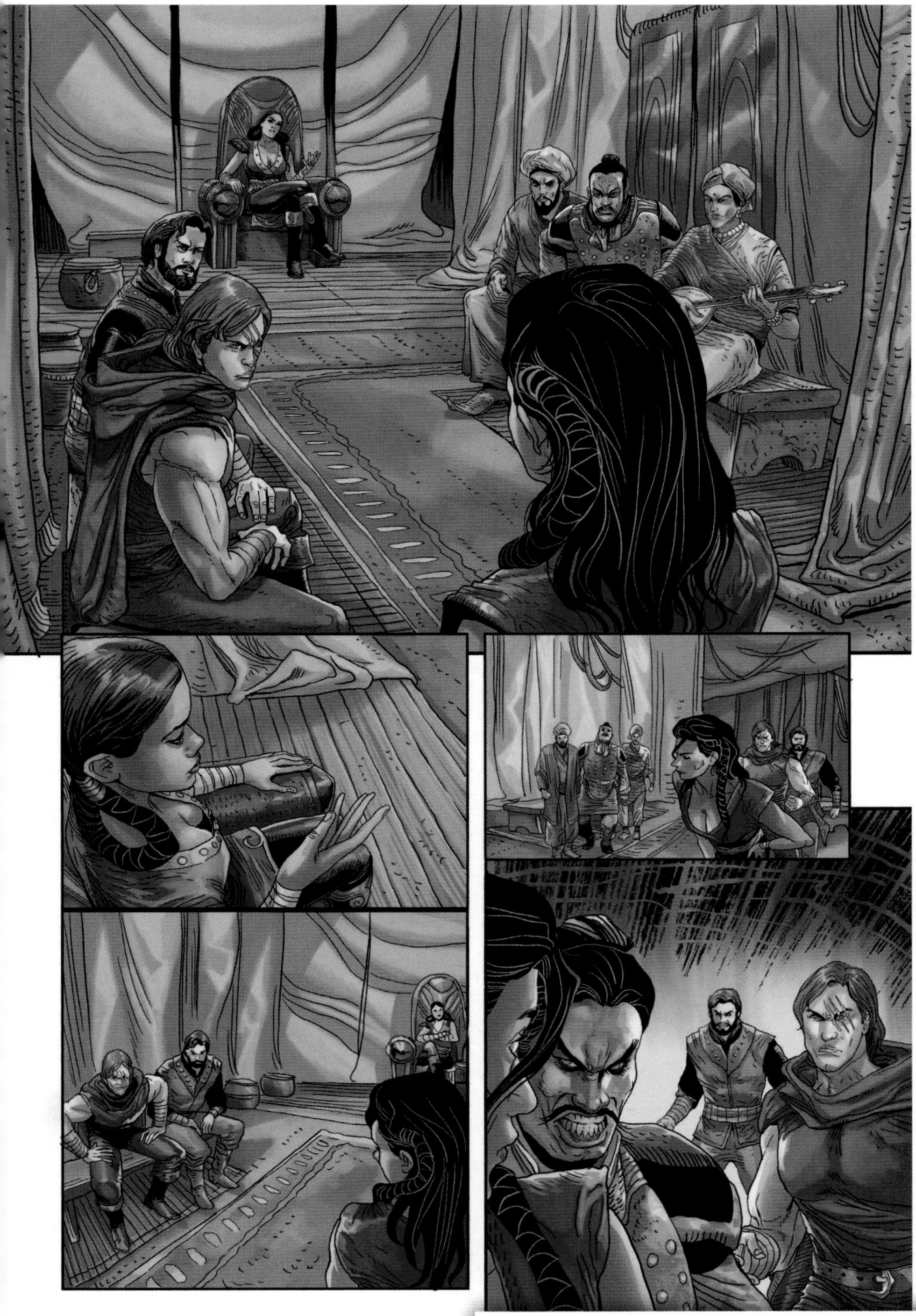

Khutulun sits there with this era's Unity – Marco Polo and some other heroes of this era that make up Unity. GILAD (The Eternal Warrior), and three new figures (all male). There is a 13th-14th-century Muslim scholar, a 13th-14th-century Indian poet mystic with a tanpura on his back, and a Chinese terracotta warrior – dusty, muddy, but still human-looking. Maybe a LITTLE dead. He's OLD, much older than these folks here. 200 BCE. He's not immortal, but I imagine he got recently animated.

THE FORGOTTEN QUEEN #1 COVER B
Art by VIKTOR KALVACHEV

THE FORGOTTEN QUEEN #2 COVER B
Art by VIKTOR KALVACHEV

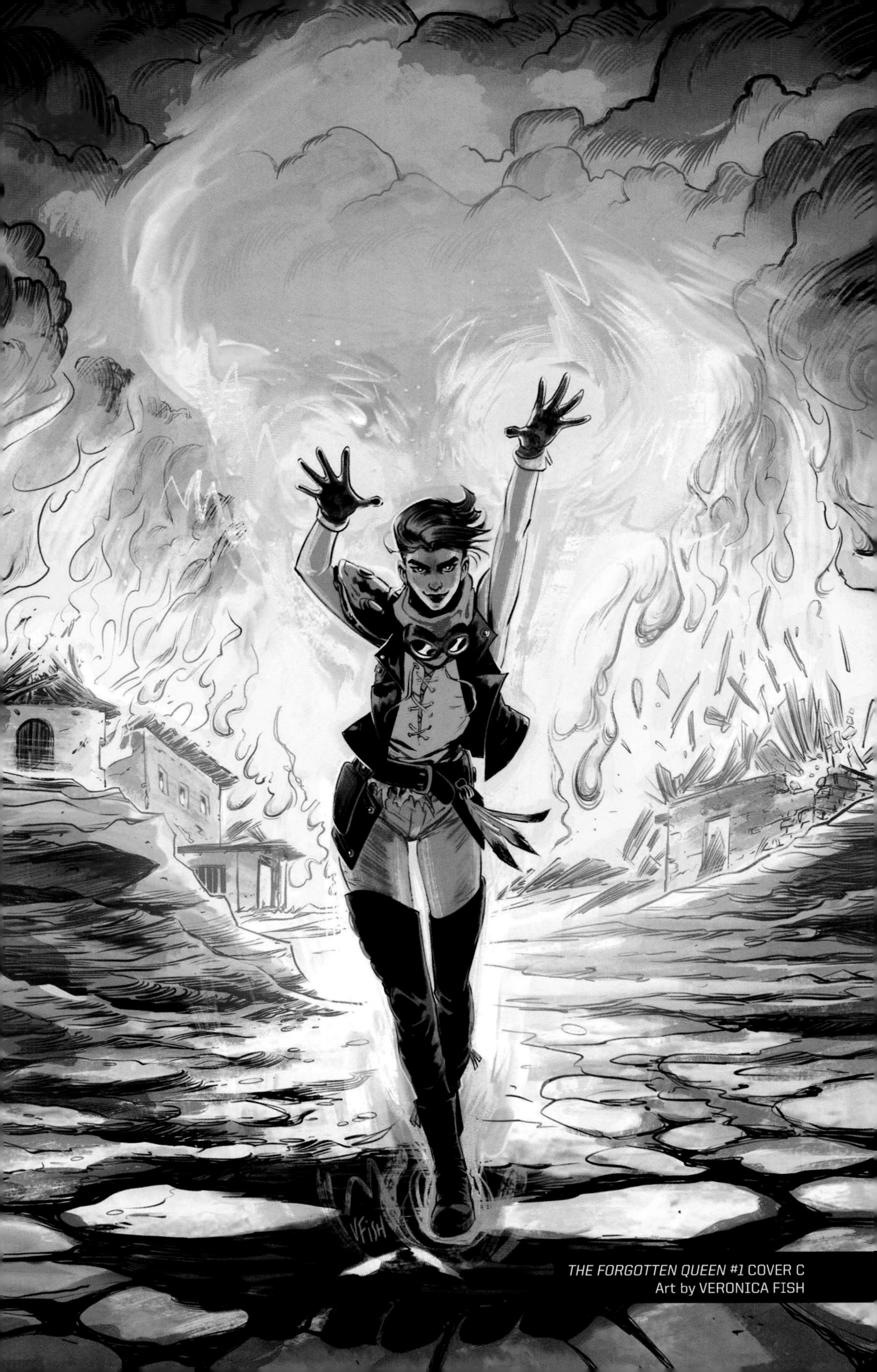
VFISH

THE FORGOTTEN QUEEN #1 COVER C
Art by VERONICA FISH

THE FORGOTTEN QUEEN #2 COVER C
Art by MIRKA ANDOLFO

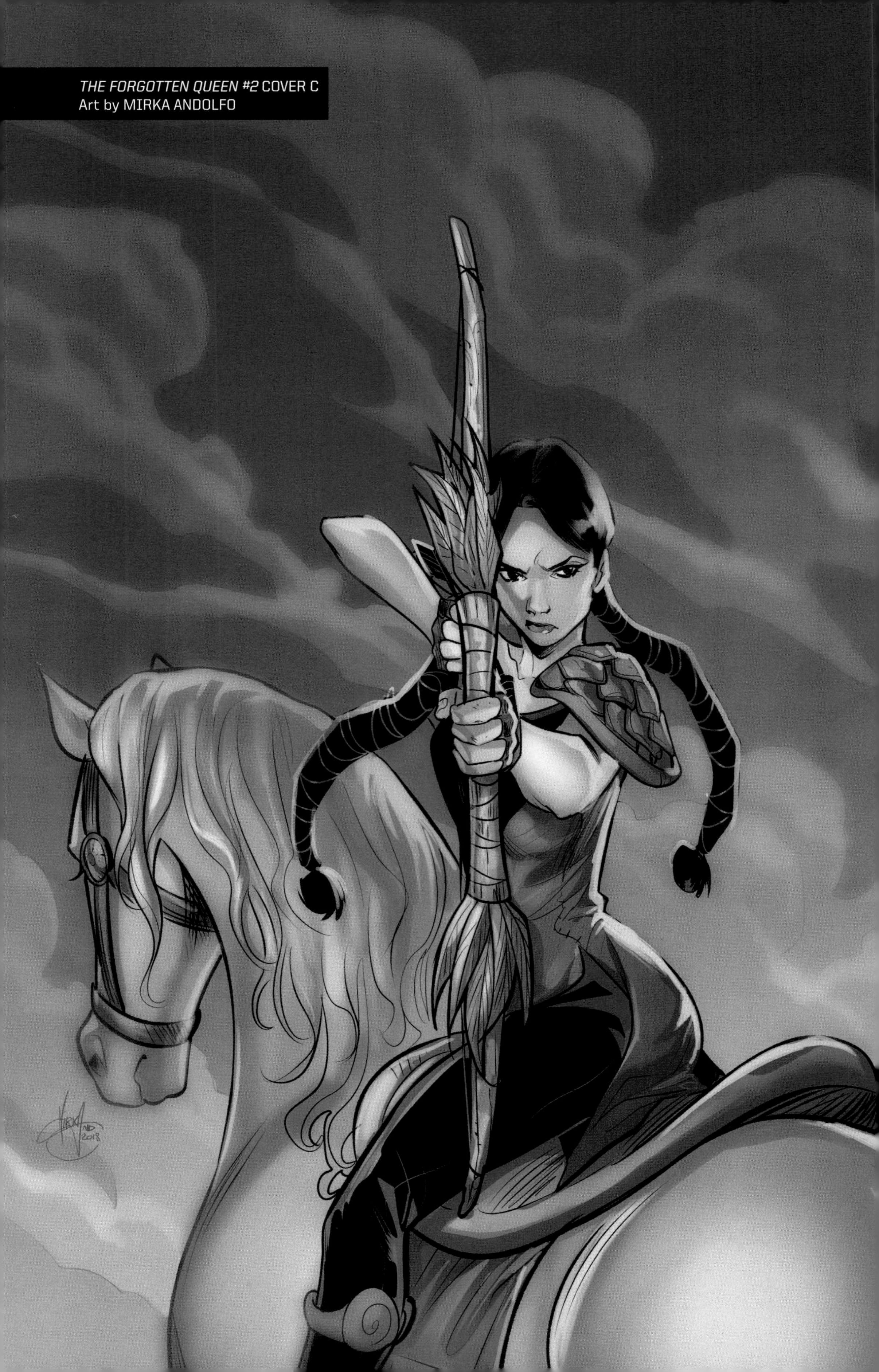

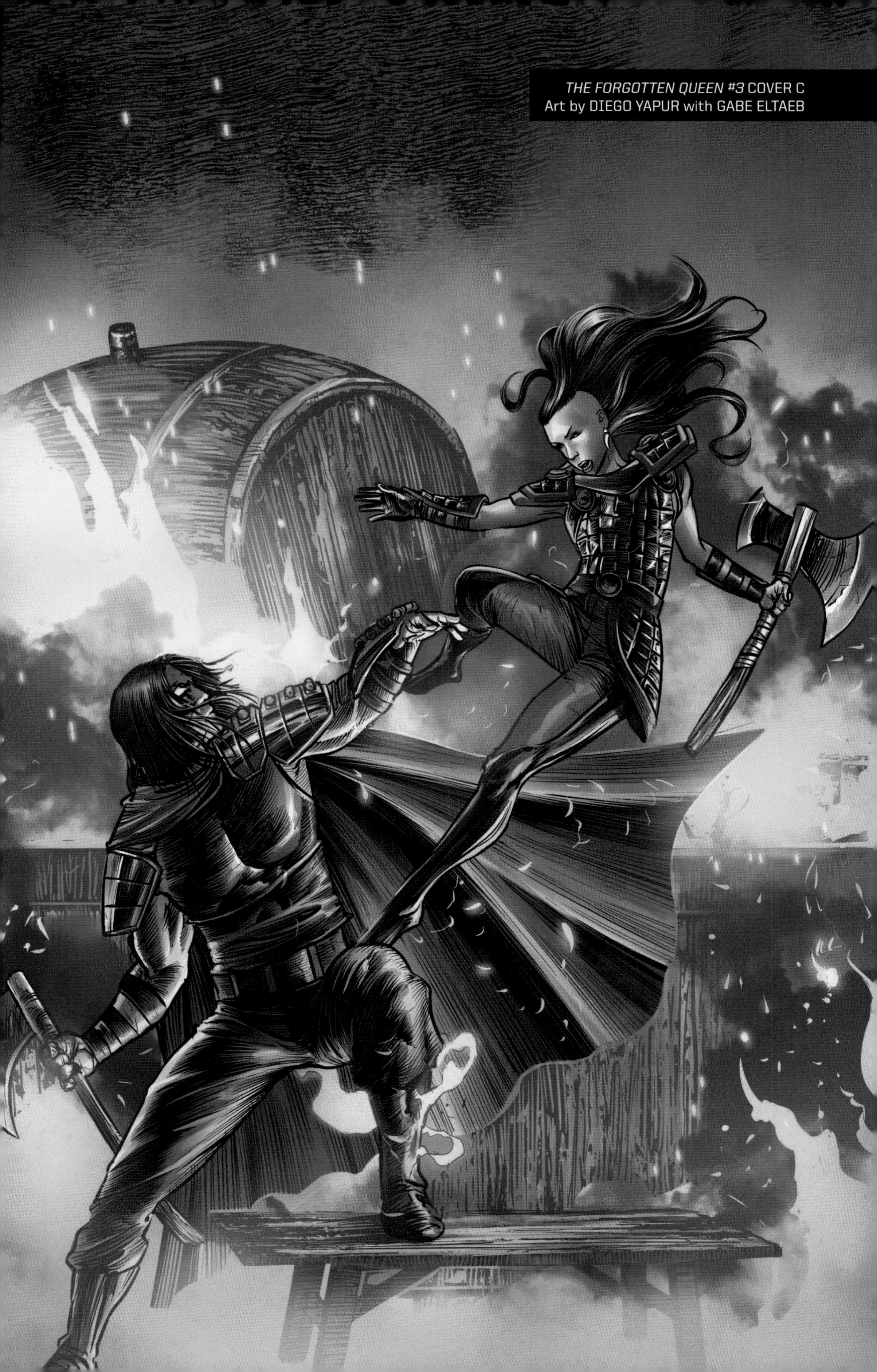

THE FORGOTTEN QUEEN #3 COVER C
Art by DIEGO YAPUR with GABE ELTAEB

THE FORGOTTEN QUEEN #4
PRE-ORDER EDITION COVER
Art by AMILCAR PINNA

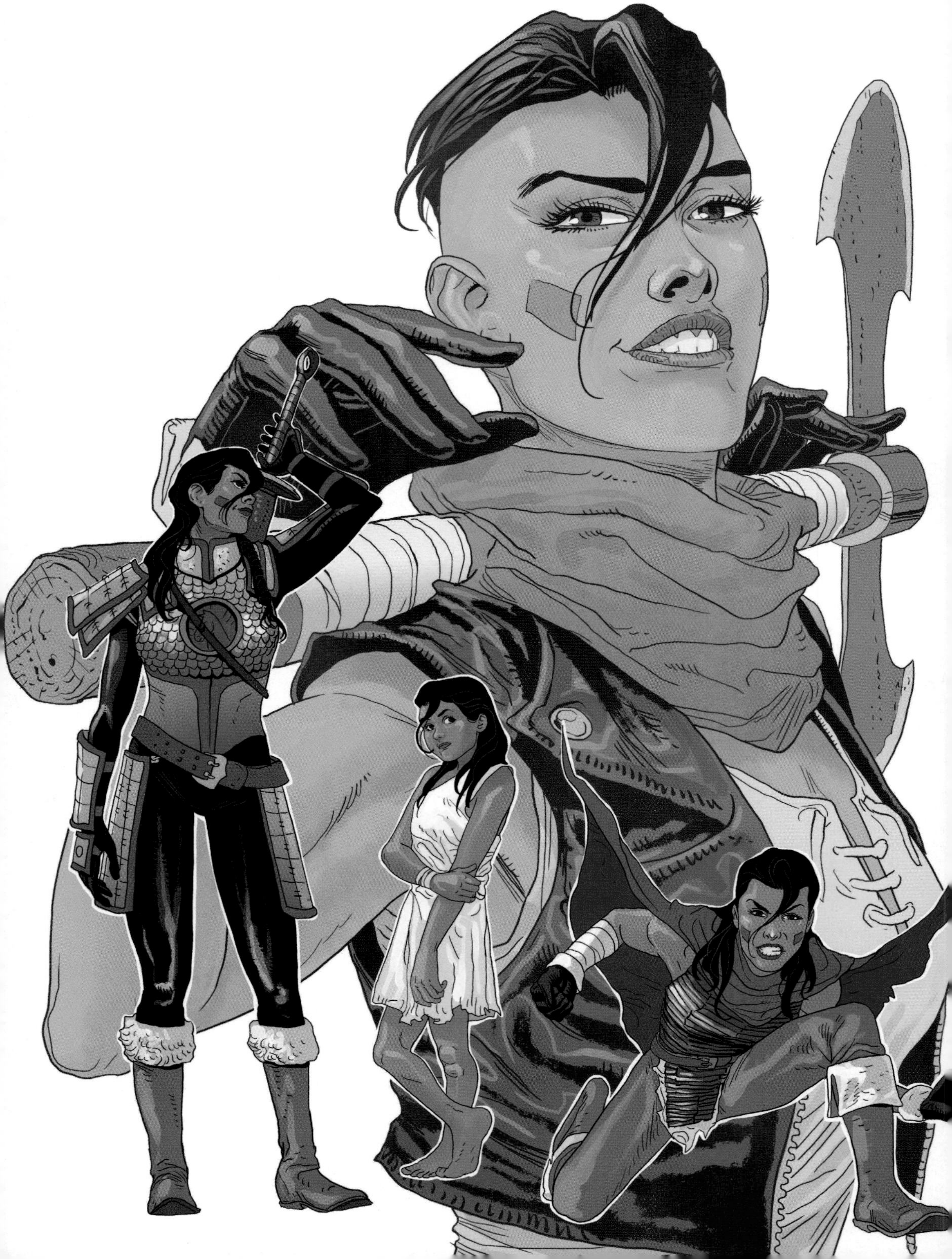

THE FORGOTTEN QUEEN #1, pages 1 and 2
Art by AMILCAR PINNA

THE FORGOTTEN QUEEN #1,
pages 18, 19, and (facing) 20
Art by AMILCAR PINNA

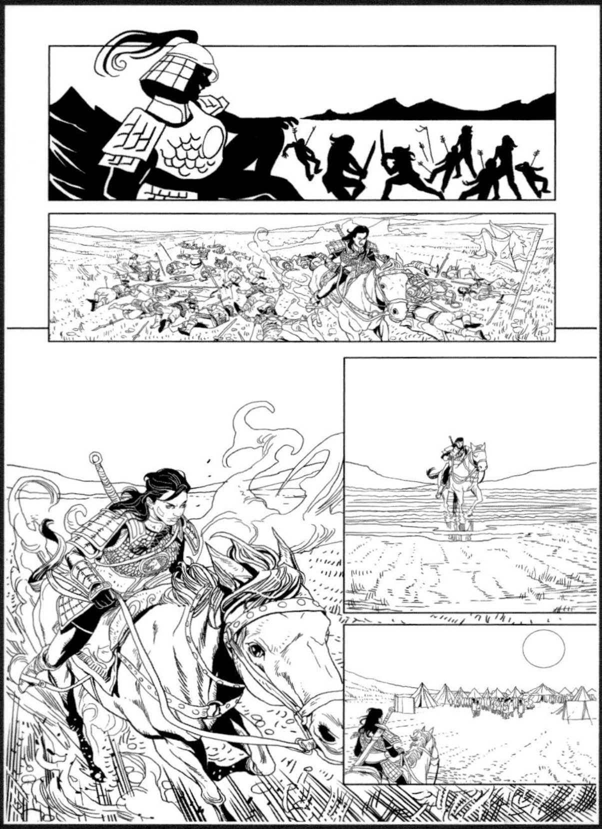

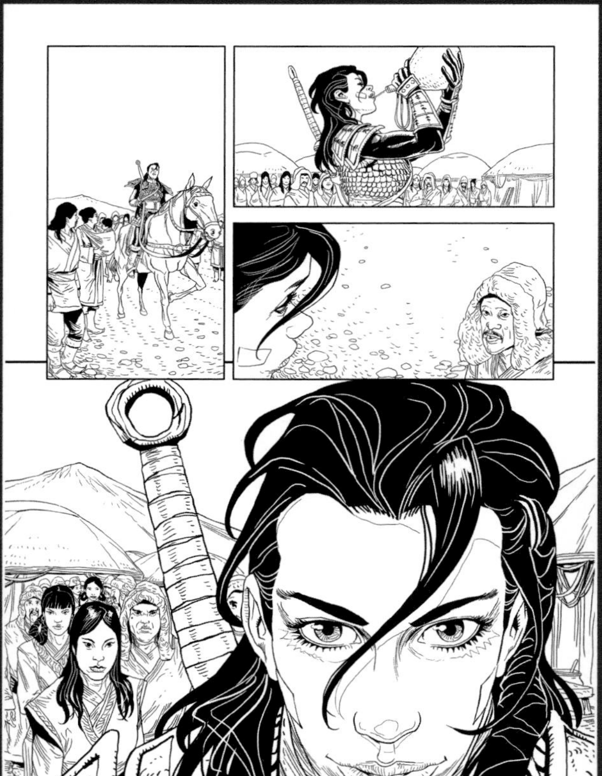

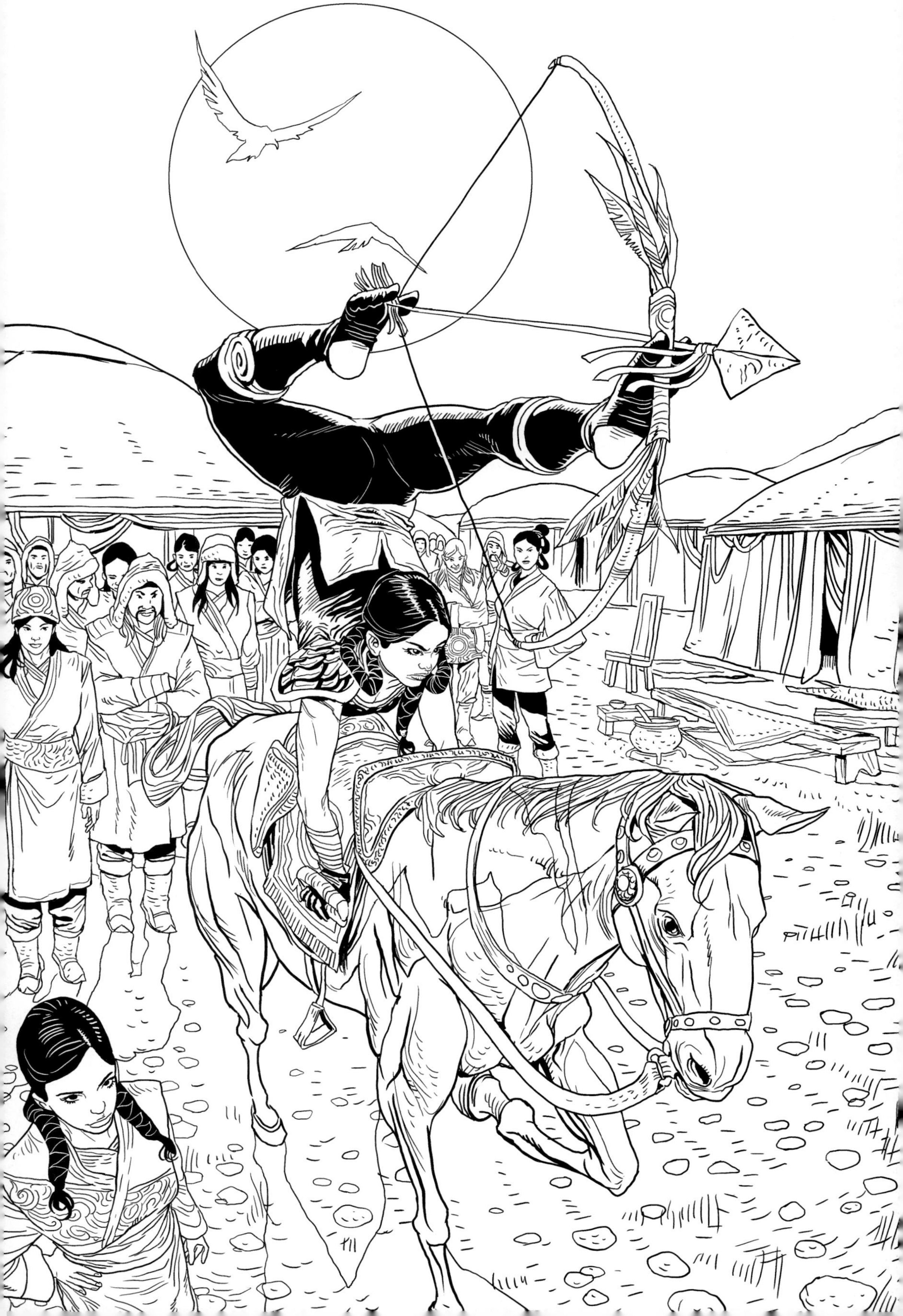

THE FORGOTTEN QUEEN #3,
pages 17, 18, and (facing) 19
Art by AMILCAR PINNA

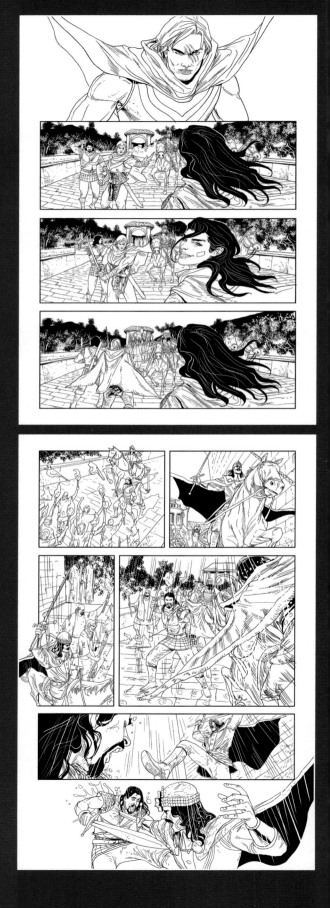

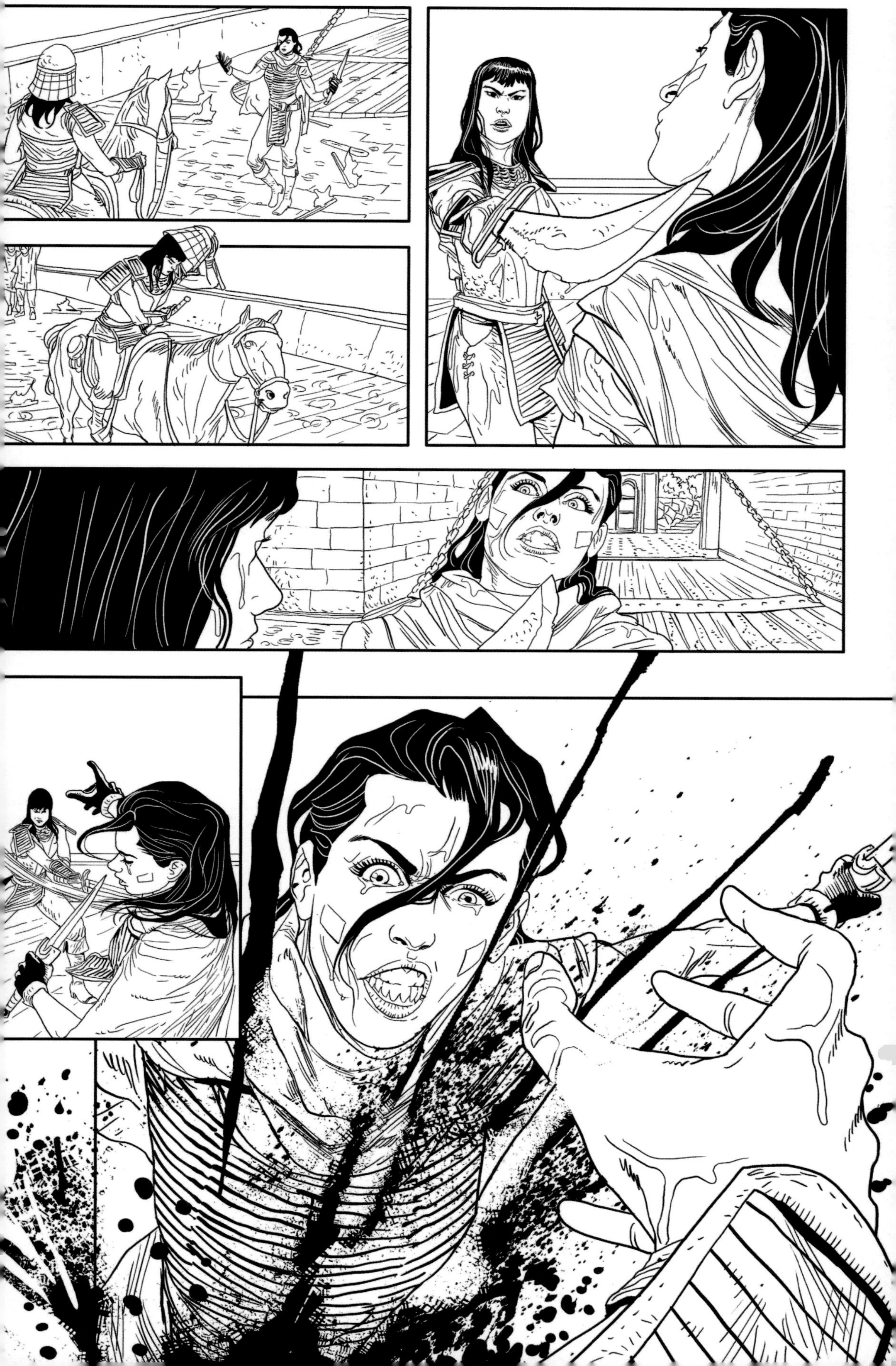

EXPLORE THE VALIANT

ACTION & ADVENTURE

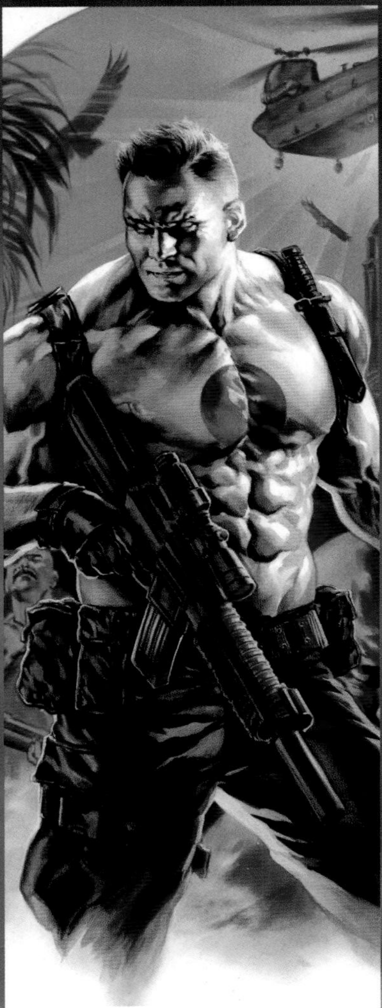

BLOODSHOT SALVATION VOL. 1: THE BOOK OF REVENGE
ISBN: 978-1-68215-255-3

NINJA-K VOL. 1: THE NINJA FILES
ISBN: 978-1-68215-259-1

SAVAGE
ISBN: 978-1-68215-189-1

WRATH OF THE ETERNAL WARRIOR VOL. 1: RISEN
ISBN: 978-1-68215-123-5

X-O MANOWAR (2017) VOL. 1: SOLDIER
ISBN: 978-1-68215-205-8

BLOCKBUSTER ADVENTURE

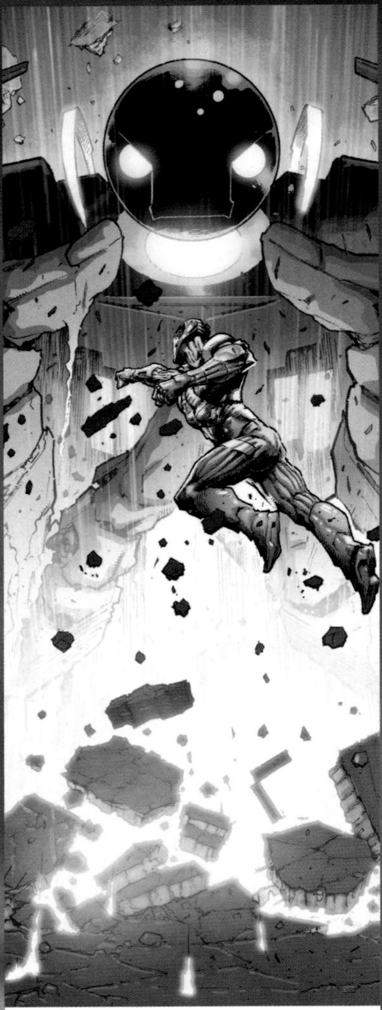

4001 A.D.
ISBN: 978-1-68215-143-3

ARMOR HUNTERS
ISBN: 978-1-939346-45-2

BOOK OF DEATH
ISBN: 978-1-939346-97-1

HARBINGER WARS
ISBN: 978-1-939346-09-4

THE VALIANT
ISBN: 978-1-939346-60-5

COMEDY

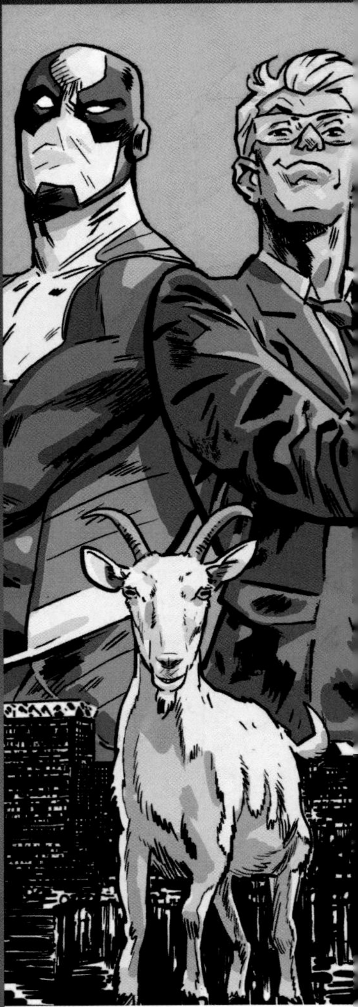

A&A: THE ADVENTURES OF ARCHER & ARMSTRONG VOL. 1: IN THE BAG
ISBN: 978-1-68215-149-5

THE DELINQUENTS
ISBN: 978-1-939346-51-3

QUANTUM AND WOODY! (2017) VOL. 1: KISS KISS, KLANG KLANG
ISBN: 978-1-68215-269-0

NIVERSE FOR ONLY

$9.99

HORROR & MYSTERY

SCIENCE FICTION & FANTASY

TEEN ADVENTURE

Discover the entire Valiant Universe of titles at VALIANTENTERTAINMENT.COM/ALL-SERIES/

VALIANT®

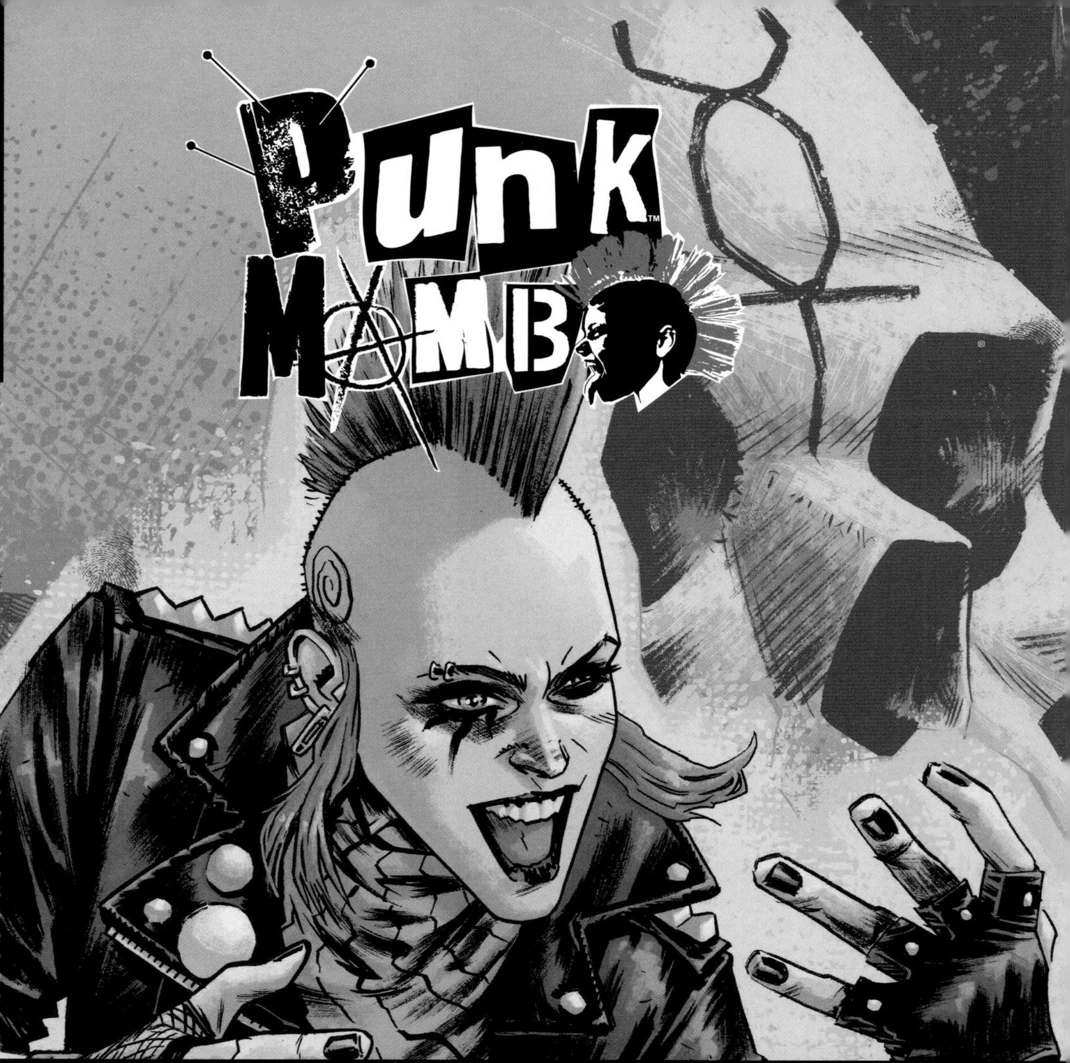
PUNK MAMBO

GO PUNK YOURSELF!

Punk Mambo is a hard-living voodoo priestess who grew up in London, then relocated to Louisiana's Bayou Country. Now, she's a mystical mercenary-for-hire. In her first-ever solo series, Punk Mambo investigates a series of abductions in the New Orleans gutter punk scene, stumbling upon a deadlier mystery that takes her to the haunted shores of Haiti.

From writer Cullen Bunn (*Venom*) and artist Adam Gorham (*New Mutants: Dead Souls*) comes this hilariously horrifying breakout adventure for Valiant's fan-favorite mystic malcontent.

Collecting the complete PUNK MAMBO five-issue limited series, along with PUNK MAMBO #0 from writer Peter Milligan and artist Robert Gill.

TRADE PAPERBACK
ISBN: 978-1-68215-330-7

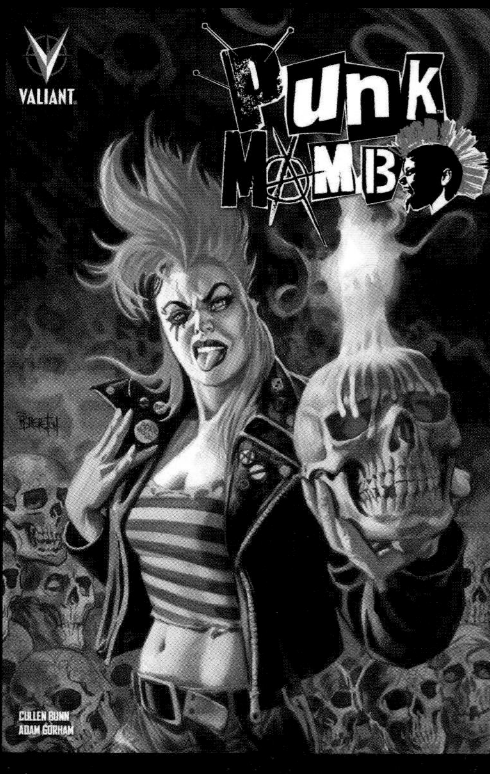
VALIANT
PUNK MAMBO
CULLEN BUNN
ADAM GORHAM